MOLDERS
OF THE
AMERICAN MIND

MOLDERS
OF THE
AMERICAN MIND

*A Critical Review of the
Social Attitudes of
Seventeen Leaders in
American Education*

NORMAN WOELFEL, 1895—

OCTAGON BOOKS

A DIVISION OF FARRAR, STRAUS AND GIROUX

New York   1974

Copyright 1933 by Columbia University Press

Reprinted 1974
by special arrangement with Columbia University Press

OCTAGON BOOKS
A DIVISION OF FARRAR, STRAUS & GIROUX, INC.
19 Union Square West
New York, N. Y. 10003

Library of Congress Cataloging in Publication Data

Woelfel, Norman, 1895-
  Molders of the American mind.

  Reprint of the ed. published by Columbia University Press, New York.

  1. Educators — United States.   2. Education — Philosophy.
  3. Education — Aims and objectives.   4. United States —
  Civilization.   I. Title.

LA210.W6   1973   370.1'0973   73-19823
ISBN 0-374-98707-6

Printed in USA by
Thomson-Shore, Inc.
Dexter, Michigan

TO

THE TEACHERS OF AMERICA

ACTIVE SHARERS IN THE BUILDING OF ATTITUDES

MAY THEY COLLECTIVELY CHOOSE A DESTINY
WHICH HONORS ONLY PRODUCTIVE LABOR
AND PROMOTES THE ASCENDENCY OF THE
COMMON MAN OVER THE FORCES THAT
MAKE POSSIBLE AN ECONOMY
OF PLENTY

INTRODUCTION

THIS study grew out of a conviction that the philosophy of education has come increasingly to be a matter mainly of discussions of theoretic educational issues with numerous citations of authorities pro and con. A content literature of enormous proportions concerning these matters has grown up in recent years, and textbooks covering the field have come in rapid succession from the press. The background of more general philosophic thinking appears not to have been adequately explored. The following pages endeavor to show that views about theoretic and practical problems in education depend to a very large extent upon the way the social scene as a whole is contemplated. With this end in view the author has analyzed the materials published, since approximately 1925, by seventeen prominent leaders in American education. In the cases of Finney, Snedden, and Rugg, each of whom has written a single volume incorporating his idea of the relations between society and the schools, the same attempt to analyze all available published materials since 1925 has not been made. The three volumes in question—Finney's *A Sociological Philosophy of Education,* Snedden's *School Educations,* and Rugg's *Culture and Education in America*— were taken as the chief sources of the presentations made of the substance of the thinking of these men. The selection of the seventeen names chosen has been influenced to some degree by the fact that the particular men selected for study have most affected the author's professional thinking. There is, however, reason to believe that the thinking now current in professional educational circles is traceable in large degree to the writings of these men. The list is obviously not exhaustive and another student undertaking the same task would most probably make a somewhat different selection.

In the first Section an attempt is made to read the implications of some things that are happening in American society at the present time. Certain centers around which American institutions have been built up seem in process of disintegration. There appears to be evidence for believing that new centers are in process of crystallization. The inference is drawn that traditional institutions are undergoing major changes. That these are matters which American teachers at all levels and in all fields should be vitally concerned about cannot be over-emphasized.

With this necessarily brief analysis of the contemporary scene as a background, in the next Section the attempt is made to show how the points of view of the educational leaders under discussion are oriented. Various classifications of the thinking of these men might be made; the one here used is defended merely as one possible classification. In Part One the views of men who seem most concerned about traditional values are presented and briefly discussed. The author is, of course, responsible for the particular statements made; he has, however, earnestly attempted to enter sympathetically into each man's thinking and to present, somewhat in the style of the man himself, what seems to be of most importance. The men in each classification differ variously and no attempt is made to obscure these differences. The classifications are not regarded as ironclad, and the author would be the first to acknowledge that the inclusion of a particular individual in one classification rather than another is made on somewhat doubtful grounds. After the discussion of the views of men who are oriented mainly in the direction of traditional values, Part Two presents and discusses the views of men whose writings seem to indicate a belief that Science is an ultimate guarantor of progress. In Part Three the classification is on the basis of an orientation toward the philosophic thinking characteristic of American experimental naturalism.

In the third Section the author criticizes and interprets from the basis of his own convictions the views analyzed in Section Two.

The fourth and concluding Section of the study suggests an orientation to certain vital considerations for educators during a period of transition and outlines some major educational strategies for the immediate future.

Lest it appear that the author has in the course of the analysis, criticism, and discussion of Sections Two, Three, and Four of this study unduly assumed the inferiority of the older analyses and methods of education and the superiority of so-called Progressive Education, let it be confessed that this issue is not argued at all. Indeed it may be considered very doubtful whether this issue can be argued to any effect in this day and age, for it is a technical question that must await more significant experimentation than has so far been practiced. The aim here has been to point out the connection of general and specific educational thinking with typical underlying philosophies of the present day. The interpretations made throughout the study are, of course, influenced by the viewpoint of the author. He believes that modern experimental naturalism offers a substantial basis upon which a new and distinctive American civilization can be built.

The author is especially indebted to Professor William H. Kilpatrick of Teachers College, Columbia University for encouragement and counsel in connection with the study. He wishes also to acknowledge his indebtedness to Professors Reisner, Counts, Raup, and Childs of the same institution for helpful criticism.

N. W.

Columbia University
May, 1933

CONTENTS

SOME IMPLICATIONS OF CONTEMPORARY
SOCIAL CHANGE

SOME IMPLICATIONS OF CONTEMPORARY SOCIAL CHANGE

Prefatory Note

UNDER the headings—"Factors in the Decline of the Christian Tradition," "Factors in the Decline of the Business Régime," "The Beginning of Cultural Distinction and Independence in America," "Resources for Social Reconstruction," and "Bearings of the Contemporary Social Background upon Organized Education"—an attempt is made to build a picture out of factors which are obvious to any one who cares to look for them, of what seems to be happening in America today.

The analyses are not intended as complete. Together they are meant as calling attention to the phenomenon of the disintegration of one set of traditions in America and the emergence of another. Such matters are all too frequently omitted in educational literature.

I. Factors in the Decline of the Christian Tradition

It has long been part of the tradition about the founding of the American nation that one of the great ideals of those ancient days was religious freedom and religious toleration. The conception of our noble ancestors as crusaders for complete religious liberty, although greatly overdrawn has, nevertheless, a substantial basis in the longing of many of the colonists for freedom from persecution as they worshipped within the sanctions of particular sects. The later idealization of this longing by popular historians into an almost universal desire for tolerance in religious matters bespeaks admirably a certain type of patriotic pride but reckons without fundamental considerations. The people who had come to America were of almost solid Christian stock and those few who actually expressed ideals of religious liberty were, of course, referring to liberty within the Christian fold. Actually the heritage of repression which Europe had written into the souls of colonists was too strong in most of the colonies to permit even this degree of liberty. Minority sects had trouble everywhere. The tale of religious persecution in early America is too well understood to need further comment.

When the Federal Union was formed the influence of eighteenth-century European rationalism upon the minds of the more intellectual framers of the Constitution is evidenced by the inclusion within that document of the proverbial guarantees of the Rights of Man. These rights have remained a solid tradition in American life up to the present. They have been the source of political oratory and idealistic diatribes all down the years. But the early dominantly Protestant Christian coloration remained upon the mass mind and under the influence of a laissez faire economy became a great unifying cultural influence as the Federal Union grew into a great modern state. The Catholic, the Jew, the atheist, and the member of any sect which was markedly different from the Christian Protestant dispensation, while nominally free to enjoy most of the common privileges of community, have ever remained under a kind of covert suspicion, if nothing worse. Political and social bars have been drawn against dissenters from the commonly accepted, if not constitutionally established, faith of the great dominant majority since the days of the founders. The Catholic and the Jew, both biblically within the same essential tradition, gradually have attained fuller recognition, although even today "whispering" campaigns are not unknown. The Atheists and the members of other radical sects were continually regarded as queer people, oftentimes more to be feared than foreigners.

Such cultural products as were natively developed in the period of America's growth were nicely within the permissive sanction of the Christian religious faith. American literature, American scholarship, American recreational customs, the American stage were all measured by Puritan moral standards. The American school has always been carefully nourished upon the universal and fundamental Christian beliefs despite its latter-day professions of secularity.

Since it was so firmly established in America there has never been very much intellectual consideration or analysis of the Christian tradition itself. The common thought has unconsciously accepted and assumed Christian preconceptions. In barest outline, the preconceptions of the Christian tradition were that God is the Father and nurturing Protector of the universe, that the life of Jesus Christ, his divine Son, is the eternal model after which every life should be patterned, that the Ten Commandments are final and complete ethical standards, that the Church and its appointed leaders are God's surrogates on earth, that some kind of immortality in heaven follows after the end of an earthly life which the church is willing to approve, that the Sabbath day should be dedicated to worship, that the Bible, written by prophets under the direct inspiration of God, is sacred and infallible. So solidly were these and their many subsidiary minor tenets packed into the background of the American mind up to and beyond the nineties of the last century that they even became an important part of patriotism. This nation in the minds and in the public utterances of its leaders from all fields of endeavor was the realization of a great dream. The combination of Christianity and democracy was assumed to guarantee the permanency of American institutions as they had been evolved.

In the physical environment, in the work-day occupations of the people, in the racial constitution of the population, tremendous changes were going on while the nation was expanding in size and in significance. The change from an agricultural to an industrial economy, the flood of inventions following in the wake of the scientific and industrial revolutions, the growth of large cities, and the spread of education seemingly affected everything but our religious tradition. Christianity had become a matter of course, the church a dominant and necessary institution; its meaning and significance under these major changes were never inquired into. It is the intention here to discuss certain fairly obvious social phenomena of the recent past and of the present which seem to have a bearing upon the ultimate and largely unquestioned permanency of the Christian religious tradition in the American scene.

The picture as above briefly sketched is no longer a true one. Everybody today is troubled about ideals, and there seems to be a profound disturbance of inner complacency in the American spirit. Something appears to have snapped among the forces which bound the people together into a nation of stable ideals and institutions. The triumphs of a glittering material advance are not matched by a satisfied national soul. Modern life no longer operates under any real guidance or supervision of the Christian church. There are more churches than ever, but they carry on in an isolated sphere. Congress still opens with a prayer, and persons still are forced to take an oath upon the Bible, but such outward forms mean next to nothing in the onward rush of the varied activities of daily life. Who in politics gives a thought to religion beyond uttering now and then on auspicious occasions a few pious words or beyond sharply calculating the voting strength or lobbying pressure of church groups which have learned the techniques for exerting influence? Where in the intricacy of business, financial, and industrial activities is there a sign that man has a religious nature? On what occasions do the pursuits of leisure give evidence that the Puritan moral code still functions? Did the nation during the World War, despite the utterances of some of the clergy, declare in any convincing fashion that God was on its side? Did the soldiers or the civilian population demand this consolation? Do American colleges, the greater majority of which were established in the interests of some particular Christian denomination, make any serious effort to defend and propagate the faith? Are the public school teachers, who are forced by law or school regulation to make their pupils repeat verbatim the Lord's Prayer or to read from the Bible each morning, possessed by the militant Christian missionary spirit? How many church or Christian organizations of one kind and another are vigorously fighting to make God and Jesus and the Bible once more the integrating center of American cultural life? Such questions as these bring to a focus the actually disintegrative tendencies that are already well in motion. Let us look a little more closely at some further phenomena.

During the nineteenth century the Christian faith proved itself incapable of making a rapid and adequate adjustment to the results of earnest scholarship applied to biblical literature. The so-called higher biblical criticism which developed in Germany established beyond peradventure of a doubt the actually varied and sometimes contradictory sources of the Christian Bible. Most of this research was undertaken by Christian scholars themselves within the tradition. Intellectual and moral integrity demanded that organized Christianity accept and positively embody the results of this research. This was not done until too late; rather was there vigorous and continued opposition supplemented by new defenses of divine origin and of unquestioned unity of content. From another angle modern scientific workers in various fields, themselves within the Christian tradition, were building up an increasing store of tested knowledge, some of which by its very abundance began at length to seep into the minds of the clergy and of the populace. But the Christian church was not equal to the challenge of Science. Such a hue and cry was raised over the damage threatened by scientists to biblical infallibility and canonic doctrine, that some of the echoes are still ringing. These issues are today no longer pertinent, higher criticism and Science have both been haltingly accepted, but how those needless controversies have broken the grandeur of inherited Christianity!

The various sects and cults within the Christian tradition are also an evidence of fundamental disruption, for most sects have arisen over hair-splitting issues of received doctrine, rather than over anything really fundamental in the religious life. The long-standing division of the tradition into Catholics, Protestants, and Jews is today often only superficially descriptive. The many sects are mostly too narrow and esoteric in appeal to bear promise of permanent stability and growth. The haphazard way in which science and pseudo-science have been incorporated into many religious sects shows lack of inner integrity. The recent attempts at unity within the Christian fold by means of community churches of an interdenominational tone, from their relatively small success, seem to have come too late to save the essential solidarity of the Christian tradition. The tendency towards disintegration or dismemberment promises to go on until it approaches as a limit personal religious independence or spiritual anarchy. Although the Protestants and the Jews give evidence of most serious internal disruptions, the more rigid understructure of the Catholics is also observedly weakening. The Catholic Church preserves an apparent external harmony, but actual differences on matters of doctrine and policy and divergence in the direction of the social sympathies of its leaders are fairly obvious. The recent Papal encyclical on the state of Christian marriage, reaffirming a permanent defensive stand at the Augustinian formulations, makes an interesting background upon which to throw the available data on the patronage of birth-control clinics by Catholic laymen.[1]

The Protestant churches that are really alive today are so by virtue of powerful personal leaders, of whom the Reverend Dr. Harry Emerson Fosdick is an outstanding example. People attend church and participate actively in organized religious

[1] M. Sanger, The *Nation*, Vol. CXXXIV, No. 3473, 1932, p. 102.

undertakings in the degree to which they are touched by the genius of their pastor. If he be hail-fellow-well-met, whose appraisal and penetrating appreciation of the contemporary social scene respects the intelligence, but does not molest too much the fundamental Christian preconceptions, he will have a following which does not leave his church as empty as the majority. But what a puny holding-power is this personal leadership compared with the pomp and authority of Christian doctrine during the previous centuries!

Of late from among Protestant theologians of the more modernistic turn of mind there have come active and persistent discussions of the concept of God.[2] Who of devout religious observance, in days not so far gone, would have ever desecrated the name of God by referring to it as a concept? But of more moment than this, some among these theological sticklers over modernity actually agree that the concept of God is a purely poetic or mythological one! How far from his undoubted place at the very center of great philosophic systems has God traveled during the few brief years of this century!

It may be relevant to mention in this connection the strange constructions of the personality of Jesus that have come out of the social upheavals which have broken Christian religious hegemony in America. For the benefit of business men whose urge is for sociality and for the self-approval which comes from participation in constructive social efforts, Jesus has been painted as a kind of successful, benevolent, modern business man. From more sensitive quarters for the sake of a clearer conscience while functioning in modern life, some Christian leaders have pictured Jesus as the first modern Socialist. The earliest preserved traditions about Jesus indicate that he was an other-worldly character who, in his concentration upon the problem of salvation in the life to come, formulated the purest love ethic that the world has ever known. Making the character of Jesus a focussing

[2] H. N. Wieman and others. *Is There a God* (Chicago: Willett), 1933.

center for biblical literature and inherited mythologies the organizing forces in the Christian church gradually built a powerful and controlling religious tradition. That the essential Jesus was frequently lost amid myriad creeds and forms and doctrines of established Christianity has given rise to numerous revolts and splits within the church in the course of its development. Always in the past the Christian tradition has been able to reform its doctrinal lines and to extend its sway in one form or other over humankind. These modern sensitivities and tribulations are, however, of another order. The old power and glory of Christianity would never have stooped to philosophic disqualifications of God or to completely modernized versions of Jesus. The Catholic Church clearly recognizes this, as do some Protestant fundamentalists in their efforts to retain in rugged splendor the whole cloth of the tradition.

If we look outside the folds of the church we are struck at once by the fact that modern life differs in most essential details from that of Christian Rome or medieval Europe or nineteenth-century America. The shortsightedness and the stubbornness of leaders responsible for carrying on the Christian tradition has caused it to become almost completely irrelevant today. The standards of conduct and the moral sanctions in contemporary society do not issue from within the body of this tradition. The highly respected Puritan code of the last century is laughed out of court today. Expressionism runs riot to such an extent that some have already constructed it into a cult. The movie, the stage, the press, the radio report, the manners and customs that are most current, and the pulpit when it actually disapproves, merely confirm our suspicions. The younger generation is on its own and the last thing that would interest modern youth is the salvaging of the Christian tradition. The environmental controls which technologists have achieved and the operations by means of which workers earn their livelihood need no aid or sanction from God nor any blessing from the church. Human power is everywhere manifest and when its anarchic management creates a national calamity like the present economic depression, the church, if one may judge by newspaper reports of sermons does little more than capitalize on human misery by referring to the increasing godlessness of the populace. Despite this questionable tactic there appears to be no stir on the part of the masses to fill empty pews and to learn the much neglected neat doctrinal truths that stood their forebears in such good stead. The sacred Sabbath has become a day of outing, of recreation through sports and games, of entertainment at great movie palaces, and of speeding automobile trips hither and yon. National prohibition, which some sections of organized Christianity fought for so strongly by methods sometimes not overly scrupulous, is not only increasingly under universal condemnation, but has placed institutions of law and order in a precarious position. Christian religious reverence and conformity have not thereby been increased.

In the ranks of labor the organized associations, which attract the more radical elements and which during the present economic depression are gathering to themselves large cohorts of discontents, are openly anti-religious. The American proletarian movement is relatively insignificant as yet; if it develops in any measure after the European pattern, the disintegration of the Christian tradition in America will be complete. It has been suggested that proletarian churches be established while the movement is still young and in need of sympathy. Such churches might conceivably reinvigorate Christianity with the spirit of the common man as he begins to assert himself under the conditions of industrialism. Their establishment seems too much, however, to expect from a highly organized institution which is already conscious of having made many concessions to modernism.

Man today is as fundamentally spiritual as ever he was. In fact, inventions have so lessened the hours of necessary labor for all that the stirrings of the human spirit have begun to emerge perceptibly in every individual. How are these universally felt spiritual needs being satisfied today? Certainly not in the churches, for the flood of new spiritual energy has come with such a rush that the narrow, traditional, religious channels could not hold it. These wider spiritual needs of today have been sustained by forces some of which have been already mentioned as providing modern standards of behavior and conduct: the cinema, the drama, and the novel with their eternal picture of changing good and evil, the newspaper with its varied human appeal, the revivified periodical catering to human impulse, the popularized versions of esoteric knowledge in cheap books, the blatant radio, the adult education movement in its various manifestations, and the wider environment made possible by the automobile.

Under breaking traditional mores, the confusing miscellany of contemporary standards of conduct, and the increasing insecurity of life for the common man in a pecuniary economic régime, personal problems have multiplied manifoldly. Not only the organized church but the very resources of the Christian tradition itself seem inadequate to give the understanding and the consolation essential to personal integration. Some of the clergy have sensed the seriousness and the difficulties of modern problems of personal adjustment, and there have been noble efforts made from within organized religion to move in the direction of the reconstruction and the expansion of traditional duties and services. But it is fairly clear that the vast majority of personal readjustments that are being continually made today are without benefit of clergy. Social welfare agencies, domestic relations courts, public clinics, teachers, practicing physicians, psychiatrists, lay personal advisers, the increased intellectual resources of individuals themselves (not to mention the psychological racketeers that ply their trade so profitably on a basis of partial insight and pseudo-science), all effectively supplement, or entirely replace, the work of organized religion. And there is no questioning the fact that government in its local, state, and federal activities is increasingly, by means of various related agencies, bringing the fruits of a rapidly developing social science to bear on the problems which, without any stretch of meaning, can be called spiritual.

It is important to mention the rôle which the modern rapid spread of enlightenment has played in this field of problems of personal readjustment, an area which was, until fairly recently, a clear monopoly for the church. Increased literacy, the main contribution which the public school has made to American life, feeds on the glare of publicity that modern devices of communication give to events of human interest. All varieties of problems, personal and otherwise, are continually thrust upon the consciousness of the masses. The masses are driven by the very nature of mind to think and to feel about these problems and to arrive at desired solutions for them. The tremendously increased and varied stimulation and the consequent increased complexity of response characteristic of modern society make the personal emotional life of the common man no easily charted territory. Wholesome integration is far more difficult to achieve. The simple but irrelevant panaceas which issue from the pulpit fall consequently upon minds far too sophisticated to be corralled within ecclesiastical sanctions. The common man, although far from understanding his own soul, has been able to build independently a set of convictions and an outlook which for the most part gets him by.

Philosophy as taught in American universities and colleges up to the beginning of this century was a justification and a validation of the Christian faith. Christian idealism was presented as the grand culmination of the history of philosophy. Since most teachers of philosophy were Christian ministers, and since many of the higher institutions themselves were denominational, this was entirely appropriate. Christian philosophy for the intellectuals who pursued a college or university career was the keystone of the arch of a solidly Christian nation. The picture is far different today. The teachers of philosophy are scholars and specialists; some may be disciples and special pleaders, but relatively few are ordained clergymen. Independent philosophic formulations from different centers of learning have come upon the scene. Idealism in one form or another is probably still dominant, but it is no longer so obviously a system of Christian apologetics. Pragmatism with its practical and iconoclastic tone has become increasingly influential. Humanism, a modern rendering of classic Greek and Roman values, has had some vogue as a kind of antidote for the assumed materialistic leaning of pragmatism. Experimental naturalism, just appearing over the horizon, seems actually to lay the foundations for a completely relevant modern synthesis of outlook.

It is not assumed in this brief analysis of some of the disintegrative factors at work upon the Christian tradition as it has been known in America, that the tradition is anywhere near complete collapse. Christian preconceptions, though not operative in life today to the degree that they have been in the past, are still essentially unquestioned in the minds of the great majority of the people. Critical attacks on fundamental preconceptions like God, Jesus, and immortality still bring powerfully emotionalized rejoinders in factory, market-place, and office, The atheist is still looked upon as a kind of sinister influence; his associations have not received the people who have drifted away from the church. What has been happening is not of the nature of a war upon the Christian tradition. Had that been the case the church might have been gloriously vindicated and brought into closer relationship with modern life. No, the Christian tradition as it has been known, seems at present to be moving rather slowly but inevitably off the stage of modern America. Whether the process takes from fifty to one hundred years, or whether a social cataclysm some time in the next generation telescopes the process, may make little eventual difference. If the Christian tradition, as we have known it, passes, it probably will not be missed, because the infinitely numerous complex and penetrating influences of modern society will have imperceptibly replaced its functions. Future historians may look back at the period of America's Christian birth and youthful upbringing with great curiosity, for it will seem strange that such utterly complete indoctrination should have failed so signally to guarantee a healthy livelihood to a tradition which had buffeted the storms of nearly twenty centuries of development in the Western World.

It is interesting to speculate upon what will happen to the various churches and church organizations now still so earnestly engaged in salvaging operations. Will the very sincere and noble efforts of many Christians to promote broader social welfare and ennobled conceptions of the individual life continue to operate when religion ceases to be coterminous in America with Christian preconceptions and with churches? May we conceive the possibility of a happy harmonization of all such efforts with the efforts of other agencies engaged in wide diffusion of the significant cultural attainments of man to promote a happy, a constructively expanding, an artistically and aesthetically fruitful future American social life? If so, the fate of the Christian tradition will be a happy one and all its great and lasting contributions to the spirit of man will be saved as a chastening influence upon the cultural development of the future.

II. Factors in the Decline of the Business Régime

American democracy from the time of its establishment has always been under the domination of business (agricultural or industrial) and financial powers. Even the farthest reaches of the imagination of a Jefferson did not contemplate extension of the suffrage to the masses of men in cities. Today the battle for universal adult suffrage has been won except in the case of the negroes in the South and the newly emergent drifting unemployed. Years of experience with universal suffrage have, however, been long enough to demonstrate that a mere increase in the number of qualified voters is in no sense a guarantee of real democracy. The early vital connection between economic interests and political sentiments has not only continued but has been strengthened while the raw continent was gradually beaten into submission. The passing of the agricultural era with the Civil War transferred economic control from landed proprietors, who exercised some degree of personal supervision over their laborers, to great industrial corporations operated on the principle of absentee ownership. Government has been carried on largely in the interests of pioneering captains of industry, whose retainers in one form or another have amply salved the consciences of some of the great names of American history as they directed that one policy rather than another be written into the fundamental law of the land. But in large measure such tactics were unnecessary since the personal financial interests of legislators were intimately connected with the progressive expansion of one or another branch of private business enterprise.

In fact, all American cultural traditions were built around the classical economic preconceptions brought over from England during the period of heaviest colonization. Some of these in essence were that man in his economic activities is guided by the principle of self-interest; he knows what he produces; his participation in economic activities of society as a laborer, or as an employer of labor, is evidence that he is receiving a neatly balanced return for his endeavors, for if he were not, he would not continue; government exists essentially for promoting the orderly and efficient working of established institutions; private property is a natural right which must not be interfered with under any conditions; the protection of capital is to the best interests of all; competition for private profit is of the very essence of human nature; business activities are productive activities; and labor unions are in unqualified opposition to the very interests of labor itself. Such tenets along with many deductions from them are summed up by such generally descriptive terms as "laissez faire" or "rugged individualism." They were fortified in America during the nineteenth century by the dominant Christian religious tradition and taught in our colleges and in our lower schools along with Christian ethics as the fundamentals of common sense upon which individual success and national prosperity depended. It is small wonder then, that when captains of industry needed large supplies of cheap labor, immigration policies were adjusted towards that end; that when the resources of the West were thrown open, private initiative should be allowed to develop them in the interest of profit; that the Federal Government should underwrite the great private railroad ventures which went along with the winning of the West; that when labor or the farmers on occasion revolted under the ruthlessness of large-scale private industrial or financial operations, the resources of the courts and of effective public opinion should succeed in branding them as revolutionary and un-American.

Nor is it strange that during the present century when the real triumphs of Big Business were becoming evident to the populace and the dream of becoming a captain of industry occupied the mind of every enterprising youth, American universities should set up colleges of business administration and of finance. Leaders of public education were not slow in joining the parade, realizing quite suddenly that education also was big business and required for its practical efficiency many intricate techniques of administration and organization modeled after prevailing business ideals. The dogged insistence that our elementary schools concentrate on a narrow literacy and a facility with number, and the mushroom growth of a very illiberal commercial and vocational training in our secondary schools have an obvious relation to the business tradition. The scientific and the engineering schools of the country have so deliberately limited the more broadly cultural aspects of their curricula that their graduates, who in a very real sense constitute the main technological resource of the machine age, have given themselves almost to a man in the cause of Bigger and Better Business. Large-scale commercialization of college athletics could take place only under a régime in which business men may dictate educational policies.

The boastful assurance of the business régime that efficient production of needed goods was its special forte was bluntly challenged during the World War when public management and control were temporarily substituted under the guise of war necessity. But Business came back into new glories during the decade of the nineteen-twenties when an unprecedented expansion in old and new lines of corporate enterprise took place. America was in the vanguard of the whole world, and nearly every citizen had put on a capitalistic front by participating in some small degree in the glories of absentee ownership.

Most of the above absurdities are under a cloud today when a much chastened nation is confronted with the sinister results of rugged individualism in its economic life. One need not go into statistics of stock and bond depreciation, of bank and business failures, of unemployment, of governmental insolvency in states and municipalities, or of inadequacy of public and private relief funds. The situation is such a desperate one that the President of the United States issues almost daily a public message or announcement of some kind. The necessity for any radical readjustment has, of course, not entered the closed minds of business and political leaders. The effort is to bend all available energy in the direction of resuming economic activities at the earliest possible moment in anarchic full blast as before. But there are reasons for believing that the present economic depression has brought to a focus a number of trends which indicate that economic and social normalcy in the future will be conceived in far different terms than those of capitalism.

A veritable tradition of social legislation reaching back almost to Civil War days, has grown up in America. Every gain in this direction has been contested, and in many instances final victory for a specific measure was gained only at the cost of several previous defeats. The complete liberty and self-sufficiency of business to do as it pleases with regard to natural resources, labor, flotation of securities, and production of commodities, have been gradually sapped by increasing degrees of governmental regulation of one kind and another. The masterly and vehement dissents of liberal Supreme Court Justices in cases involving the unconstitutionality of social legislation are no small monuments along the road to a changed economic order. The idea that government may, under stress of an emergency like the present depression, come to the rescue of business by adopting far-reaching policies aimed at quick recovery is still with us, but the anomaly of that idea is becoming increasingly apparent to a wider section of the public. The supposed dependence of the working man's full dinner pail and the farmer's solvency upon a high protective tariff is a principle that can never have the effectiveness before the public in the future that it has had in the past. The widespread public derision which early in the present depression greeted statements of the President and of political and financial leaders that business conditions were essentially sound, was a shocking phenomenon to business idealists. The publication in popular magazines of facts about the extent to which the government actually underwrites private business, even in normal times, is not calculated to augment continued public deception by such catch phrases of apologists for the business tradition as "Keep the government out of business."

Organized movements among the churches, such as the Federated Council of Churches, the Catholic Welfare League, and others, have for some years been calling attention to social evils and deficiencies attendant upon the way the nation's economic machinery was being run by captains of industry. Recently in a middle western state the ministers of one whole denomination went on record as definitely opposed to the present economic set-up and as calling for socialized control of industry. Such tendencies are indicative of a belated recognition that nominally Christian business men have long been neglectful of the meaning of Christian love in the relations between capital and labor and producer and consumer. They portend also the recognition that churches in America have been subtly influenced by generous benefactions to keep religion pure and uncontaminated by discussion of major social issues. This recognition marks the beginning of the end of an alliance that has been exceedingly profitable to the business order—an alliance that made it possible to construct the much-flaunted image of the successful business man as the ideal American citizen.

The social order in Russia today is about as near a reversal of that in America as could be conceived. When the changes resulting in the establishment of the Soviet Republic were first inaugurated, not only did this country officially participate with others in adding to the initial difficulties of Russia's revolutionary organizers, but the American press was flooded with atrocity propaganda and with tales about social life under the revolutionary régime properly calculated to horrify the dominant American middle-class frame of mind. Business and political leaders made speeches and offered press releases predicting the early downfall of an economic régime whose theoretic foundations were obviously contrary to human nature. But Russia survived and was temporarily forgotten in America during the boom days of the twenties. When the Five-Year Plan was announced to the world, it was hailed in America as the thunder which precedes the dawn of a return to common sense, property values, and private enterprise. It was believed to be the last stroke of a group of fanatics who were losing their grip on Russia's helm. Not long after, however, when Soviet emissaries began to visit among captains of industry in this country and to flash huge orders for machinery, tools, and equipment, they were actually welcomed. Despite a disapproving governmental administration which haughtily refused recognition to the worker's republic, shipments of American products were made, and the Russian gold received in payment for them proved as genuine as any other. American newspapers began to show interest enough to send special reporters to Russia and to accept special articles from visitors to Russia. American engineers, technicians, and scientists, apparently regardless of their wonted allegiance to the ideals of private business, responded in increasing numbers to invitations from Russia to assist in the realization of the great Plan. Today what trained worker or chastened captain of industry in the United States would turn a cold shoulder to a tempting offer to labor for the Soviets? The news reports of what is going on in Russia are beginning to approach accuracy; magazine articles and radio talks discuss the Russian situation with increasing frequency; there has been a veritable flood of popular books about Russia. It may be that the hide of the business régime in America is too thick to be penetrated by these shafts from within its own ranks, but that remains to be seen.

Since the beginning of the present business decline a great many economists and a few far-seeing business leaders have become more and more sensitive to discrepancies in the gospel of unlimited freedom for business enterprise which in the past has been accepted as the basis for attaining the good of all. We have a new phenomenon in the talk among business men of plans for coördination and careful systematizing within industry to avoid over-production and consequent unemployment. But equally strange to our scene is the picture of the foremost theoretic apologists for the American business system, the academic economists, falling over one another to insist that social control in industry and careful national economic planning in some form must be established within a comparatively short time. To be sure, the current discussion of social planning is usually carefully explained as having nothing whatever to do with the great Russian experiment and as emanating entirely from our own World War precedent. These obvious rationalizations do not detract however from the value of the mental shake-up which has apparently taken place.

Graft in politics in America is an old story, so old in fact that the public today is little stirred by further damaging revelations of betrayal of public trust. Such things we all know about, and we have come to regard them as almost inherent in the present system. It has been customary to hear leaders of public opinion declare that if the government could be run after the manner of business, graft and corruption would be unheard of and efficiency would reign supreme. What a revelation therefore is it to be informed, as we are today, that the graft within business itself is so pervasively dominant as to be almost basic to the very carrying-on of business activities![3] Integrity of character in the full sense has become virtually impossible to business "technicians" in positions of responsibility in the various privately managed productive enterprises. In governmental malpractice involving misuse of funds, it is at least customary when guilt has been established to remove culprits from office. In business life, however, the prevailing practice seems to be the reverse, namely, advancement in office providing the activities in question can be shown to have contributed to profits.

The depression has ushered in another phenomenon unfamiliar and startling to earnest defenders of traditional economic life in America. The classic theory maintained that troubled times or rifts in the even run of prosperity were due either to

[3] S. Chase, "The Luxury of Integrity," *Harper's Magazine*, CLXI, Aug. 1930, 336-44.

unexplainable acts of God or to the fact that there was not sufficient understanding of basic economic principles among the people. The only thing to be done about hard times was to endure them grimly, learn a little more thoroughly the lessons of self-interest, thrift, and competition for profit, and then wait for the sun of prosperity to shine forth in greater glory than ever. It was unnecessary usually for public agencies or government to make provisions for those people who suffered to the point of actual want. That recourse was painted as un-American; the American way was for those who had more than enough to share generously with those who had less than enough. This type of charity was possible in days when town life was such that everybody knew everyone else and actual misery could not be easily concealed from view. Today, because of the large centers of population and the consequent impersonalization of life, private relief has had to be organized on a large scale and administered in a Big Business way. Everyone with a surplus or a job has been called upon to contribute until it hurt, and in many cases employers, public and private, have taken measures to assure the concurrence of their employees in this laudable, charitable endeavor. It was, however, evident very early in the present emergency that private charity was not enough to allay distress among the populace, and huge doles were forced out of municipal and state treasuries, so that the bankruptcy of local governments has become a fairly common contemporary phenomenon. The power of the Hoover administration was almost universally used in promotion of the raising of relief funds from private sources, and little or no account was taken of the obvious failure of this policy in practice to yield adequate relief. What the new administration can do remains to be seen, but it seems probable that the theory of public relief by private bounty will be pushed aside as irrelevant to the actual situation.

More and more attention is being given in public discussion to the mounting inequalities in the distribution of the national wealth. These inequalities have resulted from the way American industry has been managed in the past. Social theorists are doubting the supreme wisdom of a system which brings such small returns to the great masses of people and such large returns to comparatively few people at the top. In 1928 and 1929, for instance, of the national income of about ninety billion dollars only slightly more than half went to forty-seven million workers, whereas the remainder went to one million substantial owners of property. Always in the past the class struggle in America could be referred to in a figurative sense only, such facts as these point in the direction of grim literalness.

It is only in modern days that the real irksomeness of labor has become apparent among large masses of workers. Technological improvements and inventions leading to extensive use of intricate machinery and of mass production methods have increased specialization to the point where the effects of monotony have completely reversed the normal curve of individual productivity as measured by industrial psychologists. The reflex effect of monotonous labor upon social activities during leisure hours has already given deep cause for concern to moralists and social commentators of an ethical turn of mind. When this factor of labor which is dominantly monotonous is coupled with the insecurity of employment, to which under modern American conditions even skilled workers in all fields, including the professions, are subject, further evidence of an inevitable trend toward far-reaching economic readjustments in the future is suggested.

The lobby which Big Business has been maintaining at Washington for a long time past (the activities of which among our legislators have caused the defeat of much industrially regulatory legislation during the past several decades) no longer possesses a clear monopoly of the lobbying field. Its methods have been amply copied by all sorts of organizations interested in various particular pieces of legislation. By the very pressure of different interests represented in the lobbying activities of today Congress cannot give the same type of undivided attention to purely business needs and desires as in the past. The successful pressure by veterans' organizations on behalf of unprecedented doles from the public treasury for ex-soldiers was an extremely complicating factor in the lives of representatives of the Big Business lobby. The People's Lobby although its activities have barely begun, has succeeded in keeping unsavory facts about the business world before the eyes of Congress and before large sections of the public. It represents another sharp thorn in the sides of the business régime. How unfortunate for the business powers that techniques and policies of lobbying worked out and refined through long experience should so easily accrue to the benefit of irrelevant and opposed interests!

The full effects of the disappearance of the frontier on American life and institutions have not worked themselves out in the brief period since the early nineties. There have been complicating factors such as the completing of an industrial structure more than adequate to the economic necessities and demands of the population, the emergence of the American imperial state after the Spanish-American War, the closing of the Open Door to foreign immigration, American participation in the World War, and the speculative orgasm of the nineteen-twenties— to mention only a few major ones. But it is an interesting speculation to wonder now that the frontier is no more, what avenues of expression the increasing number of malcontents among the population will take in the future. Political radicalism has not so far been popular, for the only apparent effect of the close approach in policy and outlook of the two historical parties to each other, and the consequent lack of any clear issues over which real political battle might be drawn, has been widespread lack of interest in the use of the ballot. The Socialist Party, which has been the only significant opposition force in American political life in the recent past, despite marked lessening in doctrinal rigidity, has not shown any steady increase in vote-getting powers. The Communist Party is profiting considerably in some highly industrialized sections of the country by virtue of the depression, and also by virtue of a number of unduly repressive tendencies on the part of the courts, such as the Sacco-Vanzetti case in Massachusetts, the Mooney case in California, the Scottsboro case in Alabama, and the case of the soft coal miners in Kentucky and Tennessee. Organized labor has been both conservative and non-political in tendency, and in recent years it has suffered a heavy decline in membership. Attempts at crystallizing these and other centers of thinking more or less opposed to the established order have been proverbially unsuccessful in the past, and the more liberal or radical members of the Democratic and Republican parties have so far preferred to remain aloof from such efforts. However, if present tendencies in social life continue their undirected movement a new frontier may be created in politics by a realignment of forces along clearly drawn radical-reactionary lines.

The influence which may prove most effective in promoting the demise of private business as the dominant force in American economic life is the modern racketeer. His activities are constantly in the spotlight of public attention, and the logic upon which he pursues them is the logic of competitive business. He carries the main principles of the business life to their logical extreme and demonstrates their essential absurdity. Like the business man he is interested in gain, and like the business man he believes in doing the least to get the most, in buying cheap and selling dear. Like the business man he believes in attaining a monopoly by cornering the market whenever possible. The chief difference between the racketeer and the business man is that the business man's pursuits have about them an air of respectability given by customary usage and established law. He may pursue them in the open, advertise them in the public press and over the radio, whereas the racketeer must work under cover. There is a little more chance in the business man's activities, because he is never sure despite much advertising chicanery that the particular commodity which he markets will continue to be in public demand. The racketeer is never in doubt on this score, for he corners human life itself when necessary to exact his tribute. It is not in the evidence that the methods of racketeers are any more brutal than those of our lauded business men, financiers, and captains of industry. Is it more brutal to smash up a barber shop and shoot the proprietor because he refused to pay for "protection" than to extract constant tribute in the form of profit from millions of workers receiving less than a proper living wage? Who but the marketer of small arms, ammunition, and sub-machine guns supplies the racketeer with his equipment? Who lobbies against legislation which would stringently limit or abolish altogether public sale of firearms? Under an economic régime based upon the profit motive, as our business system unquestionably is, it is simply impossible to draw a hard and fast line between those who prey legitimately and those who prey illegitimately upon the public. The sensational methods of the racketeer seem liable not to stimulate the forces of public law and order to adequate action, for that already has been proved virtually impossible; rather, they seem destined to awaken a public conscience which will not be satisfied until all phases of economic life are socially controlled in the interest of all.

It has been the intent of this discussion to call attention to certain fairly obvious factors in American social life which are damaging the inherited economic system controlled by private interests and operated for the sake of private gain. The present unfortunate business and financial crisis only too easily gives rise to prophecies of doom, and there is no desire here to add to such a stock. Business may quickly recover and bring once more a modicum of prosperity, but it seems a patent fact that the old days of laissez faire are definitely gone, and that sooner or later there must develop through the forces generated by industrialism itself a broader public recognition of this fact with consequent adequate public action.

III. THE BEGINNINGS OF CULTURAL DISTINCTION AND INDEPENDENCE IN AMERICA

It was not to be expected that a people engaged in the tasks of founding a republic by means of revolution and then building up the new nation to the first rank in size, equipment, and influence, and enduring a civil war in the process, should have made any great contributions to culture in the finer sense. America in the past has made few such contributions. Her cultural life has been necessarily scanty, and what little nurture the higher spirit of man demanded was easily supplied by cultural importations from abroad. It is also no great cause for wonder that when a polyglot population found itself burdened with increased leisure and at the same time possessed of a great array of stimulating, time-passing nick-nacks from cross-word puzzles to automobiles and aeroplanes, there should follow a period of recreational frenzy such as the world has never before seen. To judge, as some have, that America is undergoing the beginnings of an inevitable cultural decline is to lack appreciation of the stupendous material task that has been wrought in the comparatively brief period of its status as a nation, and it is to be blind to those stirrings of creative genius in various fields which have already demonstrated their significance.

It is a commonplace that schools were founded for the purpose of inculcating the elements of Christian truth and morality among the young, and that colleges were established as training grounds for the Christian ministry. As the people turned more energetically and more seriously to the business of material success on the continent, the dominantly religious purposes of our educational institutions gradually subsided. They remained in the background, however, and operated to prevent any open violations of the tradition. Teachers had to profess Christianity before being hired, and community elders watched over their out-of-school activities with a severely circumspect eye. The colleges and academies, while gradually widening the scope of their studies throughout the nineteenth century, held fast to the aim of Christian indoctrination, and even in the growing state universities any instructor who was in the least degree sceptical of prevailing mores had a hard time of it. As late as 1892, when the new University of Chicago founded by John D. Rockefeller started to function, fourteen of the thirty faculty members were connected with theological work of one kind or another. This Christian tradition in harmonious and profitable alliance with the business régime based on classic economic principles of individualism and laissez faire, gave America during the nineteenth century such a rigid cultural crust that the tiny flame of indigenous intellectual or artistic creative freedom could scarcely be kept burning at all. As is well known, geniuses like Poe and Melville received their first acclamations from abroad. As late as the nineties and the early years of the present century the difficulties of such an accomplished political economist as the late Thorstein Veblen in finding congenial employment among our universities bear eloquent testimony to the strength and permanency of this cultural incrustation.

However, the free thinking of Jefferson, the agnosticism of Paine, the artistry of Poe, Melville, Whitman, and Emerson, the signs of native genius in painting, sculpture, and architecture, the philosophic formulations of Peirce and James, the ringing economic dissents of George, Bellamy, and Veblen have attained the respectability of earnest cultivation in the minds of increasing numbers of Americans. The genteel tradition in American culture, in which the Christian-Business alliance was such a large factor, has definitely ceased even to call vigorously for a return to the old solidarity in which values seemed so stable and ideals so permanent.

A spreading, sprawling educational system in which fifty-two per cent of the adolescents of the nation are already in the secondary school, and in which intricately varied programs are offered, cannot be kept within the neat bounds of any traditional formulations. Under modern conditions and especially in large urban communities no kind of supervision can be successfully exercised over the leisure-time activities of school teachers. With new psychologies and philosophies breaking into the professional schools of education in the universities and into the lower teacher-training institutions, confusion reigns supreme at the very heart of public education. Teachers in elementary and secondary schools are torn between following a prescribed course of study, itself somewhat removed from the tradition of *status quo* apologetics, and the desire to do something really vital. The greater freedom and the wider social participation in the Progressive schools, along with movements like the Parent-Teacher Association, are influences which have perceptibly modified the rigidity of the public schools. Constructive forces from inside the system of schools such as higher standards of teacher qualification, the beginnings of the serious application of science to education, the inclusion of vocational and aesthetic activities in the curriculum, and personnel guidance work, have also contributed to the increasing sophistication which pupils bring from the schools. Out of the hordes of youth crowding into the colleges and universities today a larger and larger proportion of the intellectually and artistically talented is being selected and directed into channels of independent creative endeavor, while the great majority, for whom as yet such a happy culmination is impossible, are nevertheless forever rendered immune from shouting the glories of traditional institutions. Although during the war there was in university circles, as elsewhere, some recrudescence of an intolerance of intellectual activities and opinions out of harmony with accepted attitudes, the battle for freedom to pursue any line of research whatever and to hold opinions of whatever nature has been very largely won. Organizations like the American Association of University Professors, The Teachers' Union, the American Civil Liberties Union, and the National Education Association have been strong stimulatory forces in the development of greater public tolerance towards teachers. In a Southern state recently, when the Governor proceeded to pack the State University with his own political adherents of questionable qualifications, activities of the professional standardizing agencies, of the American Association of University Professors, and of other associations of educators, forced him into a hasty and ignominious retreat. Policies of institutions denominationally founded seem to proceed in all directions almost regardless of the original fundamentally religious aims. And even the theological seminaries have on occasion been known to foster a social and religious radical. Professors of philosophy openly present such unvarnished truth as research has yielded upon the classic philosophers and imply intelligent scepticism towards every accepted value; professors of history and government frankly betray the facts about American history without bothering overmuch to idealize the acts of our great men and the beneficence of our inherited institutions; professors of economics hammer away, not altogether ineffectually, upon classic individualism and upon the sacredness of property. These free and vigorous intellects, along with their fellows in many other subject matter fields are, of course, in a decided minority among the profession as a whole, but that they are openly tolerated and thereby encouraged is a fact of great significance for the future of American culture.

The philanthropy of millionaires has led to the creation of great foundations for the promotion of research along various lines, and while the attractive scholarships or fellowships which are dangled before the eyes of interested and qualified scholars undoubtedly favor the development of research along certain lines with consequent neglect of other perhaps more important lines, the sum total of the efforts of these foundations is heavily positive. They guarantee that increasing numbers of men and women shall have had the experience of productive endeavor unmolested by the fear of economic insecurity. The many large donations to college endowment funds, and to permanent scholarship funds all over the land, have helped markedly to open college and university life to more and more deserving young people. Thus the unearned increments which are skimmed off productive industry to build great fortunes are in some small measure turned to a social use that breeds a type of mind in which the very thought of large private fortunes must become increasingly uncongenial.

In recent years college and university students in America have given signs of a self-conscious maturity and independence which in the past has been almost completely lacking. This displays itself in varied forms: in increasing discrimination in choice of courses to be taken; in more active and more sincere participation in class discussion; in campus discussions involving the content of courses studied as well as of current affairs; in clearly voiced opposition to military training in the college; in more critical and serious college newspapers and periodicals; in calling national student conferences upon the problems of youth; and in participation with organized associations outside the college upon significant constructive undertakings. This kind of thing is aided and abetted by the apparent inclination in administrative circles of higher education to experiment in some measure with the accepted curriculum. There is no higher institution of learning in the entire land but has been influenced in some degree by this tendency. Experiments range from reconstructions which reverse completely the setting and the program of college education as it has been known in this country, to slight alterations in individual courses, entrance requirements, or other administrative details. It may be that much of the impetus behind these changes has come from administrators rather than from teachers and students. Nevertheless, the thing which stands out is the fact that what proved adequate for so many generations is today openly recognized as inadequate. In practically all the reforms in process there is contemplated increasing degrees of student freedom and closer adaptation of administration and instruction to student needs and to the problem of student orientation in the changing modern world.

For many years associations of scholars within the several fields of modern learning have promoted coöperative and individual researches and investigations along scientific, literary, or philosophic lines. The sum total of these activities as found in the yearbooks and accredited journals in the various technical fields presents an imposing array of independent American scholarship. It has been unfortunate that inter-associational undertakings have not been more frequent, and that the tendency in the past has been to increase specialization and the formation of subsidiary associations to such a degree that proper cross-fertilization between the different fields of knowledge has not been possible. It is also unfortunate that the various scholarly associations have not until very recently been particularly sensitive to real problems in the social life of which their members are a part; and that so far there has been no great consciousness among scholars that any need exists to de-technicalize the fruits of scholarship for the benefit of the public at large.

These shortcomings, however, represent but future possibilities; the labor of erecting a machinery and technology of independent intellectual research has been, in the main, accomplished. Illustrative of the type of association referred to, are: The American Association for the Advancement of Science, The American Historical Association, The American Philosophical Society, The American Economics Association, The National

Education Association, The American Psychological Association, etc.

Extension and correspondence education is increasingly carried on under the auspices of large private and state universities. The chicanery that has been characteristic of many correspondence schools is definitely on the wane as the higher institutions of learning adapt themselves more generally to the cultural and vocational needs of adults. In some institutions, interesting types of local community cultural projects have been undertaken; many are beginning to carry on reading and instructional programs with their alumni. The work carried on under the Smith-Lever federal legislation is a fine example of highly secularized and yet dominantly cultural education based upon the expressed desires and the coöperation of adults in small local communities. The Adult Education movement as a planned associative endeavor has only just begun, but it has back of it leaders in many lines of endeavor, and it contemplates a program of broad and penetrating scope calculated to affect in positive constructive ways people all over the United States. Within what is customarily known as our public school system there are many other organized educational forces which have proved sensitive to the changing needs of the times.

Mention should be made of subsidization of scientific research by the Federal Government in its Bureau of Standards. Here a small society of scientists highly trained along specialized technological lines is at work upon the complex problems of pure science and of modern industry. These scientists work for comparatively petty salaries, and as a consequence the Bureau has been rudely preyed upon by Big Business, which by means of attractive financial offers to individual scientists of renown has been able to attract many to the technological laboratories of private industry. The Bureau has been much criticized in some circles for its relations with private business and also for its failure to meet the bewildering needs of the lay consumer of industrial products. But that its independent research should have obtained any foothold whatever under the watchful eyes of the business and financial oligarchy of the past is at least a starting point for future extension of its activities more concretely in the public interest.

Of late years another indication of the distinctiveness and quality of American intellectual effort has been the increasing flow of students from foreign countries to American colleges and universities. These students come in all sincerity to sit at the feet of American men and women famed all over the civilized world for their accomplishments in different fields of study. Formerly the movement was all in the other direction. American students who wished the finishing touches of a real education went to European universities. American students in large numbers still go to Europe for study, but they go for specific purposes and in the spirit of international good will and exchange, not out of an innocent and fawning reverence for European learning as such. International recognition of American creative activity is by no means confined to academic or scientific lines. That it has come mainly in these lines is true, however. This was to be expected from American concentration upon material triumphs. The list of American literary creations which have been translated into one or more foreign languages or republished in England would be a very long one indeed. American philosophy, American drama, American music, American painting and sculpture, American architecture, even American cooking—the American movie perhaps most of all—have their appreciative audiences in every civilized land. Nobel prizes have graced Americans in all five classifications of award. Although these foreign reverberations of our culture are nothing over which intelligent Americans will greatly thrill or have reason to feel superior, they are phenomena which have come largely out of the present chaotic age and are very certainly not evidences of national spiritual decline.

An analysis of the American mind, of democracy, and of the possibilities of American civilization was first clearly indicated in the eloquent discourses of Emerson and the anarchic and almost pagan singing of Walt Whitman. These inquiries into the American soul were extended gradually, chiefly by William James and John Dewey, into a rounded synthetic foundation for an American philosophy. Because this native philosophy incorporated into itself the method of modern science and because it accepted modern industrialism, it has been severely criticized by both the adherents of traditional cultural standards and by the self-styled proponents of new native artistic ventures as having surrendered completely to the insistent vagaries of a mechanical civilization. From other more appreciative sources it has been criticized chiefly for giving a decided over-weight to purely intellectual endeavor as opposed to aesthetic appreciation and artistic expression. Whatever may be said of it, however, this philosophic attitude variously termed pragmatic, experimental, or naturalistic, is universally conceded to be an indigenous product. The literature produced in its name is already substantial both in its critical and its constructive aspects. Its adequacy or inadequacy in the face of the many serious problems of American social life in the present and in the future awaits the verdict of a wider public examination than has yet been accorded to it.

The multiplication of such cultural influences as schools of all types, museums, art galleries, libraries, exhibits, expositions, conventions, and the like during the first three decades of the twentieth century has been an obvious stimulus to individual cultural growth among the American people. The rapid increase in the number and miscellaneousness of independent organized associations of the type of clubs and societies, religious sects, propagandist agencies, study and discussion groups, and self-styled research or fact-finding agencies in the public interest is indicative of active response to new opportunities for expression and coöperative effort. The drama has never come into its own as a powerful force in American cultural life and it now faces new obstacles in the movies and the radio. But genuine American drama built out of native lore is just beginning to appear; dramatic societies and Little Theater movements were never so alive and critical as they are today, while university study of the dramatic art is well established.

That there is no end to the making of books was never better illustrated than in contemporary America. Novels, poetry, short stories, essays, criticisms of life and letters, popular science, guides to the spiritual life and to parenthood, ancient and modern classics, biographies, treatises on philosophy and psychology, reports of travel, explanations and manuals on sex, not to mention technical monographs, textbooks, encyclopedias and book sets flow in unending procession from the press. Even the drug store, the tobacco store, and the corner grocery are aiding in the distribution of books at suitably low prices. One can only speculate upon what is happening to the circumspect little library of the average American home described in the *Middletown*[4] of a few years ago. That there is much trash, pornography, and pseudo-science in all this mass of literature goes without saying. Nevertheless, the volume of material printed bears testimony to powerful expressive and absorptive tendencies in social life. Censorship has been literally hooted down, and every further legal test results in a new burst of riotous literary creativity, or another resurrection of long-suppressed "classics." In the popular magazine field much the same expressive voluminousness and heterogeneity is found. The field for critical journals of opinion is still a very narrow one, but the nucleus of intelligent, informed, and liberal minds which feed upon them is a decided asset in these changing, precarious times. The marked alteration in content and format of well-established

[4] R. S. Lynd and H. M. Lynd, *Middletown* (New York: Harcourt, Brace & Co.), 1929.

monthly and quarterly journals is a significant phenomenon for art, literature, and opinion in America. The dominantly critical and analytic tone of articles published in these substantial periodicals contrasts strangely with the finesse, the prettiness, and the complacent smugness of articles in the same magazines a decade or two back. The native artistic vitality of their short stories and of their poetry is also in sharp contrast to what has been customarily published in the past.

The urban daily newspaper has become literally a popular home university library. This is not to ignore the fact that its miscellaneous content is seldom of high quality and is always acutely calculated to increase circulation figures so that merchants will spend more for advertising. The newspaper like every other business in America is operated on the profit motive, and it is to be expected that only policies that bring the desired return will be continued. Corporate organization has actually lessened the number of dailies in large cities, editorial differences are less prominent, political sympathies are often obscured; these are distinct losses over a former day. But these obvious faults are beside the main point. There *is* a daily newspaper market for reviews of serious books, for the comments of special editors of liberal sympathies, for quasi-literary columns, for special informative and interpretive articles from the domestic and the foreign scene, and for worth while syndicated material. There *are* schools of Journalism over the country in which technicians in newspaper work are being trained to higher standards than the old apprentice system in journalism could ever boast.

The radio in America has been allowed to gravitate to almost exclusive control by big business interests. It is viewed by them as a new and profitable vein of advertising revenue. The absurdities and banalities which such control and such a purpose have turned loose on millions of radio listeners almost beggar description. These are fundamental and obvious facts; only a blind optimist would deny, or dispute, or justify them. They call for swift and far-reaching reconstructive effort by the public. In the present state of public confusion, such efforts will probably not be immediately forthcoming. Let us look, however, at the positive and genuinely constructive aspects of radio. It has brought good music, even a small amount of the finest opera singing in the whole world, into all sorts of appreciative American homes. It has brought home to Americans generally swift news of national and international events, intelligent discussion of domestic and foreign affairs, a high standard of good English diction despite some peculiarities of announcing technique, the voices and the comments of famous as well as of somewhat notorious characters, a great deal of genuine amusement, fun, and helpful information. Especially noteworthy are the programs which were sponsored during the 1931-32 season by the National Advisory Council on Radio in Education. It seems a conservative prediction to say that such programs will grow in time allotment and scope of subject matter and in more general appreciation in the future. The special committees on psychology and economics (during the season referred to above) have brought into coöperative popular educational endeavor some of the foremost leaders in these fields. The challenge to say something significant in a forceful and understandable way seems to have been surprisingly well met on the first large-scale test. The economics series proved especially significant because the speakers focussed almost unabated attrition upon traditional and currently accepted economic principles and were in practically universal agreement upon the advisability of some sort of national social planning.

Any attempt to discuss forces in American life tending toward distinctive and significant cultural achievements must not omit some comment upon the prevailing state of mind found in ever increasing numbers of persons. Machine civilization has put an end to the simple unsophistication of our former lives.

We are harassed at every turn by innumerable distracting and disturbing influences. The even tenor of the old life when hard work was followed by short periods of easeful leisure has gone. Labor is no longer so hard and the lengthened periods of leisure are far from easeful. There are too few satisfactions to be derived from the old religion and only too truly we know not what to do nor whither to go. The occurrence of a major war only a little more than a decade ago, the oppressive insecurity of the armed peace which has followed, the more sinister nature and the spreading extent of modern crime, technological unemployment, and the depression are only a few of the matters that plague us. Against such ills mechanical playthings like the automobile, the aeroplane, the radio, the movies, and the thousand minor luxuries cast off by the machine afford little relief. Neither jazz music nor the plaintive classical alternative can soothe our troubled souls. Education makes us burn only the more with dissatisfaction. Many of us sentimentally seek a return to the old cultural solidarity which in retrospect seems really to have had a touch of genuine beauty. More of us manage somehow to lose ourselves in hobbies, sports, religion, literature, art, esoteric sects, or even in politics. Most of us, however, live merely from day to day, snatching what peace and joy we can from the steady attrition of events. The pervading restlessness and untempered sophistication characteristic of the American soul of today may be the sign of a hastening decay, but as one gains in perspective it seems more likely to be a gathering matrix out of which centers for a new and more democratic cultural solidarity may grow.

A great many more influences making for creative distinction and independence in the contemporary scene would deserve discussion if an adequate inventory were attempted. There can be no guarantee that the comparatively small total to date of original native works and of opportunities among the people at large for independent creative effort will grow. The point of this discussion is simply to insist that a beginning has been made and that the odds against future efforts to build a culture equal to American opportunities are not overwhelming.

IV. RESOURCES FOR FUTURE SOCIAL RECONSTRUCTION

America during the nineteenth century, in the minds of the great majority of its citizens, did display genuine cultural solidarity. The American outlook was that of patriotism, business, and Christianity. No one knows what has happened to genuine, deep-seated patriotism. "One hundred percentism" was but recently in our midst, to be sure, but one cannot help feeling that all the blatant shouting in its name was a sign of a somewhat troubled heart. It is exceedingly doubtful whether American business, after the present crisis, can recover the former splendor of its rugged privacy and profit-seeking. Those things seem to have been in some measure on the wane since 1890 anyway. And the Christian religion, though many of its traditional tenets remain in the background of our mentality, has ceased to be of significant public influence. For large part, the churches cultivate only a small corner of the average citizen's soul and seem to have almost no hold on the younger generation. Intellectual and artistic freedom from the old cultural complex is attained in increasing degrees, but American life as a whole seems to be in a very confused state. If it is to move toward new centers of cultural integration, what resources are there at hand?

One is reminded of classic Greece, of imperial Rome, of Florence during the Renaissance when one looks at the stock of available materials in modern civilization. Those older distinctive civilizations were built up when the spirit of man in conscious assertion moved forward to new construction. They were preceded by cosmopolitanism, confusion, unhappiness, and the bursting asunder of inherited traditions and customs. Their brief splendor and eminence was due to the way in which use was made of the available elements of all cultures with which various contacts had been made. The reverence which the Greeks, the Romans, and the Florentines had for former civilizations was demonstrated in the adaptations which each of these civilizations made to its own time and place, and not in meek deference or blind imitation. What are the conditions which face the modern American today? The anthropologists tell us that physically we have built a new race. What has that race to work with? Never in history did such a spectacle confront man! Culture upon culture opens up its unending array of treasures; knowledge about the past is seemingly inexhaustible and ready at our elbow. All the great intellectual achievements, all the great art, all the great literatures, all the great religions open at our touch and display in amazing truthfulness the details about great geniuses and about great nations. Dare we also leave aside deference and imitation and construct something to our native taste and genius out of the richness of a past which modern scholarship has revealed?

Science and technology has bound the world into a single great society. The marvels of modern transportation and communication literally make neighbors for us at the ends of the earth. Our diet, our industry, and many of the cultural products which we enjoy are already international. Our machines make possible the provision of organic needs, cultural necessities, and luxuries in abundance for all. The Malthusian law of population becomes a faded specter before the influences of social selection as exercised in use of contraceptives and in other equally effective ways. Determinism of any variety cannot stand the glare of modern Russia. Universal education has already been worked out among the American people with some degree of effectiveness. The beginnings of native creativity along many lines are even now apparent. A democratic tradition affords some sense of direction. And we stand confused! Perhaps the vision is too dazzling and American men and women will shut out part of it to satisfy themselves with smaller benefits and a shorter destiny. That remains to be seen. First let us be certain that all may view and have the chance reflectively to contemplate the possibilities which lie before.

Something like contemplation of great possibilities for man in the future was quite widely entertained during the period of the Eighteenth Century Enlightenment. It is in fact a fairly unforced imaginative project when human beings wax optimistic and prophetic over new instruments of control. Science has been on the human scene for a few hundred years however, and nothing very remarkable has happened. Certainly modern America is far removed from any semblance of Utopia despite the fact that technology has reached its greatest fulfillment there. And democracy has had a ragged appearance since the war settlements. Political internationalism is now under a dark cloud. All these things are true and many more like them. They deservedly fill the modern generation with the tragic sense of life, and cause many serious minds to wonder whether progress is not some will-o'-the-wisp after all. Is the fundamental situation any different today from former times? The problem is to master the materials of our own and of other cultures. Is it an affair of intellect alone? Was it ever? Did Greece ask such a question, or Thirteenth-century Europe? Or did either conceive its triumphs in advance and bring them into being by means of concerted action? To ask such questions is to answer them. The golden moments of history, the records of which constitute what we are wont to refer to as "classics," occurred out of fortuitous concatenations of circumstances among men and women of virile stock. The instinct of workmanship, perennial in humankind, functioned to produce noble works by means of individuals who happened to be situated so that they could make the best of their opportunities. It is with conditions basic to human cultural expression that modern man in some small degree, has learned to operate. That powerful intellectual tool, modern scientific method, bears within it techniques capable of mastering always larger portions of the earth's surface. So much has been already proved to the satisfaction of even the most profound critics of science. The basic environmental conditions which led to the few short historic moments of brilliant human achievement occurred by chance. *These conditions can now be analyzed and created at will by man.* Man's efforts at such creation in the few short generations following the perfection of science and technology have been complicated, however, by a host of unfortunate contingencies. Nothing in inherited ideals or modes of thought contemplated any such extensive power in the hands of man; the authority of tradition forced scientific endeavor at first into areas of life where it would supposedly be harmless and later, as daring increased, it was pressed into the service of especially privileged classes in society. Today, as Russia has discovered, science will equally well do the bidding of the common man. The increasing consciousness of this discovery *is* something new under the sun, and though it be probable that tragedy and frustration are never absent from the human scene, they need not in such full measure come out of the prostitution of science!

A tempered sense of the possibilities of man emerges. He will not soon again be free to dream as wildly as some sons of the Enlightenment have done. The difficulties of implementing democracy are enough to occupy his capacities and his energies for a long time to come. Mayhap as modern man bends his efforts to this task, drawing in full measure upon all his resources in good Greek or Medieval fashion, the finer and more characteristic products of human civilization will appear in even greater abundance than the Golden Ages of the past could show.

V. Bearings of the Contemporary Social Background upon Organized Education

What has the preceding cursory sketch of some aspects of the American scene to do with teachers and with the problem of public education in the United States today? That, of course, all depends upon how education is viewed. In the past, American society has been largely content to let the schools function as a kind of aside to life, necessary to be sure, but irrelevant to the sweep of larger affairs. And the schools themselves have been in the main content with such a rôle. Schoolkeeping has matured from an avenue into other occupations to a profession in its own right. The American faith in providing for youth, together with years of unparalleled business prosperity, has led to such a growth in school machinery and equipment that professional educators are now managing or mismanaging a veritable cultural giant. The figures in the Biennial Survey of Education for 1927-28[5] show that out of nearly thirty million persons who enrolled in all types of schools from the kindergarten to the university, twenty-three and a half million were in kindergarten or elementary grades, over four million in secondary schools, and over a million in higher institutions of learning of all types. This horde of modern youth is taught by somewhat more than a million teachers and housed upon property estimated in 1930 to be worth over seven billions of dollars. The total cost of education for the year 1930 was nearly three billions of dollars. In 1927-28 about two hundred seventy-five thousand students were enrolled in normal schools and teachers' colleges, and more than five hundred thousand students in all were pursuing teacher training courses.

A direct cultural agency of such proportions deserves careful study and clarity of aim and purpose if it is to lead to significant achievements. During the first three decades of this twentieth century, a vast educational literature has been produced, the beginnings of a science of education developed, and the whole traditional philosophy and psychology of education called into question. As a consequence largely of the latter phenomenon confusion in both practice and theory prevails today throughout the educational system.

[5] U. S. Office of Education, Washington, D.C.

The possibilities of education loom larger than ever before because of a cumulating tested stock of knowledge about human nature and about social institutions. Education in the widest sense, including all the influences shaping human nature, is the very lifeblood of modern civilized society. Organized education, properly conscious of itself as the integrative agent of all socially educative forces, holds the key to social stability, social decay, or social progress. Exceedingly few of our million teachers seem to be vitally conscious of this primal fact. Most of them ply their trade more after the fashion of the modern machine tender than like creative artists in human nature. They do this because of the heavy weight of past traditions and because of modern administrative systematization of educational organization and of instruction. These two influences work hand in hand to dominate the outlook and the functions of teachers in a very effective way.

In institutions for teacher education increasingly highly selected young people are brought into contact with a number of differing, often conflicting school practices and theories about education. It is to be gravely doubted whether much is being done to explore the more general social theories or philosophic points of view which lie back of these same practices and theories. It is much to be doubted also whether our present institutions for the preparation of teachers give any serious attention to problems of personal integration and outlook among students, so that almost universally initiates into the teaching profession have little insight into fundamental problems of life in American civilization.

In the following two sections of this volume, the author analyzes and discusses the views of seventeen present-day leaders in American education. The brief survey of some aspects of the contemporary social scene in America, which has been attempted in the foregoing pages, provides a background of conviction against which the thinking of contemporary educational theorists may be cast.

ANALYSIS OF THE VIEWPOINTS OF AMERICAN EDUCATORS

ANALYSIS OF THE VIEWPOINTS OF
AMERICAN EDUCATORS

PREFATORY NOTE

C LASSIFICATION of men and of ideas is a dangerous enterprise. Men and ideas are what they are and should be
valued in and for themselves. Classification obscures individual variability which always must remain the basic fact.
Classification is itself the effort of an individual working under
the influence of certain ideas.

The reader is therefore forewarned about the classification of
contemporary educational philosophers, reformers, and theorists
made in Section Two of this study. He is urged in his own
thinking to attempt a classification more adequate or at least
a clear way of looking at the views of the men here under study.
The classification used here seems objective and valid enough
for the general purposes of the author because he deeply appreciates the individualistic variety and richness of the thinking
of the men themselves. He will not hesitate in the future to let
his thinking about these men evolve with his further interpretations of what they shall continue to write. Their views are presented, it is hoped, as accurately and as clearly as possible. No
attempt has been made in writing the individual accounts to fit
the classification which has been used. The accounts were written
from extended lists of quotations gathered under the following
five headings:

1. General Viewpoint and Its Relation to Education
2. Nature of Practical Proposals
3. Estimate of Current Educational Practice
4. The Nature of Learning
5. Reactions to Other Points of View

It is believed that each man's thinking has been shown to be consistent enough under these various headings for classificatory purposes. The classification was, however, hit upon afterward. It need not be added that the classification into Tradition, Science, and Philosophy involves no invidious distinctions of any kind and no mere glorifying of one group rather than another. The variety of thinking in American educational circles as in American life generally is regarded as a sign of vitality and of conscious search for ideals adequate to a new age.

Tradition is the record of man's accomplishments and when he ceases to use it consciously he moves back to the primitive. Science is the precious tool by means of which man has attained a grip upon himself and upon his world—for him to scoff at it is the cult of futility. And philosophy, age-old urge to see things in truer and more meaningful relationships, is man's opportunity to mold into a dynamic synthesis his inheritance from the past and his techniques for creating out of the present a more desirable future.

I. Educators Stressing Values Inherent in American Historic Traditions

The men whose points of view are presented in Part One vary in the emphasis which they place upon traditional values. They seem, however, in one way or another, to indicate that the values embodied in American historic traditions are preferable to values derived either from modern science or from what in this study is called modern naturalistic philosophy. The particular order in which the men are presented indicates what seems like a progressively decreasing stress upon the values of the past.

HERMAN H. HORNE

General Viewpoint and Its Relation to Education.—In Herman H. Horne a stanch transcendental Christian faith estimates the modern world, defines its major problems, and constructs a philosophy combining what he sees as the best of the past with the best of the present. He is convinced that this type of enlightened traditional Idealism is capable of guiding a troubled America into a new and better ordering of affairs. In this philosophy God is the prime center of reference. Jesus Christ is the symbol of the kind of life a pious man may strive after and the assurance of God's benevolent attitude toward man. An ultimate Christian Utopia is present in God's vision, and man's conscious efforts towards the eventual realization of this Utopia here upon the earth guarantee his attainment of the ultimate goal of life, Immortality. In the course of his endeavors man discovers truths about the universe and about himself, and thus enters into the mind of God where everything is already clearly written out. Science is this process of effortful discovery of pre-existing truth, and philosophy is the divine privilege of contemplating the incomprehensible. The social institutions under which we live, the home, the school, the business world, the state, and the church, are based each upon a divine idea and serve to guide us towards the inherent ideal possibilities of our personal natures. Through them have developed the moral ideals of the race and through them all future changes may be safely regulated within the bounds of ideal sanction. Capitalism, modified to remove its present obvious deficiencies, seems written in the course of events. Democracy as an ideal for humanity seems a kind of earthly projection of the Kingdom of Heaven. Education is the process whereby we become adjusted inwardly and outwardly to the vast universe about us—from nature through our fellow beings and ourselves to God. The processes of change, growth, and development, through which we attain this adjustment, take place against a stable background of inherited culture, social institutions, moral ideals, and organized subject matter, all of which in essence are Absolute. The school working more consciously but, nevertheless, supplementarily to other institutions organizes itself under the guise of this Idealistic viewpoint to make clearly evident in all men its implications.

Nature of Practical Proposals.—Horne comprehends the nature and meaning of things in general and is satisfied that the Idealistic outlook is inclusive of all the factors of life and in harmony with the nature of man. His practical thought about education seems fully in line with the accepted first principles. Given an authoritative tradition the realization of whose implications is dependent upon man's understanding and coöperation, education becomes primarily a transmission of this tradition. Self-realization is fully attained only in and by means of the Christian tradition as it works itself through the *status quo* to a contemplated ultimate Utopia. The ends thus set in philosophic speculation, it becomes incumbent upon educational scientists to assay the resources in knowledge and techniques and to arrange a curriculum best fitted to their realization. In substance this amounts to a hierarchy of organized subjects or bodies of knowledge and a set of general guiding principles. Broad culture, deep appreciations, social efficiency, and high character are important aspects of personal adjustment to God, so that the apparent bareness of the educational formula is fully in accordance with richness of content. The content and the method of education are evaluated entirely in terms of whether they lead to the realization of pre-conceived individual and social ends and therefore have only incidental intrinsic worth. The teacher is conceived of as a sternly sympathetic traveling companion pointing out the highways and byways which must be explored along the journey to the transcendent final adjustment.

Estimate of Current Educational Practice.—From his Christian idealistic vantage point Horne must needs decry modern materialism as it gets itself expressed in the schools. The cult of success, the appeal of vocations technologically conditioned, the increasing secularity in our schools, are all tending to reinforce American society and culture where it least needs reinforcing. The new philosophy behind the Progressive Movement in education, he feels, has not penetrated deeply into the consciousness of teachers despite an apparently widespread glibness of verbal acceptance. On the whole, Horne has little to say regarding the actual practices of the schools beyond pointing out that in general progress is evident.

The Nature of Learning.—Horne maintains an epochal developmental psychology. This consists in an analysis of the growth of mental life into a series of steps from the sensation and movement of infancy through the development of imagination and memory and relational thinking in youth to the philosophical thinking of adults. Accordingly free play is the method which best aids development in kindergartners. This should be followed by increasing emphasis on the work attitude as the school takes over the serious undertaking of training children in right thinking and right habits of action by means of a systematically organized curriculum. Since the center of education lies in preconceived ends, the process takes on an artificial character and a virtue is made of the necessity of external discipline. The good teacher will temper this discipline by tactfulness, artistry, and contagion of personality. Eventually, it is assumed, the content of education and culture will take on interest of its own account, as the individual begins to see the transcendent vision of the meliorative trend in the course of events and emerges into the true freedom that is tempered by self-control. The modern emphasis upon activities and upon the appeal to the intrinsic interest of children is recognized as a positive supplementary aid in realizing the primary aim of education.

Reactions to Other Points of View.—Just as Horne sees clearly the vision of his own ultimate philosophy and consistently adheres to it in discussing the problems of education, he also clearly discerns the nature and meaning of another philosophy whose triumph would result in the passing of the authoritative Christian tradition and the Idealistic analysis. He is so much concerned about the point of view represented by John Dewey that in his latest book he has attempted to indicate that his own philosophy includes, within its wider scope, all that is worth while in Dewey's naturalistic emphasis. He has found neither God, the Christian tradition, nor the realm of Pure Ideas in Dewey. He misses pure philosophy in the speculative realm and the concepts of duty and conscience in the practical realm. He sympathizes with much of Dewey's trenchant criticisms of the present social order, but misses constructive remote goals toward which present reform may be directed. He feels that Dewey's philosophy is heavily loaded on the scientific side to the neglect of the aesthetic side of life. Naturalism to Horne is a pure assumption and an inadequate one in that it denies the natural interest of men in what transcends experience. The full adoption of the philosophy of naturalism by the schools Horne would regard as a misfortune. It would mean the neglect of great areas of the social inheritance, the loss of any criterion of valuation as between different subject matters, the domination of education by the experimental attitude of problem-solving, the depersonalizing of teaching, and the introduction of soft pedagogy on a grand scale.

HENRY C. MORRISON

General Viewpoint and Its Relation to Education.—The social change and civilizational movement which Henry C. Morrison recognizes has shown definite progress. In personality development man has expanded tremendously, essentially because of the broadening scope of civilized social institutions and technological advances. Morrison would deny that in the course of the last hundred years any changes have occurred in science or in general outlook which markedly alter the direction of man's thinking. There has been a gradual extension along all lines of thought, but the *fundamentals* have always and will always remain the same. True at present generalized lay thinking lags behind the scientific, political, and economic advances which followed in the wake of the Industrial Revolution. This but denotes the problem for contemporary educational statesmanship. The long ages of man's climb to civilization have witnessed many types of social experimentation of which the best in institutions and in moral standards and ideals has come down to us. The truly civilized and cultured person, nurtured on these inheritances, is, in essence, the same everywhere and at all times. Capitalistic economy is one of these inheritances, and Morrison finds in it the seeds of a social order in which everyone may be a capitalist, and in which prosperity may continue forever. At this point the universal school enters the picture. The fruits of the Industrial Revolution and of modern technological development have ripened to the point where, under proper management, the common man may share them. Youth has been released from the necessities of productive labor to attend school, and age, likewise released, may search out the benefits of retirement. The financial basis of modern schooling in our economic régime is sound and holds the possibilities of even greater development provided that professional school men meet the challenge of systematically transmitting thrift and refinement to the masses. The aim of the school is the initiating of individual pupils into the richness of our physical, social, and spiritual inheritance. The production of a citizenry so initiated would guarantee intelligent choice of leaders and thoughtful followership by the public. It is the task of a science of education.

Nature of Practical Proposals.—Morrison is clear as to the educational machinery necessary, under modern conditions, to fulfill adequately his general educational objective. The program of education must be conceived as a whole and must possess unity throughout its various parts. The lowest level, consisting of the kindergarten and primary grades, is oriented towards the equipment of its pupils with the essential working tools of further education, the three R's plus social adaptation to school conditions. The next level, the secondary school, represents the main business of providing an education, for during its years the most essential content of culture is transmitted and habits of independent study, choice, and taste are built up by means of a closely supervised study-teaching program. The product of the secondary school so conceived is considered to be an *educated* person. Should this person attend the university, he would do so as a free agent independently pursuing advanced intellectual purposes.

For the learning units, which in Morrison's thinking take the place of lessons in school subjects, a careful sifting of the whole cultural inheritance in its various aspects is suggested. In view of the fact that secondary education will complete the education of most people, only such units shall be retained on that level, as will demonstrably, when mastered, result in the desired thrifty and refined citizen. Morrison suggests a classification of these external things-to-be-learned into various types according to applicable teaching techniques, as, for instance, the science type, the appreciation type, the practical-arts type, and the pure-practice type. It is the function of every officer of the educational organization to look upon himself as a teacher interested primarily in producing educated human beings. All other interests are subsidiary to that. The special function of the classroom teacher is to study ways and means of presenting his subject matter to the particular groups under his charge. In place of the grade-promotion plan of advancement Morrison suggests his mastery formula, namely, *pre-test, teach, test, adapt teaching procedure, teach, test, etc.*, until learning and the sought-for personality change has been irrefutably demonstrated. In the course of experimentation towards the educational end proposed, all courses are to be properly organized and validated. Thus the beginnings of educational science are made manifest.

Estimate of Current Educational Practice.—Morrison believes that, instead of a great public-school system engaged in building citizens for our self-governing state, what we have had has been a series of private schools maintained at public expense. The height of this anarchic absurdity in schoolkeeping is reached, according to him, in the present movement for state-supported infant schools. There has been an obvious failure on the part of professional educators to meet the challenge of the authority and responsibility in school matters which the public has delegated to them. Administration has been too readily conceived in factory-management terms, to which, of course, the subject-grade promotion system easily lent itself. Our teaching force remains amateurish and casual, while children and youth of promising capacity graduate from our schools in an intellectually and culturally starved condition. The curriculum is crowded with material unteachable because of its lack of any significant connection with modern life. Our educational research so far has been engaged in statistically validating the various parts of a system of education which is thoroughly antiquated.

The Nature of Learning.—Morrison conceives of children as natively egoistic, and of normal educated adults as altruistic. He therefore counsels the destruction of native egoism as preliminary to building up normal altruism. The education of children should proceed from a beginning in complete dependence upon the teacher to a consummation, at the end of the period of schooling, in complete intellectual independence. As a warning against intelligence-test determinism, Morrison insists that learning capacity increasingly depends on what has been previously learned.

The objectives or eventual products of learning are those attitudes and abilities best suited to adapt the individual to modern life. The only final test of whether or not they are present in individuals is in the habitual reactions which individuals make in everyday life. As has been previously indicated these objectives are attained through the mastery of selected units of the cultural inheritance of the race. The way to such mastery is complex. Since learning is dependent upon an inner drive towards the particular adaptation represented by a teacher's subject matter, the first function of the teacher is to establish a proper motivation in the pupil. The pupil is thus saved both from adaptive inertia and misdirected curiosity. It is upon the basis of the immaturity of children and young people that courses are organized. As teaching proceeds, external motivation becomes less necessary because original purposes and intrinsic motivations develop in the pupils themselves. After establishing motivation for the mastery of a new subject matter unit, the teacher uses an exploratory test in order to obtain cues for the first real teaching exercise, namely, *presentation*. Presentation is an art which any intelligent teacher can acquire if he be but duly observant of the effects of his own efforts. It is essential that the concentrated attention of pupils be held continuously and that the presentation proceed only to the point where the responses of pupils indicate that they have caught the *drift*. Presentation is followed by a check-up test which furnishes the cues for reteaching. It is frequently necessary to reteach three times before proceeding to the supervised study exercise of *assimilation*. In assimilation it is the aim to have pupils immerse themselves so deeply in subject matter content that it becomes integral to their intellectual orientation. Assimilation is also followed by testing, which is understood always to be for diagnostic, and not for grading purposes. After assimilation the class meets for a teaching exercise called *organization* which takes place without access to books, notes, or charts, and in which individuality in composing the argument of the particular unit is encouraged. Finally, in *recitation*, the pupils reverse the original presentation of the teacher by themselves presenting the mastered unit to the teacher in the rôle of audience.

In units of the appreciational type the technique shifts to a somewhat different basis, since the aim is so to present the good, the beautiful, and the true that they become part of the pupil's stock of values.

To the possible remark that this analysis of learning involves constraint and repression of pupils Morrison replies that these are normal processes in civilization.

Reactions to Other Points of View.—Morrison holds it infinitely more constructive and worth while for professional educators to entrench themselves upon the present line of educational advance by sharper discrimination of policy than for them to attempt the formulation of far-reaching plans of educational reorganization. He is extremely critical of the many educational catch-phrases now in circulation. The slogan of making public education *as wide as life* seems to him representative of a peculiarly naïve logic. The view that educational motivation can be successfully based upon natural curiosity alone is to him a serious misapprehension, since the period of childhood is not as long as the history of the human race. Subject matter must be depended upon to furnish motivation, or else we drift to a soft pedagogy and a doctrine of self-indulgence in the place of discipline. To be sure, some Progressive schools achieve effects which appear startling, but closer examination usually discloses such effects as essentially noneducative. Morrison considers it ridiculous for pupils to discuss moral and ethical problems which even a philosopher might shun. The disparagement of obedience as a character builder he labels pure demagoguery. Homogeneous grouping of pupils on the basis of intelligence test results represents to him a repudiation of the very possibility of education.

WILLIAM C. BAGLEY

General Viewpoint and Its Relation to Education.—William C. Bagley suggests that we are facing one of the great turning points in social evolution. The unforeseen consequences of the progressive development of automatic machinery and of technology generally have brought on a serious crisis in our social life. Our fundamental moral controls seem to have lapsed in the face of material advance and the increasing mobility of our people. In the field of social philosophy there has been a strong and popular tendency to discount or deny older traditional standards. This has added confusion especially to educational machinery already taxed to the breaking point by the practical difficulties of realizing the universal school. We must return to fundamentals. In the face of mounting crime ratios, increasing divorce rates, prevalent intolerance, spreading materialism of outlook, the lack of great creative manifestations in our culture, and a narrow cult of Americanism, we cannot go on haphazardly. Light may be thrown upon our problem by European experience. In countries like France, Germany, and England where universal education under the disciplinary ideal has reinforced common cultural and moral standards, social development has continued in a positive direction. In countries like Italy and Russia where universal education was openly neglected there have been violent social cataclysms. It would seem, therefore, that the key to future stability and progress in our own country lies in making effective our program of universal education. The continuance of democracy depends on an *educational program* that recognizes and builds against degenerative tendencies, that raises the mass of people to a new level of enlightenment in a pervasive common culture, that meets the demands of modern industry for stepped-up intelligence, and that provides adequately for the increased leisure of modern life. In short, we must make our educational system the source of a rigorous mental and moral discipline for all. The realization of such an ideal Bagley sees as the next step in social evolution.

Nature of Practical Proposals.—Bagley calls upon educators to gain an understanding of social and economic factors in our life in order that their meaning for educational policy may be discerned. The social barometer registers the effect of the public schools, and it is the duty of the educator to balance the comparative freedom in which he operates with this larger social responsibility. Bagley calls for the thorough revision of contemporary educational ideals (which come very largely from what is known as the Progressive Movement), in the interest of the development of more virile ideals. He suggests as a compromise between hard materialism and soft sentimentalism the slogan "Through Discipline to Freedom." The main challenge which the schools of the nation must meet today is that of adequately planning the education of the masses. Bagley is definitely out of sympathy with the aristocratic tradition of concentrating on the production of leaders. He demands serious and patient labor at the task of making educational opportunities at all levels attractive and profitable. This means a certain degree of national uniformity in the grade placement of crucial subjects and topics, especially in the elementary curriculum. Only as all curriculum materials are integrated around such a central core of subjects can we hope to make progress towards the desired common culture. Standards of intellectual performance must be kept high enough to challenge real effort on the part of everyone. Bagley finds the heart of the educational process in the direct personal contact of the mind of the teacher with that of the pupil. Teaching is to him a fine art even more complex and difficult to practice adequately than that of the physician. He looks, therefore, to the progressive upgrading of the teacher-training institutions and particularly to the development within these institutions of teacher-scholars whose consummate art in teaching subject matter shall be contagious to students working under them. Bagley expects the teacher-training institutions by their manner of dealing with differing educational theories to act as stabilizing forces within the profession. He pleads for more general appreciation of the fact that there can be no "humble" posts in teaching, and he urges the breakdown of the invidious distinction between executive officers and teachers. As a safe mode of progress in education he suggests that only experienced teachers of proved stability shall try out new proposals. Educational research Bagley considers the basic method by which the organization and administration of the fundamental language and measuring arts is gradually refined and simplified.

Estimate of Current Educational Practice.—Bagley believes that our schools have had a considerable share in the attainment of present high levels of health, culture, and economic efficiency, but he does not think that the schools are keeping pace with developing disintegrative forces in our social life. These uncontrolled tendencies have forced the schools into a state of unstable equilibrium, so that there is widespread confusion among educators as to fundamental aims, educational programs are congested and inarticulate, and results are superficial. Public education seems to be between two fires, on the one hand that of a narrow and hard commercialism which would grant niggardly financial support, and on the other that of a mushy sentimentality which has no defense against the specter of social disintegration.

Within the profession Bagley is impressed by the influence wielded by that modern American phenomenon, the professor of education. While this influence potentially is of great significance, the effect up to the present time has been rather in adding confusion and faddism to educational theory. It has substantially hastened the acceptance, by teachers generally, of a mechanistic psychology and an opportunistic philosophy. It has given credence to the strange theory that education can be entirely based upon spontaneous impulses. The notion that the way to the freedom which education guarantees is through the constant practice of freedom by pupils has given rise to the many catch phrases used by the Progressive Movement. One prominent effect of a mechanized psychology may be seen in the prevalent emphasis in education upon the development of highly specialized abilities, rather than upon capacities for adaptation to the needs of modern life.

Specific weak points in the schools of today Bagley detects

in the movement away from comprehensive examinations on large units of subject matter, in the neglect of promotional examinations, in the introduction of elective programs, in the use of mass averages on objective tests as standards, and in the apparent substitution of an ingratiating charm on the teacher's part for a frank attempt to develop in pupils duty, self-control, and good workmanship. Due mainly to the propaganda of intelligence testers, Bagley finds the schools still catering to the superior child. Experimental schools, he points out, have been everything but experimental in the way they have developed and multiplied.

The Nature of Learning.—In accordance with his rejection of the mechanistic psychology, which tends to explain higher-order functions in terms of lower-order activities, Bagley calls for renewed vigor in pursuit of the disciplinary ideal. He accepts the biological continuum from the lower organisms up through man, and he makes of it the basis for the emergence of distinct qualitative levels of mental activity. These he specifies as: *specific conditioning,* universal in the lower animals but least important in man; *conceptual learning,* which governs intellectual generalization in man; and highest of all, *conscience,* the fundamental determinant of moral conduct in man. In Bagley's opinion mental evolution is not yet complete. He suggests that, if we are to educate adequately, a psychology is needed which formulates laws in terms of the type of mental act which is most significant, rather than a psychology which glibly assumes that laws developed for processes of specific conditioning apply with equal force to other mental processes. He suggests, significantly, that results from recent investigations in the field of brain-localization are likely to reopen the transfer of training controversy, which all too prematurely was assumed to be closed some years ago.

Bagley finds no reason for believing in the need of substantial revision of time-honored school procedures, involving external constraint of pupils who are mastering a carefully selected and arranged curriculum. He insists that freedom can be attained only by continued mastery of abstract processes and by constant broadening of the conceptual field. Externally imposed discipline is a necessary means to freedom.

Reactions to Other Points of View.—Bagley has attempted a formidable attack on those whom he calls determinists in education. These determinists followed in the wake of the more generalized use of intelligence tests. By emphasizing the intellectual limitations of the masses they have had the effect of casting a shadow across democratic hopes. Bagley feels that the determinists have openly disregarded the possibility of insuring social progress by environmental means.

While granting that the Progressive Movement has made some positive contributions, Bagley points out that its whole emphasis is definitely bad. At a time when social life called for stalwart ideals the Progressives have sanctioned looseness. Their notion that the changing conditions of social life call for a shift in educational policies is mistaken. It is pure prejudice which leads them to deny the value of disciplinary functions. In almost deifying the *felt needs* of the learner they have encouraged children to play at the work of education. While in theory they stress individual pupil effort, the effect in actual practice is to cause the teacher to shoulder the whole burden of education. Most serious is their denial of the efficacy of a systematic arrangement of the school curriculum and of school procedure. The much-touted lag between theory and practice which the Progressives decry, Bagley testifies to be altogether illusory. He claims, for instance, that what a professor of education preaches during a summer session is all too frequently attempted in practice when school opens.

Bagley is sympathetic to Morrison's concept of mastery and to Finney's insistence on fundamental disciplinary ideals.

ELLWOOD P. CUBBERLEY

General Viewpoint and Its Relation to Education.—Ellwood P. Cubberley places his ultimate faith in the Christian religion under whose tutelage our nation has derived its moral standards, framed its laws, and mounted steadily to material prosperity. In the changes and increasing complexities of modern society he sees danger to our earlier and fundamental religious, moral, social, political, and intellectual ideals. Our social progress may be definitely checked by the presence in our midst of so large a proportion of unassimilated immigrants. Our salvation depends on the public school system. Cubberley feels that the State must change its attitude towards public education from the position of a passive taxing agent, statistician, and legislator to that of an agency consciously active in the promotion of its own well-being. The financial basis for an extensive educational program is guaranteed in our economic structure, although up to the present the actual material resources have not been pooled in the interest of equalizing educational opportunity throughout the nation. Since education is primarily for the highest welfare of the State, the State must actually determine what the schools offer. The problem is essentially that of getting the masses of the population to see and to understand what the intellectual classes know. This means the reduction of the elements of modern life to simple terms, meet for a child's understanding. It means the training of youth for useful service in office, shop, and home, as well as for actual practice in the fundamentals of political life. With universal literacy, common usage of the English speech, thorough understanding of our institutions, and an inspired enthusiasm for our ideals by all, we will be well on the way towards the dreamed-for emergence of a great American race. The increasing insistence upon social efficiency as an aim has brought about a shift in educational emphasis from mere fact-learning to functional adjustments so that the actual processes of schooling today have become exceedingly complex.

Nature of Practical Proposals.—In matters of general school administration Cubberley points to business practice as a model. The qualifications of school board members (whose function is similar to that of the board of directors of a large corporation) are broad business experience, ability for action rather than for discussion, self-confidence, courage, and tact, practice in delegating the proper matters to qualified experts, and perseverance in following out policies determined upon. He adds that their efficiency would be greatly augmented by reading a standard text on school administration. The superintendent likewise should be compared to the president of a corporation in possessing wide powers, freedom of action, deep responsibilities, and the unqualified support of the Board of Education. The superintendent's point of view should give character and tone all along the line of school organization. His rôle is to think, plan, direct, and lead. Supervisory officers and principals execute his plans and follow and support his lead. The school principals outline methods of procedure for their teachers, opening for the more reliable ones wider liberties and avenues of experimentation. Teachers propose problems to pupils and give expert guidance in the actual solving of the problems proposed. This guidance function of the teacher is the heart of the whole educational process. Promotion of pupils to problems of the next grade should depend on the combined judgment of the principal and the teacher. The function of supervisors is, essentially, to keep the whole teaching body at a high level of morale and to break up lock-step tendencies so common in the routine of teaching. Cubberley feels that the full benefits of the teaching profession can be obtained only by keeping free from political agitation and discontent such as has been evident from time to time, especially among city elementary school teachers. He looks forward to a broader professional training of teachers in the future, one which will guarantee the development of significant permanent interests in teachers, and one which will make the teacher genuinely an applied scientist as well as an artist.

Cubberley lays great stress on the importance of the improvement of rural and village education. Accepting the state as the ultimate large administrative unit, he suggests a more widespread adoption of the county as the administrative center about which rural and village education should be organized. He finds in the advances made by the better urban communities the models for reorganization and redirection of rural and village education.

Education must be recognized today as an applied science based upon findings in more fundamental sciences. It is obvious that the school must be the center of community life and that such matters as differentiated instruction, flexible curricular requirements, and the adaptation of individuals to a changing social and industrial world should be taken for granted.

Estimate of Current Educational Practice.—In many of our states Cubberley notes the lack of any clearly conceived, constructive, educational policy which contemplates the changes made necessary by social developments now taking place. Administrators unfortunately are not the great community, state, and national leaders which in the future they must become. There has been advance along many lines. In curriculum content, despite the nominal similarity of the school subjects of today to those at the turn of the century, there has been a veritable revolution. Too little study, however, has been made of instructional results and not much effort has as yet gone into the intensive study of local educational needs and of general community problems in their educational bearings. Many of our teachers maintain outworn educational philosophies despite widespread acceptance of educational science. The prime tools in the scientific organization of instruction have been the intelligence and educational tests, the broader and more significant use of which has only just begun. We seem well on the way towards a national system of continuation school education, whose fruits in better and more satisfied workers cannot but enhance the national wealth and raise the level of citizenship. Our reform schools have reëducated and reformed from 65 per cent to 75 per cent of the wrongdoers committed to them.

The Nature of Learning.—Education is conceived somewhat after the model of industry. The schools are factories, the children are raw materials, and the specifications for manufacture are found in twentieth-century civilization. The rapid advance of educational research, especially the development of measuring techniques, guarantees the eventual standardization of teaching procedures in type and amount. Specialized school machinery and better teaching techniques are rapidly being developed. Cubberley would not have too much emphasis on fixed state courses of study, because subject matter content is not a matter of as great importance as the type of teacher or the actual conditions of instruction. The qualifications of a progressive teacher are: the ability to organize a subject independent of the text, the ability to keep the class interested and under control, the ability to ask the right questions in the right order, and the ability to guide the thinking of the class to the proper conclusions. Such a teacher will give children as much freedom within the paths laid down for the school as is practicable and will choose wisely a variety of teaching methods.

The teaching function is made easier and disciplinary measures more intelligent by the recognition that human instincts manifest themselves at rather definite times and in a rather definite order. We must recognize the great importance of the first six to eight years of life in establishing a controlling set of right habits. The true fascination of teaching emerges in understanding that after these early years there is a right time in the child's life for emphasizing language, a right time for music and art, a right time for developing skill in the use of tools, a right time for developing insight into industrial relations, and a right time for stimulating hero worship and emotional enthusiasm for what is true and good and virtuous. There must be recognition of the fact that large disciplinary transfer of learning is not characteristic of the human mind. Cubberley indicates the great importance of training in attention, especially that kind of attention which requires an act of will to direct it towards the natively distasteful.

The so-called drill subjects are basic and fundamental, because in them are locked the keys to the rich content of the other subjects. Standardized intelligence and educational tests make the teaching of all subjects more definite and at the same time furnish to the public incontrovertible evidence of school efficiency. It is probable that such outcomes of education, which are as yet unmeasurable, are adequately cared for by assuring pupil success in those which are definitely measurable.

Reactions to Other Points of View.—Historical perspective apparently suggests to Cubberley that the so-called contentious issues of modern educational theory are really all of one piece. He finds that the tradition of formal *memoriter* learning, fitting for the needs of the simple community of an earlier day, is definitely losing ground to the developing tradition of an education which comprehends the needs of today. He states formally his belief that such studies as the *Cardinal Principles of Secondary Education*[1] and Chapman and Counts' *Principles of Education,*[2] together with the work of Dewey, give us a thoroughly modern philosophy adequate to the work of the school. Cubberley is sceptical, however, of any wide application of the project method, because he feels that it may lead to much waste of time and effort in subjects to which it is not adapted. He suggests that project teaching is most advisedly undertaken in English, science, agriculture and shopwork.

[1] U. S. Bureau of Education, *Bulletin,* 1918, No. 35.
[2] J. C. Chapman and G. S. Counts, *Principles of Education* (New York: Houghton), 1924.

THOMAS H. BRIGGS

General Viewpoint and Its Relation to Education.—Driven by
forces of disintegration which he beholds in present-day American civilization, Thomas H. Briggs makes himself the militant
spokesman of a democracy consciously perpetuating and promoting and realizing its own superior ideals. The rapidly declining influence of the home and of the church in public affairs,
the organized distortion of political idealism, the sinister effects
of criminal gangs, the obviously changing mores seem to Briggs
to constitute a clear challenge to every intelligent and responsible citizen who believes that the essentially American program
of life is better than any substitute suggested from either radical or reactionary quarters. Briggs points out that under the
necessities of the World War we achieved an integration in our
national life that may serve as an inspiration for a more permanent and a more constructive effort. Can we not do, in the
name of democracy, what Prussia did in the early nineteenth
century in the name of autocracy, namely, create a great State
whose leaders are in substantial agreement upon the ends to
be achieved? Need we doubt that, under the banner of democratic ideals and with the advantage of far more adequate
technical controls this desideratum is possible for us? Our main
reliance, of course, must be education, but before formulating
the plans for necessary educational reconstruction Briggs bids
us be clear as to basic principles. He proposes a national commission, or a series of state commissions, permanently set up
and adequately remunerated, to study the facts of modern life,
to discern prime modern values against a popular check, to
suggest, and to conduct necessary experimentation, and finally,
to set up a comprehensive program for the public schools. Such
commissions should be composed of the best minds in social
and educational philosophy and of qualified experts from the
various fields of learning. Briggs calls attention to the efficient
organization within business, the exact way in which all the

forces of business are integrated around the central purpose of obtaining a return upon the original investment, and the specialized and heavily subsidized research that guarantees business efficiency. Education also, according to Briggs, is big business— the biggest business of the State. It must be made to return dividends in keeping with the great investments made by the State. The children of the nation, the raw materials of this great business, are all good for something; let education make out of each a self-supporting, country-loving, God-fearing citizen. Let us upon the elementary level provide everywhere an identical training in the fundamental knowledges and techniques of citizenship. Let us articulate the various parts of the educational system so that its finished products shall be personalities unified by common ideals, common attitudes, common prejudices. Let us really attempt that dangerous education which leads youth to positive action and to profound feeling in regard to important social, political, and economic matters. Only thus can we hope to perpetuate and promote our form of society, achieve more widespread economic comforts, and make possible universal respect for common and statute law.

Nature of Practical Proposals.—Briggs constantly emphasizes, as the primary item in a reconstructed educational program, the formulation of a definite, comprehensive, and pragmatic philosophy which shall provide a criterion of the good life in a democratic state. After this the most vital need is for educators to agree upon the proper functions of the various parts of our public-school organization and upon the most efficient means for realizing the approved ends of teaching endeavor. Curriculum-making is a task for full-time experts, since it involves the constant gathering of subject-matter materials relevant to desired ends, the arrangement of these materials into appropriate courses, the adapting of courses to the age and ability of pupils, as well as to economy of presentation, and constant administrative revision as actual practice points out necessary modifications and as new conditions develop. Curriculum makers need to provide for the articulation of school activities with the out-of-school life of children; they must know the conditions of home study, and they must set the basic requirements in the way of standards of accomplishment and of permanent modifications of conduct in the direction of societal good. A large amount of expert supervision must be provided in the carrying out of the school program, both as a matter of stimulation to teachers and as insurance against individualistic departures from predetermined State plans. Since this is not possible in private and parochial schools, they should no longer be tolerated. All teachers should be required to know and to live the good, rich life; they should not only be enthusiastic about the subject matter which they teach but be capable of attracting the interests of their pupils to it; their constant aim should be to develop each individual along the line of his capabilities towards the utmost social utilization. Briggs does not contemplate any early major departure from the traditional school pabulum of the sciences, mathematics, languages, and social studies. He insists, however, that all studies be redesigned on the basis of pupil interest. The minimum essentials of learning as suggested in the curricular program must, of course, be imparted at any cost. As Briggs views minimum essentials, they are much more a matter of emotionalized mores than of factual information. Since the school cannot avoid the discussion of controversial issues, instead of allowing each individual teacher to handle such issues as he or she sees fit, the proper bias should be determined upon in advance and made uniform for the whole school system. Briggs believes it extremely important that all pupils be made conscious of their indebtedness and obligations to the State in virtue of the opportunities for education which it provides.

During the present emergency Briggs calls upon educators coöperatively to initiate plans and policies of economy and efficiency which, by their inherent reasonableness, may succeed in averting the evil of a panicky rush by public school officials everywhere to cut school budgets indiscriminately.

Estimate of Current Educational Practice.—Briggs does not lack appreciation for the very obvious improvements in the schools of today over those of yesterday, but his criticisms, nevertheless, are incisive and fundamental. Life itself has become too complicated for the public to have noted the failure of education to keep pace with the basic requirements of the State under the changed conditions of modern civilization. The educational profession has failed to meet the challenge of a great opportunity. Educators have acquiesced in our "congeries" of schools, they have allowed themselves to become confused about goals, they are thrilled mainly by the splendor of great school plants, and they seem unaware of the degree to which the school is failing in the topics which it actually attempts to teach. Briggs finds it paradoxical that a democratic state should go on providing a narrow academic type of education suited only to the comparatively few intellectually superior pupils, and that while providing amply the physical equipment for education the State should have allowed persons of limited competence to write the curriculum. Experts in buildings, in bond issues, and in the intricacies of school administration seem to dominate the whole profession of education. In the field of educational research Briggs finds almost complete anarchy with consequent irrelevance of the numerous studies already made, and now in process, to the obvious needs of the schools. An examination of the youths who graduate from our schools, Briggs contends, would show not only the lack of real social orientation, but also the lack of any continuing liberal interests.

The Nature of Learning.—Insisting that human nature has remained fundamentally constant despite the intellectual evolution that education has brought about, Briggs looks to the continued efficacy of time-honored methods of shaping the conduct of youth in the direction of the approved mores of society.

Since the peculiar slants of temperament towards radicalism or conservatism are set by nature, the schools must aim to render these tendencies less extreme by building in each person habits of action, habits of feeling, and habits of thought conducive to the utmost welfare of society as a whole. Accordingly the selected curricular content carefully provided in terms of modal groups of the population should prescribe such systematic training in the application of facts and principles as will insure continued future availability of the desired subject matter, skills, attitudes, and habits. Especially is education concerned with proper emotionalization of the attitudes which it aims to set up. The basic elementary-school training may proceed without great concern about emotionalization, but in the high school educators must recognize and deal consciously with the feelings which inevitably infuse the attitudes of young people and become the chief determinants of character. It is idle to proceed on the basis of rational controls alone. The most we dare strive toward is a series of functioning, emotionally-conditioned attitudes which are held tentatively enough to allow for some degree of revision when conditions change. In dealing with the facts and issues of life, it is impossible for teachers to be impartial, for by the very selecting, organizing, interpreting, and applying of the facts they teach, the conclusions of the young are directed along one line rather than another. Upon the recognition of these things the schools must build consciously.

Briggs emphasizes the rôle of personal influence and example in teaching, the use of precept, formal instruction, incidental instruction, experience followed by satisfaction, and ritual as permanently effective techniques.

Alongside a balanced and extended general education common to all, Briggs would introduce gradually into the school program forms of differentiated training determined upon the basis of the interests, capacities, and aptitudes of individuals. The test of successful education is found both in a homogeneous

progressive society and in the variety and quality of permanent
interests which individuals possess.

Reactions to Other Points of View.—In looking over the scene
of general educational theory, Briggs discovers two main classes
of proposals. One is the figurative or rhetorical type which
frequently enough produces attractive statements of educational
aims but has no apparent effect on practice. The other attempts
to be practically directive, but its statements are so varied in
preconception and emphasis as to further confuse practice.
Among curriculum specialists he finds three main types: the
theorist with a complete program in which, however, the
philosophy is vague or one-sided; the subject-matter specialist
who contributes much in the way of detail, but whose vested
interest in his own line is all too evident; the educational
scientist who collects and tabulates practices, but is only too
frequently blinded by *status quo* assumptions.

Briggs suggests that Dewey's *How We Think* should be more
generally recognized as a description of how thinking goes on
among the gifted intellects. He believes it exceedingly misleading if taken as descriptive of the thinking of the majority of
men.

ROSS L. FINNEY

General Viewpoint and Its Relation to Education.—According
to Ross L. Finney the all-pervasive changes in modern social
life are far from being fully comprehended as yet even by
intellectual leaders. Our industrial system has become a grossly
unbalanced affair run in the interest of a small oligarchy of
industrial, commercial, and financial investors, with resulting
low standards of living for the masses, an almost bankrupt
agriculture, and constant rumors of foreign wars. It would
seem that the very system of private ownership of land and
capital itself were doomed, if modern civilization is to be saved
from collapse. Despite modern technology and vast accumulated
stores of tested knowledge, the various problems of our in-

dividual every day lives, and the broad problems of society are still decided in traditional common-sense ways. Finney believes the time ripe for educators and social scientists to meet the challenge of the ideal society toward which evolution points. Can we not all see this vision of a super-civilization wherein applied science, "machino-facture," social coöperation, and democracy shall come into their own? It is within the power of teachers to realize this ideal, if they will but take the helm and hold the ship of state to a steady course. Society, however, must be enlightened before it will place the seat of social control permanently in an intellectual and moral aristocracy. Let the outlines of an age in which culture reaches down deep enough to humanize even the common man be outlined through the creation of a new school fit for the modern age. It will be possible to attain that solidarity basic to all great cultures only by a universal program of instruction. This means, first, the formulation of a set of beliefs consistent with the teachings of science in every field of life, and then the insistent drilling of these beliefs into youth until all alike are driven to the realization of stable and permanent social ideals. True cultural solidarity means the reduction of heterogeneity to such a point that social institutions may operate efficiently. It also means that the whole population has been nurtured upon common intellectual resources, a common art, a common science, and a common, therefore valid, set of beliefs.

Though as educators we may legitimately proceed to make the children of the poor discontented with the squalor, indecencies, and privations amidst which they live, it is important that until the emergence of a new consensus of public opinion we ward off possible revolution by instilling into our pupils the good, old-fashioned ideals of self-denial, honesty, frugality, thoroughness, loyalty, chastity, obedience, and reverence. Could but philosophy, in building upon the foundations of science, clarify for us a great cause in which as benefactors of mankind we can fanatically believe, the deepest cravings of the human heart, so frustrated today, might again be gloriously expressed. Meanwhile Finney advises that the various agencies of social control unite in defense of the existing order.

Nature of Practical Proposals.—The modern developments along scientific, industrial, and democratic lines suggest to Finney the need for a new philosophy of education. According to his point of view, educators will increasingly need to be sociological philosophers, for theirs is the function of running Society. They will have to determine what the institutional forms and relationships of the future shall be. Theirs is also the responsibility of providing Society with leaders trained in liberal arts colleges open only to mental and moral superiors. In such colleges Finney suggests that the constants and the electives in the curricula be reversed from the arrangement common today. He would have as constants the sciences, fine arts, and the new humanities, and as electives mathematics, formal English, and foreign languages. The training of educators capable of a proper directive function in society would be in marked contrast to the programs of colleges of education today. These novitiates are to be well grounded in biology, geography, anthropology, psychology, social psychology, economics, political science, sociology, ethics, history, natural science, fine arts, and philosophy. The colleges of education Finney conceives of as the generators of a new spiritual life. Their subject-matter disciplines must somehow provide the new religion of social progress.

Finney proposes universal education throughout the adolescent period. This would include an industrially articulated vocational education for all supplementary to the basic citizenship and cultural education. (He frankly recognizes that this may make necessary free provision of school uniforms and noon lunches.) The school curriculum must successfully impart the information necessary to proper functioning of social institutions under modern conditions. Social science courses would, among other things, give the facts about the extent and causes of poverty. History courses would reveal the panorama of human evolution and social betterment in such a way that youth will be led to feel closely allied with God in the realization of still incomplete phases of evolution.

Finney calls for an emphasis upon the distributive aspects of scholarship at least equal to that which in the past has been put upon productive or research scholarship. In accordance with his social beliefs he proposes that the wealth of the whole nation be used in providing cultural opportunities for all in equal measure.

Estimate of Current Educational Practice.—Present educational practice is characterized according to Finney by a number of absurd deformities. There are evident in public school programs many hangovers from the past, many freakish novelties of the present, and many serious omissions. Public opinion, largely because of bad education, is unenlightened regarding modern social conditions and requirements. The educational system seems dominated by the competitive desire of each person to rise out of his class even though this desideratum is demonstrably impossible of attainment to any except the most fortunate. In theoretic discussions the important *reproductive* function of education is not frankly recognized, and the necessity for social homogeneity as a basis for the efficient operation of social institutions seems completely lost sight of. There is everywhere an exaltation of educational method, which inadequately conceals the prevailing uncertainty as to aims and the lack of proper standards by which to evaluate subject matter. The education of educators is so over-balanced on the technical side that educators as a class are, to a tragic extent, uncultured and ignorant in matters about which they should be capably informed. In the common schools the calculated neglect of information-getting and the loudly-proclaimed stress on problem solving constitute a virtual new scholasticism.

Finney criticizes American vocational education as totally out of harmony with the requirements of industry. He finds the administration of liberal arts education dominated by the graduate schools to such an extent that there is little concern about providing teachers who can convey a contagious enthusiasm for their subject to students.

The Nature of Learning.—Finney reads almost the whole venture of human learning into the concept which he calls *passive mentation,* by which he means the essentially unreflective absorption of ideas into the mind in the course of the general processes of social life. These ideas are built gradually into an apperceptive mass which lies below the threshold of consciousness and functions in supplying the preconceptions and the stereotypes that constantly influence our behavior in unpremeditated ways. Finney would consider elementary education, most of secondary education, and a large part of college education as systematic processes of social suggestion by means of which the fundamentals of the social inheritance are imparted to passive minds. The curriculum problem becomes simply that of selecting subject matter relevant to modern life and grading it according to stages of mental development. It *is* artificial material, and on the elementary level a skillful teacher will resort to devices which at best may make it *seem* interesting to children. When this humbug fails there is no other resort except to compel the child to learn his lessons,—excellent training, incidentally, for law-abiding citizenship. Increasingly after childhood, reasons for education should appear obvious enough to render learning its own motivation.

The subject-matter of education consists of the best existing factual knowledge relating to social, economic, political, and ethical problems. Method is the instrumentality for imparting these facts to youth. Everything else in education is incidental to this subject-matter and the processes through which it is imparted. The aim is to teach children how to act and what to believe in all the typical experiences of life. This aim implies a large amount of forced feeding of the results of expert thinking. The schools must, therefore, frequently resort to *memoriter* methods and to systematic drill. The newer techniques of education may be used efficaciously only with the brighter children, for it is only the superior who may hope really to understand the knowledge which all must accept.

The system of school discipline which Finney favors is one as rigid and final as that employed in the army. Such a system is absolutely necessary if teachers are to habitualize institutional behavior in children before they begin to reason. It is necessary because the years of formal schooling prepare for homogeneity of thought on all socially important matters in adult life. It is necessary again because the vast masses of the population are biologically barred from contributory thinking and must therefore be rendered conservative and orderly. Individual differences of children are, to Finney, obstacles to be overcome in the attainment of like objectives for all.

While awaiting the plans for fundamental educational reconstruction, Finney advises that practical public school leaders continue to offer good stiff subject matter courses, logically arranged.

Reactions to Other Points of View.—Finney is concerned to point out what he calls the misleading half-truths in Dewey. He believes Dewey to have over-emphasized heavily the deliberative and conscious aspect of individual and social life. The result of this over-emphasis has been neglect of the social inheritance and encouragement of an individualism dangerous to modern civilization. A literal acceptance of Dewey's statement *that education is life, not preparation for life,* Finney believes would mean reversion to savagery. Again, Finney finds in Dewey a discounting of the passively absorptive mental processes in social life and of the importance of the more positive controls which society exercises upon its members.

Finney blames modern soft pedagogy for the inefficiencies

of our schools. He claims that the soft creed of life which the Progressives have put forward is actually disintegrative of the social fabric. Society today is in dire need of more authority and control over individuals, despite the protestations of recent educational cults. In the project method Finney sees the latest representation of pedagogical faddishness.

II. EDUCATORS STRESSING THE ULTIMACY OF SCIENCE

The men whose points of view are presented in Part Two are considered respectively as variants in the emphasis which they place upon science as the sole guarantor of social progress. Their work has been mainly in the enterprise of developing a science of education. It is therefore not strange that they should be somewhat unappreciative of broader speculations upon the past, present, or future. The order of presentation which follows is that of increasing departure from an apparent belief in the ultimacy of science.

CHARLES H. JUDD

General Viewpoint and Its Relation to Education.—To Charles H. Judd, the great fact in human evolution is the steady accumulation of language, science, and technical discovery in the face of mounting social demands. This social inheritance is in truth a new order of reality over and above the biological inheritance which by itself prepares us only for the tooth and claw existence of the jungle. Social solidarity and modern industrialism are the results of civilizational processes funded in the social inheritance. The world which man faces today, as a consequence, is one in which the active forces are far too great for him to cope with personally. He can act effectively only by means of the crystallized ideas which institutions are. Modern society, therefore, imposes institutions upon individuals and seeks to have everyone conform to social patterns of action and thought. These institutions have today reached such a stage in their progressive development, especially the methods and technological controls of science, that the most significant stages of social evolution seem to be in the future and may be consciously engineered by man. Ideally we can conceive of such an eventual coalition between science and government that statutes will be scientifically derived and substantiated, and there will be such general understanding of a perfected human social psychology that the results of group deliberation will prove always to be the most satisfactory possible.

Our present adult society demonstrates the highest form of organized adaptation that the world knows. The rules of conduct accepted by all favor industry and conservation of property. The struggles of today are social struggles for the possession of the symbols of wealth. The desires of the masses of people more readily find expression under American conditions of life than under the more rigid régimes of the old world. Such facts as the obvious changes going on in the business world and in social conditions generally, the obnoxious presence of all types of soothsayers, and the great gap existing between intelligent leaders and the common man, sum up the challenge which education must meet in furthering processes of socialization. The school must give by the most economical methods possible a systematic view of the world together with mastery of scientific principles of understanding and dealing with people and things. In short it must provide a satisfactory social training of pupils in bringing their habits of action and thought into conformity to racial norms and to group demands. It is no easy matter to insert lessons aimed to bring respect for law and economic stabilization in just the right manner and at just the right place to be really effective. Education is not complete until it embodies such understanding and control over common devices as to release the individual from the pressure of particular situations.

Nature of Practical Proposals.—Judd's call to educators is one which urges them to avoid latter-day speculative vagaries about education, and to recognize the practical seriousness and complexity of transmitting effectively our greatly enlarged social inheritance. He urges the mobilization of opinion behind the idea of establishing a responsible central body to promote the interests of educational science. The function of such a body would be to plan a scientific program of curriculum expansion and of improvement in the methods of administering instruction in the schools. Not only is it the duty of all administrators and teachers constantly to examine critically their own practice, but it is the duty of every school system to help in the discovery and organization for effective presentation of social-science materials relevant to the larger objective of socialization. The final answer to problems of time distribution within subjects, of the proper mixture of recreation and study, of coeducation, of the refinement of familiar teaching techniques, must be found in careful psychological analyses and experimentation. Meanwhile, however, every school should be an experimental center for concentrated attack on properly limited problems, the principal and the teachers coöperatively carrying on the research. Under this mode of familiarizing teachers with the meaning and significance of educational research they will be the more ready to receive experimental results from larger and better equipped centers and to adapt their classroom procedures accordingly.

All subjects and all activities in the program of the school must contribute to the social training of pupils. Direct instruction in the meaning and value of American institutions should be a definite part of every educational program. Actual curricular content should be chosen only upon the basis of real knowledge regarding the responses it provokes in children and the educational consequences of these responses. There is a danger in over-simplification in the organization of materials of instruction. The matter of drill in the accurate and discriminating use of specific terminology as a means to clear thinking cannot be over-emphasized. The emotional life of children is best dealt with by setting up right habits of response and behavior incentives which will absorb pupil energy. The school must not neglect training in aesthetic appreciation, but any attempt to develop creative ability on a large scale is bound to be wasteful of time and effort.

Judd expects great improvement in the training of teachers. Accepting the fundamental hypothesis that good teachers are made rather than born, he suggests a kind of apprentice training which will familiarize traineés with the educational system as a whole. He desires them to be trained in the tradition of systematic subjects and grades properly psychologized, however, into a natural course of study. Only by transmitting to initiates valid doctrine and by avoiding speculative theories can we hope for a progressively improved teaching personnel.

In planning for the large-scale adult education demanded in the changing social life of today Judd suggests making a new start and disregarding the familiar approaches of organized formal education. Moved possibly by the raids of public officials upon school budgets during the present depression Judd has been urging a unified stand by educators upon the legitimacy and necessity of educational extension. He sees a new social order dawning and calls upon the profession to leave aside petty matters and participate in the formulation of broad national policies.

Estimate of Current Educational Practice.—Judd heartily endorses the American educational program and finds that on the whole it has progressed with changing industrial and social conditions in the modern world. The development of educational science, stimulated in large measure by school surveys, testifies to the eagerness of the American people to determine efficiency experimentally. Judd believes that the present movement towards standardization of an educational program, made possible by the common terminology that educational research has provided, is better arrived at through voluntary groups of educators than by authority of the Federal government. There are in a democracy, by its very nature, forces which are not conducive to rapid scientific autonomy in education. The tremendous sums of money appropriated for education are a constant temptation to sinister forces in our social life to attempt control. There are only niggardly appropriations in most centers for research and there are far too few research workers.

In some educational research which is actually going on, Judd finds evidence of slipshod control over the vernacular and over simple arithmetic methods. He finds a decided overemphasis in the attention which has been given laws of learning derived mainly from animal experimentation to the neglect of studies of the kind of learning which takes place through human abstract mental processes.

As a consequence teachers lack the knowledge whereby to tell the pupils best how to study. There is little appreciation of the important general objective of leading pupils to see the value of order and systematic arrangement in thinking, or of the cultivation of general ideas of regularity and precision. While there is a great deal of science teaching being done, it is largely of a particularistic nature with little attention to generalization. Textbooks used in schools are too frequently unreadable and full of irrelevant and badly digested subject matter. On the whole our educational procedures at all levels have been well-intentioned and successful, but they will remain vague and fluctuating in definition until they can be scientifically directed.

The Nature of Learning.—To Judd, man's use of language, his interest in books, his concern with abstract ideals like Justice, set him off distinctly from the lower animals. Man is not to be interpreted in terms of internal drives alone; he is surrounded by the psychological environment of social institutions, which at least in equal measure determine his conduct. So pervasive is this social influence that it conditions even moments of apparently profoundly egoistic independence. Children come into the world bundles of unorganized tendencies, from which state of complete social incompetence they can be rescued only after long and tedious guidance whereby fixed habits are set up. This process cannot be sharply divided into a period of childhood preparation and adult realization, because the modern world demands rather a continuous adjustment and adaptation over the whole period of life.

In the evolution of teaching procedures there has emerged a solid body of principles, information, and techniques which today by means of research is being rapidly validated and extended. The tradition of distinct school subjects and their proper grade placement has resulted from the characteristics of pupils' minds as found by teachers in their efforts to organize instruction. A pupil is a collection of selves, so that it is in no way a violation of the law of nature to teach subjects as such. Judd conceives of a curriculum so systematically planned and so scientifically arranged that its administration will bring keen satisfaction to teachers and pupils. Only by such pre-arrangement of every item can the school properly direct the mental activities of pupils into advantageous channels and inform them best how to act and think in their efforts to control their physical and social environment. Beginning in the first grade by means of such civilizational tools as the alphabet, the printed page, Arabic numerals, the school schedule, property right, and punctuality, the teacher introduces the child to skilful ways of analyzing the world. School subjects are the reflection of this analytic stage of the child's growth and by means of the generalizations which grow out of all proper subject teaching he will in due time achieve a synthesis of understanding and orientation in life. Under the best teaching conditions, where the individuals in the class are of closely similar intellectual calibre, the teacher responds sympathetically to the difficulties of his pupils, and guides and directs their mental processes to the proper goals.

Since attitude is as important as subject matter, it is the business of class management to establish social decorum and to cultivate emotional conditions favorable to study. The rigidly coherent thinking required by well organized school subjects is so important that we must learn properly to discount the fact that the rewards of class work are difficult and hard to keep in mind.

Reactions to Other Points of View.—Judd believes in exercising restraint in regard to the public use of personal experience and of personal insight in dealing with important educational matters. He sees his own function in contrast to the prevailing mode, therefore, as that of urging a program of scientific attack upon the crucial issues of education. It is from such a point of view that he finds himself in clear opposition to all educational procedures based upon a specific item psychology. He believes that such an atomistic psychology is based upon inadequate data and will eventually be relegated to the scrap heap of hasty and invalid inferences. To speak of language as a mere reaction, of art as the expression of surplus energy, and to omit entirely specific reference to such a potent influence on men's behavior as money, is to leave open vast areas for further psychological analysis.

In the modern Progressive Movement in education, Judd finds a group of cult worshippers who have clearly lost the balancing influences of history and psychology. That strange entity which they so worshipfully set up as a standard, *the whole child,* is but an empty verbalism, nowhere actually to be found. A little appeal to the sound sense of experience quickly dispels their naïve notion that the school exists merely as an opportunity for the child to mature naturally. The criticisms of the present curriculum made by Progressives would seem to imply the abandonment of all intellectual life. While undoubtedly there will be recurrent proposals to displace language and number from their central position in the curriculum and to put in their stead

something called *activities,* Judd is of the firm faith that these
attempts will prove ineffectual and futile.

DAVID SNEDDEN

General Viewpoint and Its Relation to Education.—Without
committing himself to any objectives as ultimately valid
Snedden believes it conducive to practical progress if commonly
accepted values like truthfulness, honesty, gentility, industrious-
ness, loyalty, and patriotism be accepted as desirable. He speaks
of the variety of dynamic faiths in purposed progress which the
American people have demonstrated in the creation of new
types of religion, new regions for population settlement, new
commonwealths, and gigantic corporations. Thus today we are
the wealthiest of nations, our masses have most leisure, our education is most widespread, and our presses publish the most
printed materials. A culture at once fine and democratic which
has grown up indigenously and not as an offshoot of older cultural traditions seems possible of realization. Collective social
action has been growing upon us, and although American corporateness has been due mainly to coöperative non-political and
private effort, it seems to spring from the same roots as the
political corporateness of post-war Italy and Russia. Modern
civilization through applied science has become dependent upon the smooth-running operation of an almost infinite scope
of coöperations and perfected divisions of labor. The progressive decay of the small regional community is written in the
course of events and already largely accomplished in actual
fact. Such almost revolutionary changes from the status of an
earlier day are absorbed without great social upheaval because
they have been, in essence, extensions and simplifications of
ago-old tendencies, the effect of the enlargement of customary
tools. Captains of industry, college presidents, and political reformers have used mechanization and standardization of process
and regimentation of personnel so effectively that today we

are able to take somewhat of a respite and inquire seriously into the humane aspects of corporate life. Technique, in other words, has been so perfected that actual measures may now be taken towards realization of the greatest good of the greatest number. The specific tasks involved in the refinement of government, proper provisions for the national defence, planning universal education, and preventing men from falling into evil ways, along with innumerable others, are today capable of being outlined.

Education is no exception to the aspects of life which have become corporately organized. It may be freely admitted that, in the large-scale zeal for efficiency in public school organization, some of the results have seemed unduly harsh. Science may be fully trusted to bring about an amelioration. It is, however, futile to talk about education generally. Sociology breaks up this generality by sorting out the specific *school* educational processes from the broad educative effects of living. Schools may be defined as agencies used by individuals, organized groups, or the State for the transmission of valuable heritages, or for the production of specific types of trained individuals needed in various aspects of the corporate life. It is preferable, therefore, to center thinking about "educations," rather than about "education," for thereby we are forced into the very relevant and the very practical matter of pointing out the specific educational goods desired. Science is the basic tool for arriving at the objectives, for outlining the machinery of realizing them, and for judging the adequacy of the differentiated products of the many types of educations so attempted. In dealing with social and educational matters we are driven constantly to break up large concepts into their specific meanings for associated life now and in the immediate future. We are led to inquire into the kinds and the relative adequate amounts of democracy. We recognize not masses of people to be educated but discrete type groups with specific needs, such as the rank and file of office workers enjoying cultural values of questionable worth. We find that an individual has several careers, each involving distinct types of educations. Thus we are on the way to define the functions of schooling.

The Nature of Practical Proposals.—Snedden lays greatest stress upon the necessity for outlining a science of educational objectives. Such a science fully worked out would consist of a very elaborate series of lists of validated and balanced specifications for school educations. It would begin with as objectively determined a scale of social values as it is possible to achieve within a reasonable time limit by the various techniques of sociological science. From this could be derived similarly reasonably attainable educational values which in turn would yield particular school objectives. At this point educational science steps in to translate school objectives into specifications of appropriate amounts and kinds of subjects. Since it is impossible today for an individual in learning to encompass the whole of the social inheritance, such school objectives must be chosen as will conduce to collective well-being. The primary aim here must be to secure in habit the best of the social inheritance. The actual specifications, curricular elements or courses should, of course, be differentiated according to the intellectual capacities and the specific talents or defects of learners. It should be clearly indicated which curricular elements can be learned naturalistically, or with relative ease, and which are learned only with great difficulty. A large part of the learnings which fit for the various aspects of adult life can be acquired only upon a *deferred* value basis. Educational science would determine adequacy of learning in terms of demonstrated performance powers in courses basic to the exigencies of habitual producing activities on the one hand, and demonstrated capacities for superior utilization in courses basic to habitual consuming activities on the other. Scientifically derived programs of school learning, in addition to contributing demonstrably to the several aspects of collective and individual welfare, must be well-administered, must remedy clearly apparent educational shortages and must in no way be repetitious of learnings administered through other agencies than the school.

Snedden looks for no change beyond gradual scientific refinement of the nature and method of educational control as exercised today. He finds adequate and efficient the present division of professional educational workers into two groups, the few highly trained administrators, engineers, and executives who lay down fundamentals of policy and furnish the specifications for its realization, and the many with less training who must work in accordance with specifications provided them.

He calls for the abandonment of present schemes of vocational and prevocational training because of their failure to recognize the nature of vocational specialization today. In 95 per cent of today's vocations he would not begin specific preparation before the ages of 18 to 22. On the other hand he emphasizes the necessity of beginning as early as possible the training in wider and deeper utilization (including cultural) powers.

Estimate of Current Educational Practice.—American education is fortunately controlled through no one agency; neither educational, political, religious, parental, nor economic leaders monopolize the formulation of its general policies. Because of sentiments derived from democracy and from Christianity, Utopian hopes for the possibilities of education have been influential essentially in establishing uniform standards of achievement which ill comport with the facts about individual differences. Actually there has been little connection of educational aims with the people in whom the aims most need to be made effective. Unfortunately among educators there has been either disparagement or complete neglect of the contributions which non-school agencies make to basic educational objectives. They have been content to take the apparent functioning of the schools for the reality of the whole gamut of educative undertakings.

The many criticisms of school practice which emerge from meetings of professional educators and which fill the pages of a host of educational journals are a quite natural pre-scientific phenomenon. In every calling the methods of debate give way as science is more fully incorporated. We are approaching educational science in a few fields, but in such important matters as the careful estimation of the capacities of human beings at various ages and the determination of effective means and methods of reaching educational objectives among properly differentiated groups, our efforts are largely arbitrary. Specialists in subject matter dictate curriculum construction in far too many instances. Old methods are retained and new methods introduced in completely haphazard fashion, since no reliable criteria exist by which to determine true values. The gap between social needs and school achievement is nowhere larger than in civic education. Our elementary curriculum is crowded with badly assorted and poorly coördinated objectives, many of which are highly speculative. Our high school education which is not openly vocational in aim, seems clearly to defeat the cultural needs of students of average and less than average mentality.

The Nature of Learning.—To Snedden the meaning of education lies in the situation where those who arrange the social and physical environment do so in the interest of the learning of certain things rather than certain other things. The source of all learnings is in the racial inheritance, now too vast to be encompassed even in small degree by the best of minds. Persons in control of school practices must therefore make choices in terms of most necessary knowledges, attitudes, habits, and ideals to be learned. In order to avoid sentimental vagueness such choices should be made specifically for discrete and homogeneous case types of pupils. The actual curricula must be worked out in great detail, courses enumerated and course elements such as lessons, chapters, topics, themes, or even smaller entities which science shall specify as learning units, explicitly stated. The perennial problem of whether the teacher shall teach the child or the subject, science dissolves by putting the emphasis on measuring subject matter mastery in terms of the relevantly altered behavior of the pupil. In fields like medicine, for instance, educational scientists proceed to make over strategic health findings into courses capable of being taught to children between the ages of 6 to 12 years.

Specifications for educations are not ready for classroom use unless psychological analysis has indicated clearly which can be learned developmentally, or in the play spirit, and which require the discipline of pure work. Increasingly, of course, modern needs depart further and further from what may be called natural inclinations, and consequently proper preparation must be largely through the contagion of the social environment or by appreciation of deferred values. The learnings undertaken during early childhood, say before the age of nine, should be almost entirely of a *developmental* nature. Increasingly thereafter it should be plain, even to the pupil himself, that learning acquisitions must be of the *deferred* type. The educational needs of the child are those which wise and sympathetic parents, religious leaders, physicians, and educators perceive as indicative of what the future will require.

Snedden looks with favor upon a general social policy (to which, of course, educational science would largely contribute) of locating as early as possible the highest potential talent represented among individuals and deliberately making such talent the source of future creative leaders in all fields of constructive endeavor.

Reactions to Other Points of View.—There is much fair game for Snedden in current educational theories. The doctrines of those who preach the *free school* are his favorite targets. Their attempt to replace the existing curricula with activity programs seems anarchic to him and a plain abandonment of social purpose in education. He cannot find in their large and constant emphasis on growth any indications of concern for the direction which growth may take. The plea that the school should abandon any attempt to prepare children for the amenities of adult life flies in the face of all the practical educational experiences of the ages past. It is absurd to counter that in day to day living young people will show interest in evolving standards beyond those catering to the gratification of egoistic desires. Phrases like the "needs of the child" and "personality development" are worse than useless when it comes to doing the actual specific tasks of education. To speak of education as the supreme art and to hope wishfully that the social order must inevitably be democratized through the use of particular school techniques is to demonstrate extraordinary innocence of the scope and complexity of fundamental forces at work in modern life.

Snedden finds Dewey to be so deeply concerned with matters of educational method that he does not recognize the importance of careful selective treatment of the social inheritance. He believes that Kilpatrick is manifesting defeatism by emphasizing in his general thought the "unknown future." Snedden would insist that there never has been a time when the controls by which the future may be ordered have been so numerous and so ready-to-hand. The demand made in some quarters for curriculum construction by the local community, in so far as it is a demand for adaptation of means to local conditions, is legitimate, but in so far as ends are concerned it reverses the proper emphasis. Snedden believes it folly to assume that individual teachers can adapt subject matter to the needs of individuals; only trained educational scientists specialized to such a task can accomplish it.

Snedden has his serious doubts about all the modern efforts to enrich the child's experience in school and out. Fuller sciences of physiology, psychology, and sociology may some day startle us by tracing actual deleterious effects of intended Progressive benevolence to children.

EDWARD L. THORNDIKE

General Viewpoint and Its Relation to Education.—Edward L. Thorndike's deep understanding of the psychological structure of man and of the laws governing modification of that structure, makes him virtually gasp at the ruthless assurance with which modern industry and trade have built up their hierarchies of human interrelationships. The scientist guided by the insights of ethics and religion and working for the welfare of the future must be increasingly relied upon if the intricacies and passions of human nature are to be securely adjusted to the requirements of modern life. Human nature is not realized in the fullest sense unless learning is going on. Never in history has there been such a challenge to the resources of human learning capacity as today. Because America is committed to democracy, individual self-realization must be attained through such adjustment within the fields of physical work, economic affairs, social and civic life as will yield the utmost good to society as a whole. Thus education becomes the central strategy of the modern age, for it is only an informed public which can direct changes in its own interest. We must comprehensively plan a system of schooling which shall at once combine the essential learnings that productive labor in its various aspects affords with wise recreational functions and with the more stringent requirements of the higher life. This schooling must extend throughout life and be as fruitfully complete at various age levels as is consistent with the adult obligations of each individual to lead a serviceable career. Only so can the deadly dichotomy of monotonous labor and unregulated leisure be avoided in society. The school must work in close articulation with other institutions if its influence is to be felt in reducing the sum total of error, injustice, misery, and ignorance. The type and extent of learning needed by all classes of the population must be determined with exactitude in order that every individual shall be happily adjusted to the type of service that he is best able to render. It is obvious that the resources of higher education must be devoted to the education of the gifted in order that there shall be no dearth of leaders to occupy the strategic rôles in the social order.

Thorndike defines the science of education, already functioning in notable ways despite its very recent origin, as the discovery of the most satisfactory adjustments of individuals to the actual physical and social environment. The art of education, he holds, is the successful manipulation of human beings towards such satisfactory adjustments.

Nature of Practical Proposals.—Thorndike calls upon the school to broaden its scope by studying the vocational interests and abilities of pupils, by influencing the attitudes of pupils towards work and wealth, and by noting the conditions and present trends of our economic order. He suggests that fundamental improvements in education can be brought about through more analytic and open-minded thinking upon present problems, through more careful checking upon the results of present procedures, through deliberate experimentation on a broader scale, and through the development of more rational ideas about human ideals and how they may be made to function. These avenues of improvement define educational research and represent in essence the extension and improvement of observation and the discovery of more facts and better methods, upon the basis of which administrators and teachers may adequately test out their theories. The scientific study of the curriculum, for instance, would involve the amassing of data about what should be learned, about what use learners are to make of what is to be learned, and about how they are to learn it. Every subject and every method must be appraised in terms of the degree to which it contributes improvement in fundamental adjustments of human beings to increased bodily and mental health, and to greater recreational, ethical, and intellectual resources. We have great need for experimental evidence in regard to the difficulty of learning various elements of knowledge, skill, and attitude. The present apparent anarchy and the laissez faire tendency in the field of educational method can be dispersed only by means of careful appraisal and measurement of the effects of all methods and the consequent careful selection thus made possible.

Thorndike's greatest emphasis is placed upon the need for better techniques of objective measurement in all fields. He believes that the effective realization of the aims of education waits upon the further development of the measurement movement. Everything that is worth while must be more adequately known and more validly measured. The stamp of expert certification upon ideal values and upon the methods used in making ideals effective in the lives of more and more people, Thorndike believes an enhancement of the values themselves.

Self-activity to Thorndike is not a method; it is the end of all method. He wishes, accordingly, the adjustment of instruction to the needs of individuals in such measure as class organization allows. He believes that the school should provide avenues of endeavor other than the purely intellectual, and that it should develop proper respect for intellectual effort in all people. The *project* method is most fruitful when used in combination with direct learning, with systematic study, and with the development of subject matter through discussion, demonstration, and experimentation. Interest as a fundamental criterion is best applied by leading the child into studies and activities previously determined by science to be interesting. Beginning in the high school, Thorndike would attempt to bridge the gap between an over-academic schooling and an under-intellectualized living by the inclusion of productive labor in the educational program.

Estimate of Current Educational Practice.—Thorndike finds that education, like other related fields, is retarded by the undeveloped state of the science of human nature. Current theories about the school, recreation, and the higher life are blurred by the planlessness of present social life and by prevailing attitudes of abasement of labor. Educators have bent all of their efforts towards raising the age limit of compulsory education without regard to the educational implications of adult life. Despite theoretic agreement that indoctrination should be avoided, teachers in the primary and secondary school lack leisure to cultivate broad personal viewpoints, with the consequence that indoctrination in traditional religion, morality, politics, and social science tends actually to take place. In addition, the present system of schooling nearly everywhere represents an over-emphasis of the intellectual, contributes to uniformity of method and result, has constant recourse to *memoriter* practices, prescribed duties, and prescribed textbooks, and emphasizes conformity of thought. It neglects to develop habits of independence and of intelligent self-appraisal, and it fails to provide the necessary skills in learning, studying, and planning. The high school is still far from making proper provision for the experiences and the instruction necessary as the basis for a good general education. On the whole our expectations from the school in the way of rationality, morality, and high recreational standards tend to be too hopeful and unduly dependent upon verbal exhortations.

Such investigations as have been made on the utilization of school learning have indicated that relatively few of the facts and principles learned in school are used in later life. However, these findings must be interpreted in the light of present inadequate wants and not as showing that subject matter content should be unduly restricted. Thorndike finds some evidence that teachers are beginning to appreciate the fact that an educational test or scale is an objective measuring rod only, and that the use made of such an instrument is a matter of intelligent discrimination.

The Nature of Learning.—In Thorndike's estimation man is placed at the culmination of the animal evolutionary series.

Man is a more perfect and a more delicate animal than the rest, but he is an animal and not a demi-god. Learning is reacting to situations with which the organism is confronted. All mental life is constituted of connections between situations and responses of varying degrees of complexity. Progress in learning may be indicated by the selection and organization into the behavior system of those reactions which bring satisfaction. Learning is present in the strengthening and weakening of stimulus-response connections already made, in building new responses, and in changed sensitivity to situations. All learning involves changes in the whole character of the organism to some degree. The apparent qualitative advantages in man's mental life, such as the processes involved in his idealistic philosophizing and his logically exact reasoning, are in truth due to quantitative differences in the number, range, depth, and complexity of stimulus-response connections. An inventory of any man's mind which listed all of these connections would provide the data for determining what he would think and do, what would prove satisfying and what annoying to him in every conceivable situation. Nor would there be over and above such an inventory any unaccounted for aspects of mental life or behavior.

The task of education is to take the original nature of man, so extremely active and so readily apt in learning, and by means of proper techniques which science will supply, to disrupt the vicious aspects and supply useful additions. In other words, education should change original man in such a way that his wants are made amenable to the conditions of humane and rational living. The teacher's function becomes cognate with assuring a depth of motivation on the part of pupils sufficient to sustain them in whole-hearted activity. He must manage the constantly changing situations which confront him in his capacity as a teacher astutely enough to secure and render satisfying the desired response. Such principles as those of the necessary belongingness, acceptability, repetition, and identifiability of the situation, the repetition of a connection, the satisfyingness or annoyingness consequent to response, and the availability of the response, are basic to every effort of the teacher. He must, for instance, provide for careful identification of that about which facts are to be learned; he must recognize that mere repetition of a connection is futile; he must understand that satisfaction is usually far more directly efficacious than annoyance in promoting learning. He must recognize that the learner is the central point of reference in all learning and not the external situations by which the learner is surrounded. He must realize that in order to cultivate desirable reactions to real life situations, the school must be as lifelike as possible. School subjects are to be looked upon as dissociations of various aspects, relations, and abstract qualities from the total complexity of events. Since interest is the token of whole-hearted response, all subjects and activities should be interesting. By proper selection of experiences and skilful direction of the learning process, the teacher can guarantee the identification of common elements in various situations and so provide for the utmost transfer. Thorndike suggests that more reliable educational results will be obtained by the objective measurement of primary learnings than by well-meaning attempts to judge concomitant effects.

Reactions to Other Points of View.—The phrase "education is life" Thorndike reports as validated in large measure by results obtained through educating children in accordance with rather than in opposition to their wants. In much of the current emphasis upon growth by means of continuous reorganization of experience, he misses, however, any clear pronouncement upon the importance of considering the various directions which growth may take. His own carefully devised, recent experimentations on human learning are pointed to as rendering more doubtful than ever the educational value of mere experience as such. Individual perfection is inadequate as the aim of education, because it so obviously neglects to provide for the social duties and responsibilities of individuals in the closely-knit, interdependent society of today. Thorndike points out that the child's interest is not an absolutely reliable guide in the choice of subjects to be studied, and he believes it essential that teachers influence pupils away from slavish following of interest. The *project method* which stresses the immediate usefulness of knowledge, if used exclusively, would leave pupils seriously deficient in breadth and thoroughness of understanding. Thorndike accuses many educational writers of lacking skill and knowledge in educational science. He reads into what he calls the *vitalistic* approach to learning a plain abandonment of science in the interest of the unpredictable and uncontrollable aspects of life.

ERNEST HORN

General Viewpoint and Its Relation to Education.—Ernest Horn seems willing to abide by whatever principles sociological techniques of analysis may yield when directed upon the extremely complex social life of today. He believes that this analysis will point out what are the most important, the most universal, the most permanent values of life. With ideal values established it will be possible to plan an educational program in terms of them. The further research needed to make the educational program fully adequate lies in an analysis of the situations which children confront at various stages in their development. Such essentially psychological analysis provides the framework around which detailed educational procedures may be constructed. In the light of the determined permanent values or goals each specific aspect of childhood activity becomes intelligible in terms of what it leads to, and any activity may, therefore, be wisely promoted or discouraged. Horn contends that between the pervasive activities of adults and the developing interests of children there is no dichotomy but much overlapping and constant interplay. Building upon this principle the school may safely proceed to match all important groups of life values with corresponding items of instruction toward the end of assuring that children shall be directly and efficiently fitted for the important activities of life. Social shortages (one example of which is the current widespread disrespect for the property of others) are open challenges to remedial measures to be undertaken by the school. Individual freedom so constantly and fruitlessly debated as a social issue will be made clear only by resorting to principles basic to associated life. Freedom in the school is exactly the same problem and may be met in exactly the same way. Horn sums up the work of the school in terms of the legitimate expectations of children. A child has the right to expect that the school will provide enrichment of the present and preparation for the future. A child has the right to expect that the school will be more concerned about him than about its own formal organization. A child has the right to expect that he shall be given some measure of freedom to progress at his own rate in the work of the school. A child has the right to expect that sympathetic and skilful teaching service shall be rendered him individually in accordance with his needs.

Nature of Practical Proposals.—It is Horn's contention that because of the lack of any adequate scientific analysis of the values of life, the time is not ripe for setting up, even in an experimental way, a school radically different from the school of the present. He believes, however, that the thinking of at least a small group of qualified educators should be moving in the direction of a curricular organization upon a different basis than that of the ordinary school subjects. It is an exceedingly difficult task to think solely in terms of the needs and opportunities of life, on the one hand, and of the requirements of learning on the other. There are involved the creation of new materials of learning, new types of school equipment, the solution of many intricate problems of educational research, and the careful training of teachers along new pathways of method. Only as these undertakings are in their final stages may children justly be subjected to radical educational programs.

Meanwhile we are obligated by matters of practical expediency and by the very weight of a vast machinery of education constructed after the traditional pattern, to give our chief attention and effort to reforms within the bounds of the present curriculum. We can enrich the content of school subjects, we can reorganize subjects, we can promote interrelations between subjects in the interest of influencing positively, and in larger degree than at present, the life of the child in his out-of-school affairs. In all such reforms Horn believes we should be thinking in terms of what is practicable on a large scale in *public* schools. As specific proposals for the greater efficiency of the subject curriculum, Horn suggests constant study of the functioning of particular subjects in life outside the school, the clearer definition of what knowledges, abilities, skills, attitudes, and appreciations are needed to fulfill the functions of life, the determination of proper grade placement of subject materials, the organizing of more valid methods of teaching, and the development of measurement devices and techniques corresponding to each type and unit of instruction.

Horn's conception of a good school is one in which there is continuity of point of view, subject matter, and method. He would advocate an administration as simple as possible and shared in by pupils without, however, the usual elaborate technical apparatus of pupil government. Programs should be freer than at present and there should be a larger amount of unassigned time so that opportunities for educative activities outside the school walls may be fully realized. The essence of good teaching and of educative method is in a continuing friendly, social attitude between teacher and pupil. Horn finds in enrichment and stimulation the answer to the problem of educating the less gifted as well as the average and superior. The skilful use of diagnostic testing and remedial teaching in dealing with the subjects of the curriculum makes out of education a science as well as an art.

Estimate of Current Educational Practice.—The permanent and positive effects which emerge from the last three decades of advance in educational science and philosophy have been mainly directed toward the elementary school, according to Horn. He finds high school and college teaching largely unaffected by these advances. Defects in existing courses of study are due mainly to unreasoned increase in the number of subjects and failure to interrelate the elements in the program of subjects, with the result that children's efforts are dispersed rather than concentrated. School programs carefully worked out in advance are frequently ineffective because of administrative policies which seem not cognizant of the facts and principles of child psychology. Though the schools are charged with being overformal, this condition is not due to over-emphasis upon the fundamental tools of language and number, but to the failure to relate what is taught to the actual needs of child and adult life. Formalism, therefore, is as readily found in content subjects as in the three R's.

Schools which have attempted to advance considerably beyond the subject or grade conception of education have, on the whole, been less effective with their students than have the better public schools where radical experimentation is virtually impossible. The more radical schools usually fail to lay proper stress upon prime social and educational values. They provide little opportunity, as a rule, for pupils to learn that degree of self-control and that acceptance of responsibility which best conduces to coöperative learning.

The Nature of Learning.—As has already been pointed out, Horn rests his case for an education which will prepare the young for the responsibilities of adult society upon what he calls an overlap between the interests and activities of adults and those of children. The school comes in to add the refinements of psychological analysis to matters of administration and teaching method and also to add the refinements of sociological analysis to the determination of curriculum content. The triumph of educational science is in a combination of these two techniques which will yield to the growing generation the optimum development of lasting interests and of right attitudes towards learning and toward life.

On the one hand there is the curriculum, consisting of scientifically determined values which it is the school's function to teach, and on the other a body of facts and principles regarding childhood development. Between the two there is working the cohesive principle of mutual interaction of interests and functions. The curricular content by itself is no guide to method and if depended upon yields only a barren formalism. Nor are children's interests by themselves safe guides to permanent racial values, for they can yield only an anarchy of ends. Building upon the assumption that there is no conflict between these two aspects of the educational problem, we may conceive a school which realizes all the constructive possibilities of freedom and at the same time is a model of scientific systematization.

Detailed analysis of child development indicates not only the constructive interests which appear at successive age levels, but it also demonstrates the extreme variability of performance which is to be expected at different times in the same individual. Pupils can be led to see the necessity of drill and memorization when curricular content is vitally functional. They should be encouraged to share with the teacher in planning and appraising lessons, in working freely under their own initiative and responsibility, and in helpful coöperation with others on group problems. The general principle for instructional organization should be that of so scheduling the learning of curricular values that lessons or other activities have an immediate as well as a future functional reference.

Reactions to Other Points of View.—Horn is not particularly interested in philosophic speculation about problems of education. He believes that the effects of such philosophizing on actual school practices have been greatly exaggerated. Good teaching always remains essentially the same despite conflicting theories. Horn gives as a good reason for the ineffectiveness of much current theorizing the fact that theorizing has so far failed to direct itself towards actual possible changes in the public schools of today. He points out that the great stress in some quarters upon the ultimacy of children's interests in curriculum making has not been productive of any age norms for acceptable childhood living, nor has it concerned itself to any appreciable degree with the needs and activities of children outside the limits of the schoolroom.

WERRETT W. CHARTERS

General Viewpoint and Its Relation to Education.—Werrett W. Charters concedes that change is a large and rather spectacular factor in modern life, but he would insist that relative to the fundamentals of our civilization actual change is not great. We may in confidence follow through on the plans of existing society; the new adventures which the future must inevitably open up will thus be closer to ideal values than if we ill-advisedly strike out upon new social paths. Since the shifting of social ideals is an extremely slow process, it would seem a proper inference that the schools proceed to teach the best knowledge of this generation. By supplementing acquisition of the tested best solutions of today with training in the processes of clear thinking, we prepare youth for stable control of future social change. Although scientists from many fields have already demonstrated that pure science is the greatest practical force in modern civilization, Charters believes that the final answer in the choice of individual and social ideals will never be settled by scientific techniques. The philosopher will continue to compound validated knowledge in the fields of psychology and sociology into a generalized statement of the objectives of education; his function of clarification, guidance, and vision is in no sense pushed off the scene by science. Likewise curriculum-making must by its very nature continue to be the coöperative function of many agencies, rather than the exclusive concern of educational research laboratories.

As a foundation for the work of the school, Charters proposes concerted attack on the problem of working out the central core of American culture. Since in American society there exists no rules committee which irrevocably creates and hands down values, it will be necessary to select and study the truly "cultured" of the population in order to gain insight into essential ideals. This means inquiry into their interests, their qualitative evaluations of all aspects of life, their problems, and the direction of their feelings of obligation. Such is the task which confronts educators. The school is the most important of all social agencies, for by means of the school better methods are disseminated among the populace, and youth is trained to secure its satisfactions in pursuit of the ideals of society. As a matter of principle each child should be taught how to control each situation arising in his experience, but since that would be obviously impossible in practice, a selection of the most important learnings to be taught must be made. Today's standards require that all courses be selected on the basis of usefulness, the vested interests in traditional subjects and in "comprehensive knowledge" notwithstanding. Charters believes the time is rapidly approaching when the ideal of an education continuous throughout life may be realized. At such a time it will no longer be necessary to stress the learning of much purely preparatory material during childhood. The school will articulate with life as rapidly as the techniques of job analysis and of teaching method are perfected. Charters does not believe that the present depression will result in anything more than a temporary setback to the increasing volume of educational expenditures.

Nature of Practical Proposals.—Appreciating that a radical reorganization of the whole school program is not practicable, Charters advises a gradual working over of existing curricula by the elimination of obsolete materials and methods, and by the addition of new elements from a comprehensive inventory of knowledges, ideals, and attitudes. This involves mainly the addition of *project* and *problem* material to the existing stock of school subjects. What is immediately needed to promote curricular reorganization is the execution of hundreds of technical studies designed to throw light on the knotty problem of selection of materials. Here the technique of activity or job analysis is pushed forward by Charters as the most likely instrument for the purpose. Activity analysis is defined as that type of educational engineering which lays the foundations and builds the skeletal framework for all curricula. Properly executed activity analysis substitutes objective criteria for "hunches" in the determination of what should be included in particular textbooks or courses of study.

The essential steps in curriculum construction, as Charters defines them, are as follows: first, a comprehensive analysis of man's social life to set up general objectives of education; second, the breaking up of these objectives into particular ideals, activities, and basic working units; third, the arrangement of curricular elements or working units into an order of importance; fourth, the placing high on the list of those ideals and activities which are high in value for children and low in value for adults; fifth, the determination of those items the teaching of which will be the school's responsibility; sixth, the collection of the best practices with respect to the techniques for inculcating the selected ideals and attitudes; and finally, the arranging of the selected list of elements into proper instructional order by reference to the psychological nature of children. Since only teachers actually adapt the curriculum to the practical exigencies of teaching, they must always remain key consultants in curriculum-making.

The change from an ideal of information-getting to one of conduct means rapid extension of project learning, because such learning seems best to guarantee motivation deep enough to alter conduct effectively. In school practice, projects need to be supplemented by sufficient drill to yield adequate acquisition of skill in important functions. Although the school must know definitely what curricular items it must impart and must apportion these by grades and classes, the conclusion does not follow that school procedure need necessarily be a systematic day-by-day presentation of subject matter. Until the superiority of certain teaching methods over others has been clearly demonstrated, various methods should be used. It is extremely important that there be constant emphasis upon the learning of techniques of critical thinking in order to develop intellectual independence.

Charters expresses a special caution against far-reaching judgments based upon present objective educational tests. There are important areas of mental life and of personality for which no objective tests are as yet available and a great deal depends upon the exercise of a proper degree of scepticism by school people with respect to existing measuring devices.

Estimate of Current Educational Practice.—It is Charters' observation that the smug satisfaction of educators in their own professional field is fast giving way to a growing attitude of deep concern about pressing obligations to the public. The work of the school no longer proceeds on the assumption that the passing-on of information to children directly alters conduct. The actual test of successful instruction is now found rather in the degree to which conduct has been modified. It was largely because the learning of abstracted subject matter had no apparent practical implications, that the project method was formulated. Developments within education have been so rapid that the effective teacher of today must be a person of broad scholarship and deep pedagogical insight. Despite the fact that there is general agreement that moral training should be incidental to the learning of subjects, school routines, and activities, much vigorous direct moral instruction along various lines is actually going on in the schools. Charters finds that there is a strong tendency for textbook authors, lecturers, and theorists in the field of moral education to treat the development of moral character in youth on a far too abstract basis.

The Nature of Learning.—Charters accepts Thorndike's list of original tendencies in man as the most complete and authoritative. As the effective determinants of action he lists bodily structure, mental capacity, instinctive trends, and the physical and social environment. Because nature sets extremely wide limits to human action, the teacher will need to be governed by the principle of doing the best he can with his pupils under the conditions which he faces. Charters finds in children's activities the same essential core as in those of adults, such differences as exist being due to variations in abilities, interests, and character. In the interest of training children so that they shall be made capable of meeting the responsibilities of the future, adults are justified in insisting on *correct performance*. Such insistence is harmonious with the larger ends of the child's self-protection, of proper growth, and of improvement in the rules of the game of life itself. The child cannot himself be a contributor to the curriculum by means of which he is educated, although the curriculum is made for him and can be effective only if it incorporates to a high degree the child's needs and interests. The actual working units of the curriculum are far more dependent upon the nature of the learner than upon the subject matter. Training in, or mastery of, subject matter is, however, obviously not enough with which to meet the larger range of life activities. The curriculum must include all of the aspects of personality development by providing for careful diagnosis of deficiencies, for the realization of ideals through definite plans of action, for the habituation of right behavior and, finally, for such release of intellectual powers as may lead to personality integration. In matters pertaining to personality development and the cultivation of ideals controlling conduct, the curriculum must also be broken up into working units which can be mas-

tered one by one. It must be recognized that conduct and behavior are everywhere and at all times specific. Only by having
many specific experiences relative to such a trait as honesty,
for instance, does a child become capable of formulating general
rules and of adding a significant content to the concept. In this
field the teacher must understand the use of such techniques
as his own contagious enthusiasm, various forms of suggestion,
resort to rational discussion, reward and punishment, personi-
fication, and dramatization, in order that the emotions of pupils
shall be really stirred in the direction of approved ideals. Charters stresses particularly the importance of what he calls the
conduct assignment as a means to application and habituation
of what has been taught. While moral instruction and character
building must probably continue to be indirect results of education, resort to direct instruction must not be lacking whenever
serious social maladjustments occur.

In subject matter fields Charters calls attention to the fact
that education is more closely articulated with life by using
the *activity* approach in curriculum organization and in teaching. He reports that this is not practicable, however, in subjects
the elements of which are closely knit in logical relation. In
these cases the development of learning should be systematically
planned from simple to the more complex. He thus provides a
place for a core of conventional subjects and for rigid training in
fundamentals without regard to the intrinsic interest of the material or to its immediate utility. Charters suggests that the
curriculum for the moron be stripped down to the bare fundamentals of social and vocational behavior.

The recent, widely advertised findings in regard to the better
teaching results obtainable in large classes, Charters believes
should be hesitantly accepted by educators at least until deeper
analyses of such findings shall have been made.

Reactions to Other Points of View.—Since Charters occupies a
position somewhat near the center between the radical left wing
and the conservative right wing of educational theorists

the direction of his criticisms would seem to be fairly obvious. He believes in widespread discussions of opposed points of view about the aims, purposes, and methods of education. He believes the centers of enthusiasm commonly called *fads* in modern education are constructive phenomena which lift teaching to higher levels when they are supported by the development of intelligent and practical techniques. He characterizes *incidental* instruction as accidental instruction especially when attempted in the character-training field. The advocates of incidental instruction have so far furnished no comprehensive check list of functional units by reference to which gaps in character development may be quickly noted and provided for. The advocates of a curriculum which is a direct transcript of child life are really deceiving themselves, for they fail to see that in the absence of valid criteria their judgments about normality in children must be based upon either questionable preconceptions or the merest guesswork.

FRANKLIN BOBBITT

General Viewpoint and Its Relation to Education.—Franklin Bobbitt makes much of the complexity and interrelatedness of modern civilized life. For Bobbitt it is clear that man must attain a broad and balanced understanding of the forces underlying modern civilization and of the forces operative today. Our vision must extend back into the past and forward into the future, our interests must ever be alert to the shifts in affairs, our sympathies must include within their grasp all social groups, all nations, and all institutions. The deficiencies in contemporary community life are due mainly to the looseness and inaccuracy of such thinking as is done about social problems and to the apparent indifference of large sections of the population to public affairs. Society is continually engaged in recivilizing the new generation so that it shall exhibit in its conduct evolved methods of work, evolved habits of mind, evolved ideals, and evolved attitudes. The school is the specialized agency of society for carrying out this recivilizing process, but before the school can adequately guide the young into experiences of a desirable and efficient type, it must possess a criterion for judging what constitutes the good life under modern conditions. Here Bobbitt suggests the technique of a thorough-going social analysis to search out those persons in our midst who are living most adequately under the guidance of the best ideals. The assembling of all the facts about our most civilized citizens and about the manner by which they reached their high-level functioning would give us in essence the needed criteria, the objectives, and probably the most effective methods for an educational program. An educational program is to be understood basically as an outline of the ways by which conduct may be extended in range and elevated in character. Beyond a modicum of highly specialized vocational training, Bobbitt is of the opinion that about nine-tenths of education results from the general social processes in which individuals are immersed. The school in its concern with holding high the quality of present living is merely making more secure the educational effects of the Great School, life itself. A highly developed and well-understood science of educational objectives will, no doubt, show that the objectives of education are the innumerable specialized activities of living human beings. If the objectives and the processes of education are in reality one, there need be no question as to how preparation for the future is to be secured. The full, abundant life, actual wholesome behavior, is at once present reality and guarantor of future stability.

While the chief rôle of education can be rather simply stated, the complexity of modern life makes the actual administration of education extremely difficult. The educator must be a person who combines insight into life, in its various phases and on its different levels, with comprehensive grasp of life in its totality. He must be an expert worker able to fashion the school in such a way that there shall be (*a*) patterns of activities of all proper sorts available, (*b*) information needed for self-guidance available, (*c*) an awakening of interests, desires, evaluations, and ambitions, (*d*) stimulation, guidance, and supervision of the school activities of pupils, (*e*) provision for numerous and varied opportunities, (*f*) coöperation with homes in advisory capacity. With the understanding that life at each growth stage is complete unto itself, Bobbitt nevertheless concedes, in accordance with his plea for social analysis, that adult activities are strategic in the sense that they must remain the goals towards which childhood growth is guided and in terms of which it is evaluated.

The school, to Bobbitt, is not directly an agency for social reform; it is an agency whereby the young are oriented to the intricacies of modern life. That society itself shall be made better in the course of this process is naturally to be expected.

Nature of Practical Proposals.—Bobbitt would concentrate educational effort at two strategic points today. One is in furthering the development of actual objective studies aimed to determine with some degree of finality what the general fields of human action are; the other, which really follows from the first, is the continued stimulation of thinking towards definite and conscious formulation of the principles of curriculum-making. In both these endeavors the educator is necessarily driven out of the narrow and provincial field of the school to take cognizance of the deeper-moving forces within society. His understanding of life broadens and he becomes capable of seeing the problems of the school in their proper perspective. The school is not the main but only an auxiliary educational agency. The educator, possessed of detailed lists of desirable activities (objectives) drawn from life and psychologically matched to the age and ability levels of children, is able skillfully to diagnose individual deficiencies, and to provide, out of a rich store of experience, suitable remedies. This is essential educational science and every teacher can become not only a competent scientist, but can be an authoritative contributor to the accumulating scientific content of education. In the preparation of lists of objectives it is important that the short-sightedness of much that has been called *activity-analysis* in the past be avoided. The richest fields of human activity—our intellectual vision, valuation and planning, our contemplative and meditative life, our aesthetic emotions, our religious feelings, our longings and aspirations—must receive their proper major share of analytic endeavor and educational attention. Although curriculum specialists should break loose from concern over school subjects in their reconstructive labors, it will probably be necessary for some time that schools go on teaching subjects; the emphasis in teaching subjects should be placed, however, upon their instrumental value in enhancing the activities of real life.

Bobbitt believes that curriculum-making must always be a local community affair. Each community must plan an educational program coöperatively and in the light of local conditions. For after all, the finally effective curriculum in the life of any boy or girl is that which he or she has coöperated in making. The details of life in the case of individuals can scarcely be planned in advance, and only as parents, teachers, and children together face the situations of life can adequate programs of activities be drawn up. Bobbitt contends that this functional or behavioristic conception of education is not a mere alternative method to be added to existing educational lore; he believes that if it be clearly understood, radical curriculum reconstruction will follow as a matter of course.

Reference must be made to the tenor of Bobbitt's thinking in his *How to Make a Curriculum*. The above account clearly indicates some degree of shift away from the implications of much-quoted remarks from that book. For instance, Bobbitt there seemed to have no doubts that education was preparation for the long period of adult life and that the program for school education could be worked out in advance with the utmost definiteness. His plan contemplated advance specifications for work undertaken in all the weeks and months of each grade from the first on through the termination of the period of general education in the junior college. His shift since then seems to have been, not from the advocacy of detailed analyses of life activities, but in a real change of heart as to the final uses and disposition of such curricular materials.

Estimate of Current Educational Practice.—Bobbitt finds the public mind frozen around the notion that education can be carried on by means of the specialized and isolated agency of the school. Even where Progressive thought has penetrated, the tendency has been to make reforms within the school, rather than to explore and coördinate the more pervasive educational influences of community life outside. Within the narrow boundaries of the educational profession Bobbitt points to widespread confusion as to goals and the consequent anarchy of methodological proposals. Because of secure isolation, academic categories have grown to enormous proportions, whereas the functional and practical categories are all but neglected. The academic or scholastic emphasis itself is seen in that series of fragments referred to as grades and subjects. Such fragmentation of education has in turn resulted in the absence of any noteworthy coöperation or intercommunication between teachers in different grades or in different subject matter departments of the school. To ordinary observation education is everywhere identified with the traditional machinery of school administration, subjects, textbooks, recitations, and examinations. The dominant methodology is almost entirely in terms of what pupils need to do in order to master subjects or courses. Authoritative statements are still frequently given out in which the fundamental essentials of education are taken to mean those bare tools of literacy in whose interest schools were originally founded, rather than the all-sided development of individuals in respect to personal qualities, dispositions, attitudes, habits, powers of judgment, visions of reality, and assurance of future adult competence so

insistently demanded by modern conditions. The key obstacle
to any significant reform of education Bobbitt finds in the lack
of any generalized vision of education on the part of administrators and teachers.

While he notes the vigorous activity of educators in recent
years in the matter of curriculum revision, Bobbitt fails to
find any very significant progress. Syllabi are much larger in
size, but this increased bulk is still dressed up in the traditional
subject matter forms. Textbooks and curricula now being used
in the social studies are at such remove from the controversial
present that there is little possibility for students to come away
from them with any techniques or approaches of a clarifying
nature. Bobbitt notes a small but unmistakable trend among
educators away from a psychology adequate to "filling the
mind" and towards a psychology adequate to "growing a mind."

The Nature of Learning.—In the light of his later writings, the
elaborate analyses of activities in *How to Make a Curriculum*
are probably to be regarded as suggestive check lists by which
individual accomplishments may be evaluated rather than as so
much subject-matter-set-out-to-be-learned. It must be noted,
however, that even in the above-mentioned book Bobbitt insists
clearly that best educational results come from informal living.
Bobbitt looks upon human individuals as fundamentally so
different, that the particular sequence of educative experiences
leading to fullest self-realization must be determined very largely by every individual for himself. Almost innumerable motivat-
ing forces such as moods, wishes, intentions, awakened desires,
enthusiastic ambitions, likes, and dislikes, are playing constantly in the round of daily situations which each individual faces.
Any conscious teaching which is undertaken is preparatory and
incidental to these situations. Whenever it is evident that important facts are not thus being mastered, they are undertaken
deliberately by the school for definite guidance purposes. The
basic principle in learning to live and function properly in adult-

hood is to make sure of living and functioning properly at each successive age level. The proper life is an integrated one in which the various elements are so interrelated as to provide efficient keys to orientation in every situation which arises within experience. Educational guidance must therefore be constant and all-pervasive, not limited to school semesters and years. Specializations should be avoided to the end of promoting a wide diversification of interests and activities. Even in the development of proper language habits, Bobbitt would look for improvement only as language is used incidentally in the complex of human experience.

Reactions to Other Points of View.—Bobbitt takes issue with educators who seem to believe that controversial issues of theory can be avoided by promoting the use of scientific techniques whose utmost effects would be to secure more certain limited goals like the three R's and vocational efficiency. He has, however, little use for the high sounding phraseology of educational hopes which all too openly indicates a profession still ensconced in adolescence. The notion of a uniform curriculum for all, to be imposed in mechanically determinable fashion, he calls a direct violation of fundamental, individual rights. He does not believe that any progress will come from continued adherence to terms and general conceptions which grew out of totally different social and educational conditions. The objectors to *incidental instruction* seem to Bobbitt to reverse actual valuations in fearing that important matters are omitted under this type of instruction. He points out that it is only the simple and easy which formal direct teaching is capable of transmitting; everything complex and difficult to learn must come through direct participation in activities undertaken for other purposes.

III. EDUCATORS STRESSING THE IMPLICATIONS OF MODERN EXPERIMENTAL NATURALISM

The men whose points of view are presented in Part Three are considered as variants from the philosophy best represented by John Dewey, and perhaps best described as modern experimental naturalism. Dewey is considered first, and each of the others represents some degree of departure from his formulations. The particular order in which the men are presented is of no significance, for they are all clearly oriented to an outlook which finds only instrumental value in both tradition and science.

JOHN DEWEY

General Viewpoint and Its Relation to Education.—To John Dewey, man is inherently the child of Nature. Nature wrought him out of an abundantly varied fertility, provided him with broad powers, and set certain limits to his action. Man has discovered that Nature may become an object of knowledge and he has learned the secret of making Nature an ally in the realization of his ideals. This secret is called scientific method. Its use has revealed the wide extent of Nature's resources and the height of man's abilities. The protective defences in the way of religious and magical devices, which man through untold ages has erected between himself and nature, have already crashed in scattering confusion. Scientific method has proved itself the only reliable means of discovering the realities of existence: it is the new *authentic* revelation, inexhaustible in its possibilities but extremely upsetting in its immediacy. Faith in God and in authority, ideas of soul and immortality, belief in Divine Grace, stable institutions, and automatic progress have been made impossible for the educated mind of today. Applied science is so rapidly changing the underlying conditions out of which institutions arise that there is only bewilderment regarding the type of civilization which is in the making. It is obvious that most of these changes were neither planned nor desired, but it is equally obvious that they are with us and that the rate of change is steadily mounting. Some have thought science an incredible monster carrying man on into a vortex of destruction. Their minds are still oriented to a world of which only vestiges of thought and desire remain. Science is wholly passive; it yields

itself with equal facility to any purpose that man may set. Enthusiasts have even pictured the millenium just around the corner, but they are divorced from the realities of experience.
Man's endeavors do look to the future, but the future is always
uncertain despite the most careful planning. The more mo-
mentous the issue, the more telling is the effect of alien forces
and unforeseen conditions. Man must, therefore, orient himself
to a world in which there will always be a large element of precariousness, but his techniques when directed by high ideals
may yield a civilization far in advance of any yet conceived.
Values emerge in the process of conscious enhancement of human experience. As goods of experience, values occur in all
modes with no predilection towards any particular system of
relationships.

Dewey would therefore subject every institution, every belief, to the test of establishing its contribution to social and
individual goods conceived in the widest possible sense. The
fact that an institution once served as a good would not be
sufficient. Life moves on and institutions and beliefs must constantly be reconstructed in order to be continuously serviceable
to the needs of man.

The Great Society, which modern technology has bound by
technological and economic ties into a dominant reality, may, if
man so wills it, extend its facilities in such manner as to make
possible the cultural renascence of local communities. Dewey
finds the local community with its wealth of intimate interrelationships a nearly ultimate center around which the spiritual
forces of man must be ordered.

American civilization is an example of a prevailing split in
modern life. Our activities are preponderantly matter-of-fact,
materialistic; our spiritual allegiance is idealistic. We have so
far refused to let them fertilize one another, with the result that
in practical matters under the profit motive barbarism runs
riot, and in ideal matters pious verbalization holds sway. De-

mocracy, no more immune from the effects of stupidity, intolerance, "rugged" individualism, and bad education than are other forms of societal organization, has naturally not blossomed according to prescription. That public opinion, however, is becoming effective in some measure is evidenced by increasing amounts of social legislation in recent times. Native resources in the way of creative power and intellectual insight are making themselves perceptible, as oases in the desert of traditional habits and attitudes. If our thinkers would function more effectively in consensus on the task of bringing order, relevance, and clarity into the realm of ideas and attitudes, American society might readily be set on the road to some form of *public socialism*. A vision which pictures natural science and technology in the service of human life, joined with the will to proceed boldly in a course of social experimentation would soon bring order out of chaos. Danger lies not so much in social experimentation, for human nature is dependably conservative. The peril lies rather in proceeding blindly, as at present, into the very teeth of disaster. The problem in the last analysis is an educational one; not, however, one which the present system of education can effectively manage. Educational leaders today are as much confused as anyone else, and the connections of the public schools with public problems are imperceptible. Pioneering is needed in the exceedingly difficult undertaking of bringing into effectiveness the educative values of social life in all of its aspects. We are faced with the task of creating a new art by means of which the results of free inquiry may be meaningfully diffused among the masses of our people. For until a background of knowledge and insight is created, until the conditions of public debate, discussion, and persuasion are improved, there can be no hope of social integration. Until everyone is developed beyond the reach of prejudice, stupidity, and apathy, no one can be *educated* in the full sense of the term. We may well question the very possibility of education, so little do we know as yet about the forces which mold intellectual, moral, and aesthetic character. The art of education awaits the forward movement of basic social sciences. These sciences in turn depend on widespread willingness to utilize the scientific attitude in the reconstruction of the social order.

Nature of Practical Proposals.—In the impasse to which American civilization has come, Dewey places the responsibility for initiating relevant activity squarely upon the intellectual and reflective groups of the population. The duty is theirs to make the critical analysis into causes of present social phenomena which must precede new construction. Until a sense of need and a sense of great opportunity possess the minds of our most able thinkers, they and all their works must remain without social relevance. The focussing of the thought of able people on the great issues and problems of the day promises an intensification of the quality of thinking which beggars comparison with thinking emanating from occupation with traditional materials. Here educators, as members of the intellectual group, may find a center around which emerging purposes for the public schools may gather. Because of a scarcity value today, Dewey would make the development of scientific attitudes of thought, observation, and inquiry the chief business of study and learning. The small and widely scattered body of scientific workers among whom the benefits of inquiry are communally shared is a standing challenge to what could be made of the whole social order.

The universities are the proper places for the study of public problems and the only legitimate sources of oversight and direction in the general educational system. The teaching body itself must share in the determination of educational objectives and in determining what the schools shall do about social conditions. Dewey urges teachers to express their solidarity and to claim a legitimate autonomy by aligning themselves with labor groups. Only as they understand the problems of labor in all forms, can they hope to meet the developmental needs of the children of laborers. The problem of freedom is integral to the whole educational profession; especially does it concern the relations of teachers to administrators and to the public. Both educational philosophy and educational science are to be viewed as intermediate and instrumental disciplines. Philosophy evaluates and criticises practice, judging its own constructive proposals and revising them in the light of results. Science deals with the problems of practice, treats them by means of fundamental scientific disciplines, and turns over its results for the alteration of the mental attitudes of teachers.

While he believes that attempts to make master curricula for the school on a national scale would result in more formalization than we now have, Dewey urges the construction of varied bodies of consecutive subject matter which teachers may freely use in building their own cumulative plans. He urges schools of education especially to point the way out of educational confusion by studying the interrelations between subjects and their social bearing or application, and by providing suggestive reorganizations of subject matter. He does not look upon the *project* method as the sole way out, but feels that what is needed everywhere in public school situations is a will to clarify and reorganize subject matter and method in whatever way seems most promising of genuine articulation with the broad range of life activities.

Dewey suggests that the educational program for the years between adolescence and maturity may be made both more practical and more liberal by abandoning the attempt to give adequate technical preparation to students. He would have instead the aim to arouse permanent intellectual interests and to open up the scientific and social potentialities of the important human occupations.

Estimate of Current Educational Practice.—Dewey does not belittle the educational progress that has been made. He appreciates the essential democracy of the way new ideas are diffused throughout the American system of schools. He appreciates also the enriched, modern programs with the concomitant emphasis upon the development of the broader personality of the child. Subject matter is less standardized than in the past, and vocational preparation is increasingly liberal. These are all gains, but the sum and substance of them is so small that it is scarcely significant for the solution of the complex educational problem.

The chief obstacle to more rapid educational reconstruction is found in the prevailing mental concepts based upon a separation of mind and body. This dichotomy penetrates through every school subject, every method, and is basic to the whole conception of school discipline. It accounts for the clear break between theory and practice and between thought and action which is so common today. It makes our cultural education academic and pedantic and our vocational education blindly manual. The isolation of disciplines like anthropology, history, sociology, morals, economics, and political science from one another, from physical knowledge, and from social life may be similarly explained.

Dewey attacks the school-board control of education for being neither professional nor genuinely social. The school-board system has set up innumerable petty autocrats in the name of efficient educational administration and has allowed concern for physical display to throttle the schools with mass production methods. The dominant type of curriculum consists, for instance, of bundles of knowledge carefully labeled according to school grade or mental ability and neatly arranged in predetermined sequence. The hold which intellectual analysis, formalized information and technical training have upon the schools is evidence of a bias which has militated against the inclusion of valuable aesthetic experiences.

American college students are proverbially immature as a consequence of the lack of any vigorous consideration of great social issues in the lower schools. The repetitious methods used in teaching the so-called "tool" subjects are proof of a complete divorce of these subjects from social content. The increasing extent of modern knowledge has multiplied the number of school subjects, but there are few indications that the intricacy of relations between fields of knowledge so characteristic of the activities of contemporary life has affected curriculum organization. Unfortunately, even as it is taught in progressive schools, science has become just one more body of ready-made information. The idea of science as the most fruitful mental approach in all fields of endeavor has not yet affected the schools.

In many schools which pride themselves on being modern and far in advance of the ordinary public schools, a new limitation seems to have arisen, for these schools have made a veritable phobia of adult imposition, with the result that anarchy has been substituted for the lock-step.

The Nature of Learning.—Man is educable, according to Dewey, because of a wide and varied degree of organic sensitivity, and because he undergoes experiences that are varied and opposed. The extent of his past experiences determines the possibilities of the present moment for him. Organic processes represent the structure of memory and foresight as well as of affection, purpose, and meaning. Human behavior is serially cumulative activity to such an extent that it becomes impossible, except in mental abstraction, to isolate specific reactions to specific stimuli. Every experience is qualitatively unique and effects in some degree a new integration of personality as new habits are added. If there be one formula which better than any other describes the activity most natural to man, it would be that creative activity is followed by critical individual and social judgments which make possible more and better creations. This creativeness flourishes best under conditions which guarantee independence, release of initiative, and discriminative judgment.

School learning must take its cue from the basic analysis sketched above. The primary conditions would be that children participate in activities intrinsically worth while, and that in these activities they perceive the relations of means to ends. When these conditions are adequately cared for, interest in skills and techniques will show itself abundantly. In the early years the function of educators is to discover the budding needs, interests, and capacities in children, and then to secure sufficient educational exercise and application so that other more complex tendencies are generated. In the later years subject matter and method must be so adjusted that developing powers and abilities cause the emergence of still greater powers and abilities. The test of an educationally valid experience is found in the degree to which it contributes to an ordered and consecutive development of experience as a whole. In such an experience both pupils and teacher will participate, though the teacher, because of maturity of experience, will be the naturally accepted leader. Subject matter becomes whatever selected and organized materials are relevant to incorporation into present developing experience. Knowledge is the fruit of such experience, thinking is the method, and ideas are the tools. Discipline comes in the building of habits of observation and judgment which will make intelligent desires inevitable. Freedom lies in enlarging the scope of activity through more diversified, flexible, and meaningful choices.

Reactions to Other Points of View.—Dewey contends that philosophers and sociologists who think of society in terms of a uniform level of one type or another, are merely adding to the confusion of thought in which consideration for the individual is lost. He points out also that thinkers who in religious devotion to science consciously or unconsciously attempt to discredit philosophy, are thereby hindering the very development of science.

Dewey criticizes the tendency prevalent among many workers in the science of education to build a scientific content by the use of concepts derived from mathematics and physics to the neglect of biological concepts. In curriculum-making this is illustrated by the pseudo-objectivity of making an inventory of current usages and current desires, treating it statistically and psychologically, and then administering it in the schools. In psychological studies the same tendency is responsible for locating the unit of behavior in an isolated stimulus-response bond or reflex act, and then conceiving of mind or personality as a kind of totality of such isolated units. He also criticizes the current theory which parcels out the selection of subject matter to sociology and the determination of method to psychology, as omitting due attention to the continuities of the learning process and resulting, therefore, in a deficient and distorted account of personality growth.

Dewey recognizes the triviality of many so-called *projects* that have been carried on in schools, but he believes this concept of method represents a clear advance over the traditional one, and that the defects are remediable. Certainly there is no way out of present confusion in the policy of continuing instruction by means of many isolated and independent subjects while in the social situation the subject matter of knowledge and the arts are intricately interdependent. Dewey regards as stupid the advocacy (in some so-called "advanced" circles of educational thought) of the idea of turning children loose in a richly stored environment.

GEORGE S. COUNTS

General Viewpoint and Its Relation to Education.—To George S. Counts the spectacle of modern America is a profoundly disturbing one. A nation ushered into the world under the soul-stirring ideals of democracy, liberty, and toleration finds itself a century and a half later still uttering the same slogans but revealing in action an almost total negation of them. Under the challenge of physical mastery of the continent and under a marvelously developing technology, the fruits of toil have been acquisitively gathered up by a comparatively small master class possessing exceptional powers of pecuniary astuteness. Theirs has been the liberty to sequester the nation's resources and produce a virtual denial of democracy and of the so-called Rights of Man. Today this anarchic capitalism has brought us the anomaly of hunger and homelessness stalking through a nation in which, without question, there is stocked the greatest supply of material necessities and luxuries known throughout history. Yet in spite of more than a half-century of universal education, America has apparently no leaders capable of formulating plans for social reconstruction in harmony with the implications of industrial civilization.

Counts turns to the soul-stirring vision of Russia under the Soviets. He sees there not the particular Marxist dogmas under whose banners the Revolution was ushered in, but the phenomenon of the largest of modern nations, and in many senses the most backward, engaged in the supreme task of putting the billion mechanical slaves of industrialism to the service of a humane ordering of life. Counts is inspired by the demonstrated power of man's creative imagination in fashioning a Five Year Plan broad enough to grasp in its vision the implications of the maturing physical and social controls of modern science. And he notes especially what is happening to the inchoate Russian masses under the inspiration of genuinely collective ideals.

Counts challenges American educators to be done with their petty, theoretic misgivings about the possible contamination of the public school by the grossness and complexity of social life today. Let them fashion out of American traditions a new vision of democracy, collective, not individual, which will take hold of youth in such a way that another generation will not fear even revolution, if that should be necessary to rid the nation of the incubus of vested interests and special privileges for the few. Let them impose a social heritage charged with bringing into existence a civilization and a culture in keeping with the release from organic necessity that technology has made possible.

Nature of Practical Proposals.—In these exceedingly troublous and dangerous times, Counts calls upon the teaching force, in-

cluding all scientists and scholars, to scrutinize carefully the confused social situation and by formulating far-reaching plans of
reconstruction to afford a much needed stabilizing influence to
our civilization. By thus becoming a society-conscious group and
assuming the pains and the responsibilities of real immersion in
the social struggle, our educators may be able to assume tremendous power in the actual shaping of the future. If they would
meet this opportunity they must shake themselves loose from
the innocuous seclusion of middle-class alliance and boldly step
forth with a comprehensive theory of mass welfare and a compelling vision of Destiny. Instead of defensively fighting against
the efforts of various pressure groups to pin particularist faiths
of one kind or another upon the schools, teachers might become the master pressure group intent upon full realization of
the collective good. The outlook of educators and the various
techniques of educative practice will have to be vastly broader
than merely the system of schools. Under a new social order the
present loosely organized and essentially local scheme of education will probably be forced to give way to centralization and
Federal control in the interest of achieving broad social objectives among the great masses of people. Centralization also seems
to Counts the only effective way of bringing the fruits of the
recently developed educational science equally to all units of
the system as soon as they are validated. Counts is, however,
under no illusions regarding any attempt to determine objectives
of education scientifically, nor does he hold any brief for the
much heralded business management and administrative efficiency of today except as incidental to the main business of
education. He entertains serious misgivings about the current
policy of placing the early education of our children almost entirely in the hands of women and he also distrusts the increasing
tendency to use compulsion at the upper end of our educational
ladder.

Estimate of Current Educational Practice.—Counts contends
that inasmuch as the American system of education is the genu-

ine handiwork of the people, it has been molded by the same forces which have worked such havoc with the general welfare. Our schools dance to the tune of the successful business man and boast of their "practicality." Although predominantly among the populace there is still abounding faith and hope that education as we administer it will prove the panacea for all our ills, discerning observation shows teachers engaged in perpetuating ideas and institutions suited to a bygone age, and ideas and institutions already cracking under the strains of industrialism. The discussions among educators about democracy, citizenship, and ethical character which continue to go on are largely cold, abstract, and meaningless, because the profession as a whole is outside the real social situation and leans dangerously towards moral and spiritual bankruptcy. Counts credits the Progressive schools with bringing into educational focus the importance of child study, the rôle of intrinsic interest and real situations in learning, the value of varied types of school activity, and the present concern over personality and character growth, while at the same time he severely criticizes them for losing sight of social welfare. Prevailing low standards of scholarship in the United States, he attributes to lay control of the schools.

The Nature of Learning.—Counts still speaks the language of the modern Progressive movement in education in certain matters concerned with the learning process. He would agree that all curricular matter should be brought into relation with the child's interest. He criticizes the modern testing movement in much the same way as the Progressives by saying that it has tended to emphasize archaic methods of learning. He is far from agreeing, however, that the whole purpose of education can be accomplished by resorting to the child's interest alone. Most of these minute matters of educational method, Counts believes, are greatly over-emphasized in theoretic discussions of American education. He is mainly concerned with larger issues of social policy and the educational implications thereof. This leads him back to matters of educational method of more vital import. If the chief function of education today is to transmit a thoroughly relevant and appealing vision of America's social destiny to the next generation, we must call a spade a spade and frankly resort to *imposition*. Children are imposed upon inevitably and continually under every imaginable type of social order and the social impasse in which our country finds itself today is plain evidence of the manner of imposition to which we have been subject. Let us therefore openly strive to mold the child according to *our* ideal of the meaning of America—developing his tastes, shaping his attitudes, and even imposing ideas upon him. Such is the obligation of a responsible and competent profession of education and if adequately managed it is the way to great achievement. Further, let us not forget in our reconstructive educational program the importance of socially useful labor.

Reactions to Other Points of View.—Counts observes that the philosophic uncertainty evident throughout American educational theory is a reflection of the condition of life as a whole in the United States. Neither the Conservatives nor the Progressives seem to him to give notable indications of awareness of the real trend of the times. And though the educational system visibly breaks under too heavy a strain of contradictions, no satisfactory program of reconstruction is forthcoming. The Progressives see nothing in the crisis which might cause them to change their habit of preaching freedom, science, and the open mind. They fail to see the repudiation of the principle of social solidarity implied in purposing these ideals alone. The Progressive opposition to indoctrination in any form is philosophic anarchy, and it becomes in social practice the ancient gospel of laissez faire. In the Progressive emphasis upon following the interests of the child, Counts sees evidence of the lack of any robust ideal. The Utopia of the Progressives, apparently, is to be reached without grubbing down into the substratum of society to tap the deep flowing currents of social life.

The special bogies which clutter up the educational scene and so obscure clear vision today, Counts enumerates as follows: the notion that human nature in origin is both free and good; the notion that education is a kind of pure mystic essence; the notion that education can and should be impartial; the notion that the child's world and the adult's world are dichotomous; the notion that education should be primarily intellectualistic and aim at agnosticism; the notion that the school is an all-powerful social agency; and the notion that education is essentially adjustment to social change.

WILLIAM H. KILPATRICK

General Viewpoint and Its Relation to Education.—Old folkways, traditional beliefs and attitudes, and the inherited institutions of social life, according to William H. Kilpatrick, have been made anomalous by the conditions which the development of modern science has created. Actually we live in an exceedingly complex and a rapidly changing world, a world in which social integration is a necessity and interdependence already a fact. Life as every man knows it today is full of precariousness and uncertainty and strange novel events. Adequate orientation and guidance are not forthcoming from an ethics, a religion, or a philosophy based upon a logic already long outmoded by scientific discoveries. We are confronted by naked facts of human experience; dare we accept the challenge to appreciate, understand, and control them? It means acceptance of two basic elements in our civilization—mass production and standardization in the economic realm, and rapid pervasive change throughout social life. With acceptance goes the obligation to control. The precedent of human mastery set by the invention and gradual perfection of the experimental method in modern science should give courage in attempting control. Man is exalted by the possibility of putting civilization on a basis of conscious thought. In small degree he has already shown the wide limits within which human creative endeavor can shape the world. The material conditions for the great adventure of control are already at hand; the ideals and standards of coöperative living remain to be worked out.

American society of the present is penetrated through and through by changes. Unfortunately, collective intelligence has been inadequate up to now in bringing order out of widely prevailing confusion. Vested interests in religion, business, and scholarship fight strenuously against any major institutional transformation despite the obvious implications of existing conditions. Our democratic tradition, when more deeply explored and more widely extended than at present, bears within it an ethical principle capable of creating real social integration. The democratic ideal of the good life breaks down the dichotomy between individual good and social good, for it normalizes those expressive activities of the various human capacities in each person which lead to further similar but always more expansive activities of the self and of all other selves. Democracy, in effect, means a nation integrated through the variety of its sub-groups and of its individual personalities. The problem before us amid the confusions and contradictions of the contemporary scene is to combine our controlling technique of experimentation (which has made possible such unprecedented material productivity), with the democratic emphasis upon the value of individual personality. Thus we may launch an intelligent program of attack upon the tradition-entrenched vested interests. Specifically such a program will call for the abandonment of the profit motive in industry and the early adoption of a more rationally planned economy in the interest and for the benefit of all.

Such creative grappling with the situation that confronts American civilization is exactly education in the widest sense. We learn as we make clear to ourselves the actual difficulties that we face and as we try alternative ways out. The school's function is then to build personalities dynamically stable by virtue of faith in intelligence and an abiding moral vision. Educators must see to it that the experiences of childhood are those which lead increasingly to self-direction, that children's activities are increasingly self-initiated and independently thought through in the light of a broader and broader view of their effects. More specifically in the face of the confronting social situation which defines the needs, the school must move in two directions; in the first place towards deeper concern for the welfare of the whole child growing in wholesome relations to others; and in the second place towards producing in children a high degree of facility in remaking their behavior patterns as changed conditions demand them.

Nature of Practical Proposals.—Kilpatrick has been greatly concerned with clarifying the meaning of educational objectives, method, curriculum, and subject matter in the light of a point of view consistent with democratic ideals, contemporary changing society, and the developments of modern science. He proposes a school system reaching from early childhood through adult life, a system which is significantly related at all possible points to life itself. This would mean an educative environment wherein the social motive directs how the learner shall meet the progressively developing demands of the total life situation. It would also mean that the first concern of the school should be with building individual and collective intelligence capable of dealing with the threatening problems of a changing civilization. Kilpatrick proposes as the units in an educational program enterprises in which teacher and pupils together creatively work at real problems. Positive application of the fact that the future is largely indeterminable would prevent such a curriculum from being worked out in advance of actual experience. Insistence upon inherent connectivity between school enterprises and social life outside the school is expected to guarantee that variety and richness of experience without which life would remain narrow and provincial. The cumulative effects of such a succession of experiences would be measured by growth in personality in the widest sense, that is, by increasing power and control over experience. Subject matter derived from our incomparably rich racial inheritance would always be regarded as instrumental to building in learners better ways of behaving as these are called for in real experienced situations. The school is thus oriented to the problem of enriching life and of developing personality rather than to transmitting a selected subject matter. Method becomes how to deal with children, how to steer the whole life of the learner toward integration, how to widen the outlook of pupils, how to build the disposition of open-minded search, and how to lead pupils to choose experiences rich in present meaning and future promise. Study from the point of view of the learner means active attack upon the obstacles and difficulties encountered in executing individual and group purposes. School administration takes on new meaning. Its function is to provide for genuine educational efficiency by recognizing that teaching is an art based upon science and philosophy, and by creating an atmosphere in which teachers may become self-directing personalities able and eager to assist in determining educational policies and procedures. Educational research must emerge from its present extremely limited field to set up experiments instrumental in realizing more broadly conceived educational objectives. Kilpatrick does not propose immediately a wholesale abandonment of present educational machinery although it is obvious that such action is eventually called for. He fully recognizes the revolutionary nature of his proposals and the anarchy which would result from an attempt suddenly to put them into practice everywhere. But he does insist that educators face the implications of a rapidly changing universe in which precariousness is a large factor and make such immediate adaptations in their practices as will best pave the way for further adaptations in the future.

Estimate of Current Educational Practice.—Kilpatrick is duly appreciative of the fact that our sprawling educational organization has actually promoted the spread of new ideas on their merits. And he finds as a consequence that the schools have shown some evidence of an awareness of the changed modern situation by making a place for a modicum of real life experience on their programs. Due to the fascination of new administrative and measuring techniques, to alliance with conservative forces, and to the actual difficulties inherent in the management of dynamic learning, the spread of the leaven of a more progressive education is, however, effectively checked. The conservative emphasis is enhanced by a kind of academic inbreeding within the system, by the prevailing satisfaction with external signs of learning, and by attempts to use the public schools to inflict upon youth fixed beliefs and attitudes. The traditional picture of a static civilization satisfactory in its main outlines finds ample machinery in the schools whereby to prolong its existence; witness, school grades and promotion systems, recitation periods, marks, logically organized and poorly written textbooks, arrangement of school furniture, determined-in-advance curricula, *memoriter* methods, teacher "training." It is not in evidence that democratic ideals play any important part in the operation of this vast machinery of education. Unfortunately the scientific movement in education in its emphasis upon the objective measurement of abstracted and inconsequential phases of learning has played into the hands of the promoters of the *status quo*.

The Nature of Learning.—Kilpatrick looks at life biologically and sees it continuous throughout all nature. Man is the culmination of a single series beginning with mono-cellular structures. With advancing complexity of structure in this evolutionary series goes increasing range and complexity of response, until in man there appears the possibility of shaping environment in increasing degrees to suit his taste. Behavior is the series of responses an organism makes to the stimuli it encounters. These responses change the organism so that it is being constantly rebuilt during life. Past rebuildings are the basis upon which present reality is faced and the responses now made are truly creative in the sense that they have never been made before. The distinguishing feature of the human biological level appears to be that of an increased degree of complexity in the life lived, in the responses made. The consciously directed creativity called forth in every stimulating situation or behavior-upset is what is called thinking, and when this thinking is so guided that the individual expands in comprehension of meanings, complexity of self-hood, and social responsibility, it may be said that education has gone on.

The growing child builds himself from infancy onward by interaction with a subtly and pervasively effective social environment. This social conditioning of behavior is ever present and it is basic even to our most distinctive self-valuations. In human learning (defined fundamentally as the devising of a satisfactory restorative to upset equilibrium), there is going on simultaneously a unique connecting of indefinitely many parts of the situation and a remaking of the organism in indefinitely many aspects. Learning in children has therefore far-reaching effects and any attempted measurement of these must necessarily be incomplete. The only adequate test of one instance of learning would be found in the total outworking of all consequent changes in life. This consideration should guide thinking relative to existing "objective" tests of learning products.

Guidance in the process of self-building best takes place through improving the stock of meanings; this signifies making them more numerous, more widely inclusive of life's values, better defined and validated, more effectively organized, and whole-heartedly obeyed. It is to be noted that in making preparation for fullest integration within the self and toward society, we are adopting as well the best means for enjoying a rich life in the immediate setting. Freedom plays its part in promoting the child's living in his own true character, because it means the making of decisions and the acceptance of responsibility for the consequences of decisions.

Kilpatrick holds that genuine thinking and creativity are potential in all human beings. Apparent qualitative differences among individuals are matters of degree, and education must therefore provide for the cultivation of thinking and of creative endeavor in each child on his own level of ability to learn. The active purposeful experiences with which children are absorbed are conceived to be moral in the same degree to which they are adequately educative. Intelligence is defined in terms of the disposition and the ability to use existing (recurrent) elements of experience, or meanings, to build in cumulative fashion more and better meanings.

Kilpatrick, while latterly discounting the s→r terminology, still uses the laws of learning as formulated by Thorndike, but always with reference to developing situations within experience. Readiness, exercise, and effect, as he uses them, are in terms of the cumulative educative influences of the past.

Reactions to Other Points of View.—Kilpatrick directs his criticism analytically upon every vestige of traditionalism in our educational theory and practice. The traditional theory of education has been skilfully shaped into conformity with the static social outlook characteristic of feudalism and medieval religion. That which is has been so ordained and will ever remain as it is. The inappropriateness of such a view today is strikingly evident. But when we look closely at our educational scheme we find that the schools are operating under leaders the vast majority of whom are consciously or unconsciously under the influence of this static viewpoint. One needs but to perceive what is connoted in current theory and practice by terms like learn, teach, study, subject matter, curriculum, promotion, textbook, objectives, and norms to see into what detail optimistic certainty about the future has gone.

Kilpatrick opposes psychological views which assume that analytic learning must for a long time precede any attempt at mental synthesis, that one thing can be learned at a time, that learning is adequately defined as fixing in habit, and that the test of learning is giving back on demand. He opposes also the attempt to study the child wholly by measurement techniques which isolate separate items of knowledge, separate skills, or separate habits. He points out that the scientific movement in education is to a large extent allied with an anti-democratic school administration, and that the movement has been instrumental in covering with scientific approval reactionary and conservative practices. The recent trend in curriculum theory centering upon the development of so-called unit-plans, Kilpatrick puts under the suspicion of being the familiar predigested subject matter dressed up in a new name.

HAROLD RUGG

General Viewpoint and Its Relation to Education.—Harold Rugg has been intently studying the American scene for a long time. He thinks he sees unmistakable evidences of a great emergent culture. The materials of that future culture lie about us now in confused, unanalysed masses; psychological, economic, political, anthropological, and social data, awaiting a synthesis which can come only out of concentrated study. The masses of our people driven by the fear of insecurity and by the lack of personal integrity exist almost upon an animal level, herding together in large cities, pursuing intemperate pleasures to escape boredom, and lured by the siren call of property in things. Our country, however, has not been lacking in sensitive and original minds. By the very exigencies of the raw environment most of these creative minds of the past and of the present have gone into the task of the physical conquest of nature. The rich rewards of capitalistic organizations have directed the energies of potential artists into corporate material enterprise until the twin concepts of size and speed dominate American life. A few of these creative minds appearing from the native background have held a steadier course by firm adherence to the possibilities of personality in the modern age. As artists they have begun to point out to the rest of us that our civilization may be worth while only if the millions of American men and women are able to find in it the expression of their individual creativity. The bewilderment and confusion so common today among our people must give way to confidence and clarity of purpose. We must as individuals learn to place integrity in ourselves and integrity in our fellowmen at the top of our list of values. We must develop a more acute sense of social adaptability and of pragmatic critical-mindedness. A consciously reconstructed educational program is our chief reliance, but before that is attempted, much preliminary groundwork among the intricacies of the American mind needs to be done. What is needed is a creative portrait of our contemporary society that will reveal its essential internal and external make-up. This Rugg attempts to supply by recourse to the documentation of persons whom, in virtue of their matured thinking and feeling, he chooses to call "frontier thinkers." These advanced scholars have begun the exploration of the politico-economic implications of the machine age, the psychological, sociological, anthropological, and geographic backgrounds of human life, and the possibilities of artistic creation and criticism in America. On the basis of studies already available, Rugg calls for the coöperative endeavor of our most far-seeing and critical minds towards the formulation of a program for producing cultured individuals in great numbers. He believes that this can best be done by concentrating on two foci; first, an expressive theory of individual and group life based upon American cultural backgrounds, and second, a collectively sanctioned planning program encompassing economic, political, and social life. Government might thus emerge from the limitations placed upon it by the present pecuniary régime and become an enhancing and encouraging force to social and individual cultural enrichment. Rugg believes that we must distinguish philosophically between the attitude of scientific analysis and that of artistic synthesis if we would attain a proper cultural balance. Since he looks upon the school as the most effective agent for social regeneration, Rugg insists that the curriculum must be constructed around two central objectives: creative personal development, and appreciative participation in American life. He visions a school-centered community, a society in which all the institutions and productive agents are conscious of an obligation to contribute to the cultural growth of individual persons. It is plainly up to intelligent adults to create out of the richness of present resources a physical, mental, and emotional environment for adults and for children which will bring to expression the cultural possibilities of personality.

The seriousness of the present economic collapse has led Rugg to the conviction that America is on the verge of entering a new epoch. In *The Great Technology* his thought has matured to the extent of seeing the future of America in terms of three alternatives—anarchic drift, class rule, or technological civilization. He documents in striking fashion his insights into the past and present of the American scene. He is convinced that only the full working out of the implications of scientific technology in society will solve the serious problems of the present and lead to true progress. Bravely he attempts to point the immediate road which can be taken. By means of a national clearing house of forum discussion which shall focus the thought of the intelligent minority and direct ways of altering the basic mass concepts of competition and conformity, Rugg hopes that the way out of chaos will open. He is convinced that only an education as wide and as continuous as life can build the new day.

Nature of Practical Proposals.—Rugg stresses the importance of concentrating educational scholarship and technology upon the complex problem of designing a school program which will integrate all social agencies at each age level from infancy to old age. "Frontier thinkers" in education should be engaged constantly in building centers of effective adult opinion as well as in educating a progressive minority of youth. The first step in educational reconstruction is the synthesizing and the re-departmentalization of the materials of instruction. We need definitely to know what facts and principles are basic to intelligent participation in American institutions. Such a tentative core of central concepts is suggested in Rugg's series of social science textbooks recently published for use on the junior high school level. He proposes a problem-solving organization of such materials towards the development of socially valuable skills. He proposes also a richness of vicarious episodic subject matter which will stimulate genuine insight and help in the creation of a truly experimental attitude towards life. It is in the vital participation of youth in community undertakings that the basic concepts in the social sciences and in the fine arts become effective. If only a few schools in each state thus emphasized a synthesis of social understandings and skills with genuine meaningful creative activity in the community, Rugg believes the cultural level of American life might be markedly raised in a single generation.

The development of a new type of teacher-training program is part of Rugg's scheme of educational reorganization. He conceives of a faculty of truly cultured persons and a highly selected student body together making a genuine community of cultural groups. The students will grow in understanding of childhood by living with the children in a laboratory school which is under the direction of artist teachers. The students will participate from the first in research projects suggested by teaching problems. They will see demonstrated the intimate relations of the school with community life as a whole. It will be the function of the academic part of their educational program to acquaint them with the frontiers of thought in every field and to develop in them a love for good books. Through such an all-round program of growth Rugg believes the students will be led to formulate adequate personal theories of life and education.

Rugg conceives of the elementary school essentially as an introduction to community life. The secondary school should attempt to appraise culture and to review intelligently the changing trends in the social scene in order that students may be prepared actually to help in the direction of cultural evolution. Rugg proposes a school régime of activities upon a thoroughgoing experimental and creative basis. He would, however, supplement this activity program by the systematic learning of fundamental tool skills.

In *The Great Technology* written in the midst of depression, Rugg bravely calls for educational inflation. He suggests that the educational budget be quadrupled in order that effective remedies for the plight of society may be immediately applied. The money would be obtained through the Reconstruction Finance Corporation and used to promote a scientific appraisal of existing educational facilities, a scientific study of educational needs considered in the broadest sense, the organization of adult discussion groups under the leadership of Boards of Education, the development of comprehensive cultural programs integrated by Boards of Education with the national plans for social reconstruction mapped out by economic and political leaders. Rugg envisages a National Council of Cultural Reconstruction with appropriate sub-councils in local communities as the functioning agencies by which educational reconstruction may be planned and administered. He frankly recognizes the heroic nature of such an enterprise in the face of existing obstacles.

Estimate of Current Educational Practice.—Rugg sees the American educational scheme against the larger background of American life. Whatever guiding principles emerged in the course of the upbuilding of American civilization were passively reflected by the schools. In the surge of nineteenth-century growth and change when America was engaged upon innumerable material conquests, there was neither time nor inclination for taking thought about the proper design of a system of education.

Schools were built, organized, and administered in the spirit of prevailing mores. Conformity to prevailing mass attitudes and to the spirit of competition in economic enterprise were indoctrinated by means of the formalized mechanism of school-keeping. The superficial ideals of literacy and book learning represented in essence an orientation rather to past racial glories than to the present problems or cultural needs. These same ideals continue to dominate the existing school system and are, to a considerable degree, responsible for the existence of the top-heavy white-collar class which now suffers so tragically from the ravages of unemployment. Rugg points to another serious concomitant of the narrow literacy education of the past in what he calls a false hierarchy of social classes reaching from captains of industry through political bosses, professional work-ers, and skilled tradesmen to the tremendous masses of workers engaged in the manual labor required by the new industrial order. In this hierarchy, based upon exploitation, men of scientif-ic and aesthetic insight were relegated to the background, while men devoid of any insight into the social aspects of industrializa-tion rose to positions of power and dignity.

Educators have so far failed to meet the challenge of the new day; the school curriculum remains oriented to the life of the past. Education is still regarded by most professional workers as the great conserving agent rather than as the great recon-structing agent of society.

The Nature of Learning.—Learning to Rugg is maximum growth towards a known goal. Learning is a preparation for fullest living tomorrow, but this preparation becomes possible only as those who chart the learning course during childhood and youth are guided by science. Learning means first of all the reduction to routine habit as soon as possible of the many mechanical skills basic to full bodily and mental functioning, such operations as walking and talking, writing, reading, and computing. It means a program of planned experiences carefully graded to age and mental and interest levels, and so related and coördinated that growth becomes consciously a continuous progressively expanding affair. In the most effective learning the learner must himself will to learn; he must hold his mind open and at the same time direct it critically upon experience; he must be absorbed in his tasks and at the same time feel the measure of his efforts against the standard of his own inner integrity. Each unit of work or experience should be definitely contributory to growth in one or more of the following directions: power of generalization, expansion of imagination, mastery of difficult meanings and relationships, or skill in manual coördinations. The general atmosphere of the school should be one of freedom rather than compulsion. The school should be a place where a sympathetic skilled direction and guidance are constantly available and brought to a focus on developing experience. It is necessary that the first-hand observation, research, creative activity, discussion, and systematic practice of children, be supplemented by a rich assortment of vicarious experiences dealing with the natural world, with human geography, and with the historical movements of community, national, and international life, in order that the resulting fund of meanings shall cover fully the many aspects of individual and social life.

The really fundamental thing to Rugg is that learning shall culminate in every individual not only in intellectual orientation and social behavior but in a personal, mental, and emotional synthesis. Contemplative absorption in an experience as such, should be possible to all because it is the great balancing factor in life. It can come about only by making the school sensitive to the artistic and aesthetic area of life. The overflowing creativity and absorptive interests of childhood can and should be so cultivated as to yield an integrative leaven to the whole of life.

Rugg seems to be moving towards a new psychological orientation in *The New Technology*. He pleads for an eclectic psychology which shall glean from each of the major schools extant in contemporary America an essential contribution. Specifically he would include the Behaviorists, the Gestaltists, and the Psychoanalysts. He would add to these, however, the concepts of integrity and appreciative awareness which he thinks of as the special contribution of creative artists.

Reactions to Other Points of View.—Rugg is concerned, mainly, to point out that the widely prevalent pragmatic instrumentalism, as emanating today from John Dewey, is not an adequate guide to educational reconstruction. He is as fully appreciative as anyone of the constructive effects of this point of view in clarifying the intellectual aspects of life by working out *the experimental way of knowing,* and he acknowledges its destructive influence in breaking up the last remnants of faculty psychology. But he finds its defects in its very qualities. Just because its emphasis is upon problem-solving, upon the sharpening of the tools of life, and upon preparatory acts, it can offer no guidance in the realm of intuitional or consummatory or artistic experience. Life has an explosive emotional phase as well as a well-regulated, intellectual phase, and who shall say that the latter is all-important? It is Rugg's contention that this issue is paramount. Shall we proceed in the instrumentalist fashion to enthrone intellectual analysis, experimental action, social adjustment, and erudition as the objectives of education, or shall we ponder further and let the artist as well as the pragmatic philosopher contribute to the formulation of objectives? Science has just begun to validate the intuitive vision of the creative artist and American artists growing up under the pragmatic tradition have already begun to question the inclusiveness of pragmatism. It would seem then that educators should look beyond problem-solving for norms pertaining to attitudes of self-cultivation, appreciative awareness, integrity of the self, and a society of proud, cultivated persons. Let them attempt a total vision rather than accept a partial vision before planning their programs.

BOYD H. BODE

General Viewpoint and Its Relation to Education.—This modern age of science, Boyd H. Bode finds, is making over our whole civilization. The progressive release of intelligence from the bounds of tradition which is so characteristic today has made possible a vision of a continuous Golden Age to be realized some time in the not too distant future. The modern broadened meaning of democracy is now outlined clearly above the deficiencies and inadequacies of our social life. We can see, for instance, that it means a real brotherhood in which each shares in the opportunities, the accomplishments, and the ideals which are the common heritage. We can understand that democracy is truly realized only to the extent that the resources of the nation are used for the benefit of all and to the extent that there is general sensitivity to all manner of human interests. We are beginning to think that national safety lies chiefly in the better utilization of the general intelligence of citizens upon the different aspects of important social problems. These new insights may be summed up into what may be called a modern orientation to the total physical and social environment. Such an orientation would include confidence in intelligence, and joy in the release of human energies upon the strenuous task which lies ahead. Since the principal reliance must be upon education, the immediate function of educators is to prepare for a progressive reconstruction of the social order. Educators cannot continue to sit back and dully reflect the changes going on around them. They must be acute enough to perceive, for example, that the intensive programs to eliminate waste and inefficiency in industry have been in many cases anti-social in their effects. Educators should not only transmit what is valuable in the racial inheritance and develop the intellectual resourcefulness of the younger generation, but they must also imbue the young with a militant democratic faith. When the educational system works under a genuine social ideal, and when educators understand life in terms of the actual circumstances and opportunities of contemporary civilization, the road to man's triumph in a magnificent future will be open. The central emphasis of any educational program should be in developing the human power to think. Upon adequate thinking about concepts like government, force, energy, heredity, and patriotism, everything else depends. The essence of education may be found in the type of inquiry into current beliefs and institutions which leads to reformation of social aims in keeping with human worth and dignity. The discipline of thinking prepares us for intellectual independence by the recognition that there can be no ultimately valid formulation of beliefs, institutions, or ends. Bode looks upon culture as fundamentally a way of life enabling individuals to express the integrity of their personalities in and through their daily occupations.

Nature of Practical Proposals.—Bode points out that the greatest need in education today is for a controlling philosophy built out of criticism and reflection upon all the available data about modern society. Such a philosophy would give much needed clarification to the issues between educational theory and educational research. It would lead to the construction of an educational program in the execution of which each of these factors would play coördinate rôles. Theory would be concerned with the continuous refinement and reconstruction of objectives, and science with revealing the agencies efficacious in realizing objectives. Bode feels that if liberal education is to have any meaning in modern life where the call is for technical proficiency and vocational utility, there must be a thoroughgoing revision of educational subject matter and of educational methods. The new curriculum should provide for an integrated developmental program at all stages from kindergarten to college. Its central theme can be none other than *preparation for membership in a democratic social order*. All subject matter will need to be selected solely on the basis of its contributory value in building up a general attitude which recognizes the responsibility of human intelligence in making a better civilization. The school subjects must be shown in their broadest meanings and in the actual relation which they bear to each other in social life. Bode suggests that a proper recognition of the essentially scientific organization of subject matter and of democratic social ideals will give educators sufficient clues to the practical selection of curricular materials. The clue to method, he believes, will be found in a recognition of the importance of individual initiative and self-expression. The teacher, working under the guidance of clearly understood social aims, will perform functions like asking questions, suggesting relevant facts and leads, and pointing out difficulties, in such a way as to provide the utmost stimulation with the least amount of hindering interference with ongoing pupil activities. Since intelligence cannot function adequately until subject matter is logically organized, the teacher should scrutinize carefully childhood interests, vocational needs, and pure intellectuality in order to learn how each contributes to logical organization of experience.

Bode suggests the re-orientation of programs for moral education around the prospect of an experimental civilization which places the seat of authority in human intelligence. He believes the college should lay bare the underlying institutional structure and the conflicts of modern life in such a way as to leave the student free to make his own final philosophic formulations.

Estimate of Current Educational Practice.—The lack of any virile social gospel in American education, Bode thinks, is responsible for the uncertainty about educational objectives at a time when education is widely available and when the resources of life are abundantly at hand. We seem not to have inquired seriously about the meaning of education in a democracy. Bode finds two divergent tendencies at work in present-day theorizing about the ends of education. In one, preparation for adult life is assumed as exclusively desirable; in the other, the supreme end seems to be full and free childhood experience. The choice is thus between subordinating the child to adult standards and leaving the child entirely to the play of his own whims. In neither is there much provision for the exercise of intelligence. Practically we have moved in the direction of preparing children for greater social achievements by the introduction into curricula of material pertaining to man's struggles and achievements in building civilization to its present level. Educational experiments which have opened so widely the field of special talents and capacities in children are significant for thus emphasizing the possible rôle of the individual in group undertakings. On the whole, however, educational science has developed out of relation to the wider social scene and has therefore tended to reinforce the rule of tradition. While educators have neglected to widen their perspectives in accordance with changes constantly going on about them, they have at the same time let slip certain of the approved values of the past. There is little concern today for the old-fashioned ideal of scholarship as knowledge for its own sake. This represents the loss of an invaluable stabilizing influence amid the confusing trends of modern democratic life.

Bode believes that the idea of a substantive mind which is so interwoven in the body of traditional culture, has not really been given up by teachers despite apparent wholesale rejection of the faculty psychology. The drift away from general education and towards specific education which reflects the denial of the efficacy of formal discipline, will not be properly understood and controlled until we face in more analytic fashion the real significance of mind.

The Nature of Learning.—Bode defines mind as the way the organism deals with its environment. On the sub-human levels behavior is almost universally explained in terms of spontaneous activity and simple habit formation growing out of successive adaptations to changing situations. This adaptive behavior is essentially mechanical and pre-determined. On the human level behavior takes place in terms of ideas and purposes which place it qualitatively much higher than mechanical habit. Human behavior is essentially purposive, becoming so by virtue of the progressive reconstruction of successive situations. The term "mind" or "mental state" is no longer needed since behavior is autonomous. The environment, as we perceive it, changes concomitantly with changes in our reactions to it. Our reactions may be considered as a series of temporary unifications of large numbers of internal and external bodily responses. Thinking in its analytic and synthetic aspects emerges when we face novel situations for which our established habits prove inadequate responses; it is a matter of finding and testing meanings and of the construction of new, more adequate habits. Thinking is thus the essence of learning and takes place not by repetitive drill but by active attack upon unsolved problems. The conditions by means of which human intelligence is released and learning takes place are in equal measure set by environment and heredity.

Obviously the school must build far beyond the mere multiplication of specific habits in children. It must relate established habits in such manner that they are formed into wider systems of response and finally into the order of concepts adaptable to a wide variety of situations. This is the true meaning of *transfer of training*. Its realization can be assured only by cultivating in learners both social context and logical organization of experience. Since concept building must be performed by each individual for himself, school organization should allow opportunity for the exercise of initiative and experimentation by individuals. The school should provide real problems and vary teaching method in ways best conducive to thinking. The background of school subjects should be carefully developed, subjects should be connected with pupil interests, and such matters as recitations, assignments, and conditions of study should be adjusted to the end of effective, independent thinking by pupils. Only by interweaving the selected subject matter of the school with the experience of learners can we render them capable of responding intelligently and appreciatively to the variety of human needs and aspirations. Our conception of character as a collection of ideal traits must change to that of a dynamic adjustment of life's various interests in reference to a social ideal. Instead of building character by means of various isolated techniques in terms of separate traits, we must look upon character as the outcome of school life as a whole.

Bode points out that our increased knowledge about individual differences among humans in no way precludes our endeavors to attain common ends; it rather obligates us to devise new and more varied methods of transmitting the essentials of education.

Reactions to Other Points of View.—Bode has made considerable effort to give proper evaluations to various trends in educational theory. He himself thinks largely in the tradition of Dewey and therefore makes no direct criticism of the fundamental position in Dewey's philosophy. Dewey's influence, Bode reports, has so far been more in the field of method than in the field of basic ideals. He attacks rather severely some of the implications which Kilpatrick sees in the Dewey tradition. Kilpatrick leans toward letting the pupil determine his own curriculum; this Bode believes is a reversion to Rousseau. Kilpatrick also seems to imply the rather hazardous doctrine that the future should be left to itself. The *project method* as formulated by Kilpatrick, while stressing the importance of independent and meaningful action, is unsatisfactory without considerable supplementation because it makes learning too haphazard and too immediate. To Bode the project method does not give the guidance and direction to learning which clearly conceived larger ends can give.

Snedden is criticized for sacrificing logical organization and social insight to preconceptions about social needs derived from the past. The specific objectives which he sets up do not allow for adaptive intelligence or for general training. In Bobbitt, Bode finds evidences of inserting personal bias into an ostensibly objective determination of facts about social realities. Charters' development of the technique of job-analysis is criticized as being an attempt to mechanize conduct so completely that little place would be left for intelligence. In the psychology of J. B. Watson and in that of Thorndike, which are basic to much of modern educational thinking, Bode finds no recognition of intelligence as the function of re-creating and reinterpreting situations so that they take on new meaning. Both Watson and Thorndike seem to presuppose that the processes and the results of learning are entirely determinable by the teacher.

Bode attacks the scientific movement in education for its uncritical acceptance of old standards and old ideals. He sees in the scientific construction of curricula an actual threat to the development of a scientific outlook on the part of pupils.

The ideal detached attitude of traditional classicism, Bode believes, was a correct educational objective although classicism was culpable in not appreciating the obligation of learning to humanize men by the cultivation of common interests and sympathies. Likewise modern vocationalism is correct in its insistence that learning should be practically applied, and wrong in interpreting such application purely in terms of vocational utility.

INTERPRETIVE CRITICISM
OF THE
VIEWPOINTS OF AMERICAN EDUCATORS

INTERPRETIVE CRITICISM
OF THE
VIEWPOINTS OF AMERICAN EDUCATORS

PREFATORY NOTE

IN SECTION ONE the author has made clear the particular angle from which he views American social life and that aspect of it which is called organized public education. In Section Two he has attempted to present the essence of the more recent thinking of seventeen American educational theorists. These theorists were classified into three groups according as their major sympathies were interpreted as lying in the direction of inherited traditions, modern science, or modern naturalistic philosophy. In the present section the views of the seventeen men are critically interpreted from the author's point of view as more broadly expressed in Section One. The classification of Section Two is retained and its bases more specifically pointed out. The discussions of individual men follow in general the order of the topics used in the presentations of viewpoint in Section Two.

I. EDUCATORS STRESSING VALUES INHERENT IN AMERICAN HISTORIC TRADITIONS

Herman H. Horne.—There is no difficulty in determining just what it is that Horne stands for in social life and in education. He speaks out clearly and comprehensively; no questions which bother modern theorists remain unanswered in his philosophy. His philosophic training makes him stand in marked contrast in this respect to most of the educational theorists whose views are under discussion in the present study. He says with great conviction what he means about God, nature, human life, the social order, and he ties his educational theory consistently to his basic notions. He believes that his convictions have behind them the weight of centuries of civilized verification and that there is not the least cause today to doubt them in any measure.

It is really anomalous that Horne should theorize at such great length regarding public education. His thought seems more directed towards the church and towards religious education; its unbending traditionalism would at least be more appropriate in that field. How naïve today to believe that the secularism of American education, itself a departure from a not too distant complete religious domination, can be spiritualized by a philosophically purified essence of the old religious tradition! Horne builds on the obvious fact that American parents and American teachers are in large measure church members whose ideological complacency is somewhat disturbed by social and intellectual changes in the contemporary world. Most people appear spiritually cold to a Godless and experimental naturalism, and Horne would reassure them that a deepened faith in now empty and comparatively meaningless Christian idealistic terminology will bring back the old cultural solidarity. A little more scrupulous observation of the real spiritual temper of youth should demonstrate to him that Christian philosophic Idealism, as the key to life and to immortality, would be about as acceptable as mid-Victorian standards of social taste. It is perhaps because he senses this state of affairs somewhat that he makes so much of the necessity of good old-fashioned discipline in modern life. Of course, if one feels, like Horne, that the whole history of philosophy is a series of varied paeans to God, it would be hard not to judge the modern generation derelict in duty when it refuses to sing one more. The whole burden of Horne's educational philosophy rests in the conviction that educators, once they sense the real issues of modern life, will rush in eagerness to a program of education based on Christian Idealism. Christian Idealism, to Horne, is the crowning achievement of human philosophic vision. It represents the final ultimate synthesis of life's values and it affords a clear vision of the direction and the mode of future human progress. What more can man ask? Well, one really wonders whether man has asked quite so much! Do we wish to be assured in this day and generation that our social institutions are based upon divine ideas or that God has apparently so written capitalism into the course of events that all man can do is perfect it? Can intelligent people really believe that the moral patterns which have come down to us are divinely guaranteed to persist throughout even Utopia? Before nominating immortality as the ultimate end of education, in the light of which the whole program of public education should be planned, Horne might inquire deeply of his own point of view whether even immortality is the kind of thing that may be had for the seeking.

When one finds such deep reverence for a tradition like that of the Christian philosophic interpretation of the universe with all its connotations of loyalty to established institutions such as capitalism in economics and classicism in education, it is natural to expect that the practical proposals for educational reform derived therefrom will not be very startling. Horne's moral sense is outraged by the way in which materialism, the cult of success, and vocationalism have penetrated into our educational thinking and practice. He assures us, however, that these things will fade when we turn our hearts toward God and Jesus and toward true culture once more. Apologetically he explains such contemporary faults as the to-be-expected weaknesses of a nation which has undergone rapid physical development. The general scheme of education which Horne proposes to the end of a re-spiritualized America, is a benevolently authoritarian one. All the information and techniques which science has yielded to education are to be employed in the con-

160 INTERPRETIVE CRITICISM

struction and the consequent administration of a curriculum
fitted to the purpose of producing Christian citizens of a capitalistic turn of mind for the American democracy of the future.
The social inheritance in terms of compartments of knowledge
or subjects is to be reshuffled until it represents a hierarchy of
value cognate with idealistic philosophy. Education, in Horne's
thinking, appears to be wholly a technical problem, with the
issue simply what to do in order to reach the preconceived ends
of the public school. Horne urges the adoption of the principles
of Progressive education insofar as they may be employed in
serving the exigencies of technical educational problems.

There is no evidence to show that Horne has repudiated the
main outlines of the original psychology which he retains in
his recent revision of *The Philosophy of Education*.[1] He thinks
in terms of the once popular psychological insight which
describes epochs of development from infancy to maturity. This
psychology is employed to give distinction to that educational
dogma which states human mental development as a process
beginning with a kind of primitive freedom in the very young
and progressing through a period of externally imposed discipline to a final well regulated and cultural freedom in adults.
That this psychology is conceived ideally and with great benevolence only makes matters worse. Nowhere is there any indication that Horne appreciates the significance of recent developments in modern psychology, biology, or psychiatry. He sees
all science through the rosy-hued spectacles of his religious
philosophic Idealism which confidently assumes that science
reflects the glory of God. Nor does he show anywhere an appreciation of the strange new forces which move the contemporary world. It seems to be the besetting sin of all who view
the world, as Horne so proudly assumes he does, *sub specie
aeternitatis*, that the immediate everyday environment can show
nothing which is of more than passing significance.

[1] H. H. Horne, *The Philosophy of Education* (New York: Macmillan),
1930.

Horne tries to point out that there is a real battle today among educational theorists and that it rages between two poles: one, the radical naturalistic philosophy of Dewey, and the other, the idealistic philosophy of Horne. In his last book[2] he has attempted to show that the philosophy of Dewey is swallowed up in the more comprehensive philosophy of Horne. When one examines the present state of educational theory in America, it is obvious that in the prevailing theoretic confusion, the issues are not yet drawn. When the battle lines are really formed, there is little likelihood of Horne's Christian idealism representing one strong contending force. As regards the two "contending" philosophies in question, that of Dewey is an emergent one which few educators have as yet considered seriously; that of Horne is a decadent one whose followers, with the exception of Horne himself, are already apologetic about bringing it into professional discussion. Horne's instinct in opposing the implications of Dewey is, however, a sure one. He plainly dreads the revolutionary consequences of a common understanding and acceptance of the viewpoint of experimental naturalism. It means the fading of all but the memory of idealism, the passing of the Christian tradition, of capitalism, and of classicism, to all of which Horne has a strong emotional attachment.

Henry C. Morrison.—Morrison has proceeded boldly to experiment and to theorize about the method of education. He asks no fundamental questions beyond those strictly allied to method or technique. But he nevertheless answers some very fundamental questions in an incidental way. He sees mankind steadily advancing along all lines, ever pushing beyond attained frontiers in every line of endeavor. He recognizes in the Industrial Revolution man's recent and sudden deliverance from the necessity of universal and endless unenlightening toil during the extent of his natural life. Morrison's program of education is designed to

[2] H. H. Horne, *The Democratic Philosophy of Education* (New York: Macmillan), 1932.

make the consequent universally increased leisure time intellectually, morally, and aesthetically profitable. He blandly assumes that the present age with its social institutions and its moral and cultural ideals is the essential distillate of ages past. Advance we will inevitably, but along pathways already laid down. Morrison insists that there need be no more questionings about fundamental things; man's function, now, is but to perfect and expand the received distillate of cultural patterns. Although he says nothing about the Christian tradition, it is to be assumed that his objections to moral relativity are derived from Christian absolutistic preconceptions. He is frank about capitalism, and although his dream of the day when every individual will be a cultured and prosperous capitalist is distinctly out of key just now, it, nevertheless, displays the contamination of his thought by the received business tradition in American economic life. The physical, social, and spiritual inheritance into which he would initiate American youth is clearly our marvelous technological civilization controlled in characteristic capitalist fashion somewhat chastened, possibly, by the ideals of inherited American Christianity.

Morrison's specific educational proposals represent the product of original thinking about how better to do the old job in the light of the present threatened social disintegration. If the aim of permanently securing the received traditions of American life must be retained, it is easy to see that the whole school system must be conceived and controlled as a unit, and that all educational efforts must be scientized and integrated in terms of the ultimate desideratum. The technique of parcelling out knowledge into subjects, so sacred still to Horne, Morrison radically tampers with. He is closer to realities and recognizes that mass education needs to be differently conceived than upper class education. He proposes functional units of subject matter so constructed and so administered by the school that mastery by pupils of what they contain shall be guaranteed.

The graded promotion system Morrison throws into the discard as inadequate to the task of rendering our great American masses of youth properly amenable and customarily habituated to ideals whose history is said to guarantee their ultimacy. In other words, what Morrison is proposing is that all the techniques of science shall be applied seriously to the task of doing more and more efficiently what, hitherto, has been attempted in education. If the task of properly intellectualizing, vocationalizing, and aestheticizing American youth is well done, he assumes that highly integrated, modernly oriented personalities will be the inevitable result. This is a tremendous assumption and holding to it requires a deep and abiding faith in values whose disintegration is already so complete that even the usually complacent American masses have become restive under institutional forms representing those values. It is this restiveness, this outward manifestation of revolt, that bothers Morrison. He is concerned to suppress it by means of what he calls the application of the *mastery* formula in the public schools. He is not concerned to look into the values which are being flouted and disregarded; they are assumed to have been experimentally validated by past generations of men. Morrison, in other words, would bend man to the yoke of inherited institutions rather than bend inherited institutions to the yoke of emergent man. The latter alternative he would regard as sheer nonsense, because fundamentally he misunderstands the nature of the world he is living in. He misinterprets trends of continuity with the past as unalterable pathways for the future. And he misinterprets the modern manifestations of the spirit of revolt in man as obvious reversions to savagery and barbarism.

Morrison sums up human development in much too simple fashion. If properly educated, we pass inevitably from egoistic infancy to altruistic adulthood. It is perfectly obvious what Morrison means by a proper education. The ideals, as already discussed, are those inherited from the past. The educational specifications for realizing these ideals in individuals and in society at large, Morrison indicates, are a matter of technical determination. Relevant subject matter is selected for curricular content, and teaching techniques are adapted to the incorporation of the selected subject matter into the minds of youth. Morrison accepts the modern doctrine of motivation, but he restricts its meaning to a teacher-determined motivation assumed as necessary in accordance with the developmental principle stated above. The pupil's attention and interest are technically manipulated so that his behavior may be directed along chosen channels. Where the teaching art has been genuinely administered according to formula, the pupil becomes eventually a self-directing entity capable of being trusted with the responsibility for his own future. The flaw in this type of educational thinking is exactly that it reckons entirely without the modern human sciences. It is pedagogy entrenched against any possible invasion by the experimental temper of mind and against any fundamentally new theories. All of the fine things which Morrison has to say against machine-like school administration and against intelligence-test determinism go to pot in the face of his pedagogical dogmatism. Just as educators and people generally were beginning to realize that precious little is known about the great modern problems of education, Morrison gives out the startling reassurance that if subject matter be taught earnestly and intelligently enough, universal confidence and the social *status quo ante* may again be restored! Nowhere in Morrison is there any indication that the fundamentals of the teaching art of the future lie in the developing sciences of child psychology, human biology, sociology, and psychiatry, nor that the problem of education may be conceived more broadly than in terms of subject matter mastery alone.

The educational conservative is perfectly portrayed in Morrison's impatience with educational catch phrases which describe the teacher's dissatisfactions with old ways and her hopes for something new and more meaningful. Like others of conservative orientation, he attempts to make ridiculous the feeble efforts of struggling and uncertain Progressives. We are driven, however, to the conclusion that if we would earnestly follow Morrison, we should have to return to devout acceptance of the Christian moral and religious tradition as a kind of ultimate standard. It would be necessary also to revere forevermore the social, political, and economic institutions which happen to have emerged so far on the American scene. Morrison, therefore, is not inconsistent when he makes light of the brewing social storm, nor when he entrenches himself behind the substance, if not the form, of traditional education, nor when he ridicules Progressives.

William C. Bagley.—In Bagley one searches vainly for a complete declaration of faith. What he actually believes about Christianity or capitalism is hidden from view, and one must infer from the trend of his general remarks about education and the social order just in what direction his thought seems oriented. Obviously he has not the happy faith of a Horne that we are progressing with reasonable rapidity toward a beneficent millenium. Nor is there the rigid assurance of a Morrison that nothing fundamental has happened to our familiar American preconceptions. Bagley penetrates somewhat deeper; crime, divorce rates, the ominous encroachments of the machine convince him that a crisis is at hand. His appeal to Americans to learn the moral of European experience with universal education is beside the point. Just where is the moral to which Bagley points if the highly praised system of education, under which German youth has for so many years been nurtured, results in a nation submissive to Hitlerism or Junkerism, while the poor, illiterate, downtrodden Russians conceive a Five Year Plan and proceed with its execution as realistically as they have? Bagley bids us to return to fundamentals, and he reaffirms his faith in American democracy. Fundamentals, for lack of any assurance to the contrary, apparently mean the inherited Christian religious and moral traditions and the kind of democracy which capitalism permits. To demand that the level of mass enlightenment in our pervasive common culture be raised means to be so satisfied with our religious and philosophic, our social and economic inheritances that we would perpetuate their essential traditions rather than search out the meanings and the possibilities of any new stirrings in the soul of the modern American populace. Bagley would make that populace thankful and contented for what it is and for what it has. To assume that even a stalwartly conceived, an artistically administered, a scientifically regulated system of universal education can thus turn the clock of social evolution backward in this modern day, is to have faith indeed.

The key to Bagley's practical proposals for educational reform lies in his use of the term discipline. Somehow all the educational ills of the day are due to lack of discipline. Presumably we will be disciplined when over all of America there reigns a universal common culture. This means essentially that all people hold the same ideals. By default of other definition, in Bagley's case we must assume that the ideals he has reference to are those lying in the Christian religious and the business economic traditions—to which the classical educational scheme so neatly adapted itself. The common core of subjects, the unexceptional disciplinary power of thorough training in subject matter, the ideal leader-follower inspirational relationship of teacher and pupil are all concepts strictly within the old tradition, and Bagley reveres them all. Again, the necessity of making the teacher-training centers stabilizing forces, capable of calling a halt to easy experimentation in education, means assured reign for the tried and true "fundamentals." In Bagley's consideration of the subject matter of education, he places *primacy* in language and measure. Surely, this bespeaks no change in contemporary ideals of education beyond perhaps a querulous call for greater efficiency in teaching.

Naturally the classical leaning in Bagley rebels against commercialism in education as well as against new-fangled notions. The onus of Bagley's criticisms goes to the Progressive Movement in American education, the influence of which, it would be conservative to say, has scarcely touched the average American public school. Bagley sees, however, that this movement portends the dynamiting of old standards, and he would cut off its influence by concerted conservative action before it is too late. Like crime ratios, divorce rates, materialism, etc., the Progressive Movement is a sign of disintegration among revered institutional standards.

Bagley does not conceal his joy at some recent psychological experiments which have been said to reopen the controversy over mental discipline and transfer of training. Having himself never abandoned a large faith in the transfer powers of consciously held ideals, Bagley exults in this open questioning of specific-element psychology among workers on the frontiers of psychological science. He believes that scientific activity in the field of brain localization will open new vistas of the possibilities of mental evolution, especially in man. He expects possibly the exploration of the seat of moral consciousness in man, namely Conscience. Such inclusion of the mainstay of old individualistic religion in a discussion of the psychology of learning amply reveals the traditional set of Bagley's mind. The machinery which made Conscience and Duty such terrible ruling powers in individuals of a bygone age is not forgotten, for Bagley demands such external constraint of pupils as shall guarantee conscious mastery of a given subject matter content. Freedom as the end of education is conceived as adjustment to the inherited cultural traditions and ingrained methods of thinking, which constituted classical education in America.

The conservatism of Bagley does not follow strictly along academic traditions, for these traditions were essentially aristocratic and had reference only to upper class education. Bagley is a confirmed democrat. He would bring the virtues of classicism to everybody. That is apparently what he means by social progress. The intelligence testers with their doctrines of the inherent cultural limitations of the masses are anathema to him. He also despises the Progressives in education who openly call for an abandonment of classicism by redefining the meaning of education. It is from between the two opposed fires of intelligence-test determinism and anarchic educational freedom that Bagley would rescue the schools. The first means to him a denial of democracy, the second a denial of discipline. He insists we must have both democracy and discipline if an evolving America is to run true to the institutional standards by which her course in the past has been charted. What Bagley does not see is that democracy may have a deeper meaning than wide extension of traditional learning, nor does he believe that discipline may be defined more adequately than by reference to age-old educational methods.

Ellwood P. Cubberley.—Cubberley dreams of the emergence of a great American race. This sounds modern and even visionary, but his specifications for the production of such a race sound very familiar indeed. It is the responsibility of the schools to keep American social progress pure and uncontaminated. Indeed, the nation must consciously use its schools to guarantee that moral standards, laws, and material prosperity shall be under the permissive sanction of the Christian tradition. Early American ideals in every phase of institutional life are in no wise to be questioned or changed. The disturbance of these ideals caused by unassimilated immigrants can and must be remedied by the State through its school system. In the stable American economic structure Cubberley sees ample financial resources for truly national Americanization. The problem is essentially simple, and as in Bagley's case, frankly stated—the masses must be brought to the intellectual and cultural level of the upper class. Since the upper class became upper in virtue of a business system carefully idealized under the prevailing Christian tradition, it will readily be seen that the present upper class could in no better way assure its perpetuity. With youth adequately trained for useful service in office, shop, and home, and with belief in the eternality and ideality of established institutions secure, the emergence of a great American race is a prospect indeed! Ultimate matters thus simply disposed of, school administrators may with assurance turn their attention to the scientific management of details.

In Cubberley idealization of American business practices reaches its supreme height. No greater tribute could be paid an economic system than to suggest that a great public school system be modeled upon its essential ideals. Apparently in Cubberley's mind, the nearer school administration and supervision approach the forms and customs of great business corporations, the greater is their efficiency. The school board is likened to the familiar Board of Directors, the school superintendent is compared to the president of a corporation. Supervision keeps experimentation within bounds and prevents agitation among the workers. Everything runs systematically, and those teachers who conform most completely to established policies are rewarded with the greatest liberty. In Cubberley's system, teacher freedom comes by means of the lock-step formation. In arguing that the administration of rural and village education should be patterned after that of large urban communities, business idealization comes full circle, and the teacher is dominated everywhere upon the American scene by a centralized bureaucracy interested in revitalizing faded institutions. The significance of phrases like community-centered education, differentiated instruction, flexible requirements, individual adaptation to a changing world, etc., as Cubberley uses them, is that they can be used with equal facility in support of reactionary policies or of progressive ones.

When he looks critically at the functioning educational system of our country, Cubberley finds the greatest lack among administrators. Always they seem to be the key to the educational undertaking. Better training must render administrators capable of bringing the educational philosophy of teachers up to date. This means broader use of those scientific tools of education, the intelligence and educational tests. Presumably the intelligence test is the classificatory device and the educational achievement test the determiner of the degree in which educational objectives have been accomplished. The statistical tabulations and the elaborate record-keeping made possible by the extensive testing programs of educational administrators become tangible evidence that education is being run according to approved business principles.

The process of education as analyzed by Cubberley runs true to his general outlook and the way he views the national educational task. Children are run through a mill of schooling where the very latest results of educational research render teaching a highly controlled art. Teachers teach subjects over whose content they are conscious masters; they keep the children interested and under control. The proper sequence of subjects adequately taught creates the informed Christian citizen with all the rugged and homely American virtues. The *naïveté* of Cubberley in bringing to the aid of practitioners of education a psychology of periodically maturing instincts almost passes belief. The old inspirational hack of a right time for every lesson appears in its pristine vigor in Cubberley's psychology.

It is only natural to expect that in Cubberley, as in Horne, Morrison, and Bagley may be found a heavy emphasis upon so-called fundamental subjects, the basic tools of education, the sole gateways to culture. No clearer demonstration of the meaning of the traditional point of view in education could be had than this characteristic harping upon fundamental subjects. It signifies that education itself is conceived of as the mastery of a stated program of subjects or units of subject matter. The fundamentals or primary essentials obviously enough must then be those drills upon reading, writing, arithmetic, and spelling by which, it is commonly considered, the richness of content subjects is unlocked. Cubberley adds to his traditionalism in this respect the faith born of contact with modern educational science that measured achievement in the basic formalities of education is assurance enough that the imponderable values of personality and of character are also amply attained. Most measurers in education have given up this assurance. It is unfortunate that a practical leader like Cubberley, whose influence penetrates American education subtly and pervasively, should assure teachers that all will be well with the future generations if they but add techniques of measurement to their present procedures!

The extent of Cubberley's vision in educational philosophy is evident in his attempt to be both conservative and liberal at the same time. It is liberal to believe in the passing of *memoriter* learning and in the great expansion of modern education as seen in America. It is confusing to lump the *Cardinal Principles of Secondary Education*,[3] the *Principles of Education*[4] of Chapman and Counts, and the whole of Dewey into one comprehensive and satisfactory modern educational philosophy. No doubt Cubberley's emotional attachment to tradition has led him thus to make confusion worse confounded among teachers, for when issues are not clear hesitancy towards the new is increased. It is clearly conservative to be sceptical towards the project method —to regard it as another pedagogical device rather than a new philosophy of education.

Thomas H. Briggs.—In Briggs, as in Bagley, there is a constrained consciousness that all is not well in the contemporary American body politic. Briggs calls for sustained constructive effort directed to the clarification of American ideals. He sug-

[3] U. S. Bureau of Education, *Bulletin*, 1918, No. 35.
[4] J. C. Chapman and G. S. Counts, *Principles of Education* (New York: Houghton), 1924.

gests a conscious application by the State of modern technical controls towards the attainment of such ideals. Let us examine Briggs' diagnosis of the ills of contemporary society, the ideals which he reveres, and what he means by education to which he so assuredly points as the way out of present difficulties.

Briggs speaks of the essentially superior American program of life as being endangered by the declining influence of the home and the church, by changing mores, by political corruption, and by criminality. But what is the American program of life? Briggs hails democracy, to be sure, but in the light of his ideal, self-supporting, country-loving, God-fearing citizen it is fairly obvious that he has reference to the capitalistic economy and the Christian morality of the nineteenth century when America prospered so grandly as a nation. The meaning of democracy in the machine age, as something radically different from hallowed age-old institutions now passing into inevitable decay, he does not seem to comprehend. Plainly he wants to go back, and he expects that a National Commission of experts can somehow bring the loose ends of the old régime together once more into a grand synthesis of outlook labeled American democracy. A self-conscious state deliberately employing all available technology in the realization of its ends, he believes, may then make the educational system into an effective citizen-producing machine. He conceives citizens emerging as souls likeminded upon important social, political, and economic matters. His use of the big business analogy for education with its attendant phraseology indicates the close connection of his thought with the business man's way of looking at things. Briggs' constant emphasis upon the perpetuation of our institutional forms, allowing as he does for a change only in the direction of more general economic beneficence, affords him the distinction of being designated the educational prophet of a future Fascist America.

In practical proposals Briggs goes right to the heart of the problem of national preservation along essentially traditional lines. Just as experts are to formulate a national philosophy, so other experts are to take the materials of education and shape them into a curriculum minutely adapted to the task of producing an informed state-conscious citizenry. Standards and requirements in all lines of conduct are to be determined by experts. Naturally the execution of such a program requires a much expanded and a sterner supervisory system. Here the big business analogy again crops out in Briggs as he points to the supervisory arrangements in industry and business as the basis of efficiency. Boldly Briggs rules out the private and the parochial school as inimical to the best interests of the State. Teachers are to be required to lead the good, rich American life, and the right answers to controversial social questions are, evidently, to be handed to them by state authorities. This is Americanizing with a vengeance! It is a strong program and it is not impractical in an emergency like the present when vast power still rests in the hands of traditionally-minded business and political leaders. Could these leaders but be united upon something else than immediate depression remedies, there is little doubt but that they would substantially agree with Briggs on how to bring back the happy by-gone days when mores changed imperceptibly, when crime was not reported so luridly, and when extremists had little if any public. Stability after the fashion of one of our more conservative boom periods seems the aim of Briggs' social planning.

Briggs makes clear that the traditional program of subjects shall constitute the basis of systematic education in the future as in the past. His main bone of contention with the way education is carried on today is that educators fail to realize the true relation of education to the state. He is just in criticizing educational administrators and educational researchers because they do lack this fundamental orientation. The call which Briggs issues for educators to think strenuously and continuously about fundamental issues of policy, is one to which all educational workers should sympathetically respond.

The conservatism of Briggs shows itself most plainly in his repetition of the age-old phrase that human nature never really changes. His psychological insight leads him to proclaim that even the direction of social viewpoints is determined by nature rather than by nurture. Nurture or education means to Briggs a wide program of habituations designed to promote the emergence of a homogeneous society out of a heterogeneous mass of individuals. He revives the notion, supposedly securely buried by professional psychologists, that feelings only begin to infuse the attitudes of children at adolescence. In his insistence that true education is more deeply rooted than intellect and that education must concern itself with emotional development to a much greater degree than is now the case, however, Briggs has found a principle fundamental to any scheme of educational reform.

Like other theorists with whom he is classified in this study, Briggs makes much of prescription in education. The carefully planned curricula must in all cases provide for systematic training in the application of fundamental facts and principles. Since to Briggs emotions play but a small part in the lives of children of pre-adolescent years, this necessary drill is most efficiently administered in the early years of the educational program. Children, as children, thus count for little in Briggs' thinking. They are the raw materials out of which law-abiding citizens are made. The only effect of modern thinking about the period of childhood upon conservative educators in general, seems to have been in leading them to contemplate some slight alleviation of the adult despotism under which children have been forced to live. The language used in justifying long and heavy educational prescriptions has lost much of its emotional flavoring and has acquired a scientific tone. In Briggs it is "efficiency" and "future availability" which are thus used to warrant the period of forced elementary education.

With Briggs' test of successful education in an individual as the presence of varied and abiding interests, no one could possibly quarrel. The question might be raised, however, as to just how the absolute state prescription and expert-prepared curricula, which Briggs advocates for education, can meet this test on a large scale—human nature being what it is. Despite proposed benevolence and emotionalization in the educational program, the aroused temper of modern youth will not readily dismiss a certain scepticism which is part of the present age's attitude towards traditional ideals. Prescriptive education may succeed in the future as it has in the past, but certainly not under ideals which have in large degree ceased to function.

Briggs' criticisms of other points of view in educational theory are so general as to be practically meaningless. Confusion he finds and justly criticizes, but he is at no pains to point out specific objections to prominent theoretical proposals in education today. His aversion to what Dewey stands for is evident in his misinterpretation of the meaning of Dewey's "How We Think."[5] That book is decidedly not an analysis of how gifted men think; it is an analysis of the mental processes variously involved in thinking, no matter who does it. Since in Briggs' point of view thinking is of much less importance for the majority of men than unthinking habituation, he believes it misleading for Dewey to assume that thinking, as an element of behavior in all men, is important enough to write a book about.

Ross L. Finney.—Finney is prominent as an educational theorist by virtue of the radical nature of his thinking about economic institutions. He has made himself the educational spokesman of that Western agricultural radicalism which has now and again in American history disturbed Eastern financiers and business men. Among timid educators he dares to question private property in land and capital. However, as if such daring stretched his imagination to the breaking point, he snaps back into a de-

[5] J. Dewey, *How We Think* (New York: Heath), 1910.

vout traditionalism that at some points outdoes even Horne or Morrison. In philosophic outlook, Finney is apparently one of those men whom the doctrine of Evolution rescued from the nineteenth century religious slough of despond—when science had rendered the traditional belief in God impossible for conscientious intellectuals. Evolution replaced God in assuring a higher human destiny, and the old religious values thereby acquired a new guarantor. Finney thus speaks of an ideal society toward which "Evolution" points. This is the "modern" point of view within whose broad scope all tested knowledge finds a legitimate place.

All who are capable do not as yet see this vision of the super-civilization compounded out of applied science, democracy, and social coöperation. Finney issues a challenge to those who do behold the vision to draw up specifications for an immediate attack upon present social disintegration. He hopes for an educational program which aims at a degree of cultural social solidarity never before attained. Social institutions are the constant against which such a program would operate. They must not be tampered with until there is a general consensus of minds upon the social ideals which are to be realized in the Super-Society toward which all creation is headed. Against this insistence upon institutional permanence even Finney's economic radicalism crumbles. In order to ward off possible revolution he would instill the good old Christian-business virtues in individuals and stanchly defend the existing order. Like all traditionalists, Finney desires a good sized kernel of eternality in his principles. The scientifically sanctified new social order of which he dreams must exist in theoretic and spiritual completeness in the popular mind before he would tamper with a single existing institution or inherited moral precept.

Finney is an apostle of a society run by educators of a new type. The desired type of educator is a glorified sociological philosopher who appreciates the evolutionary Utopia and who can transform present society into Utopia. By manipulating the present pabulum of subjects and courses, these educators will be able to perpetuate their type in the colleges of education. Finney is not explicit, however, on how the first crop of leaders is to be obtained. Perhaps Fascist-like we might compromise on a dictator to start things off. His curricular program of prescription, instillation, and drill upon conformity to efficiently functioning social institutions smacks familiarly enough of dictatorship. It ought not be necessary to point out to a sociologist that the new religion of social progress which he craves for society cannot be a product of any rearrangement of subject matter courses in any institution of lower or higher learning. These matters of the soul which move races of men in one direction or another derive from deeper sources than an educator's curriculum of subjects, no matter how widely inclusive and scientifically valid it may be.

Finney's plea for a more genuinely socialized functioning of the wealth of the country as well as his plea for more honor to great teachers should be welcomed by all thinking educators as extremely important at the present time. His fervent language about Evolution should be recognized as a seeking after the vanished God of old religion. His faith in how a reshuffling of subjects in the curriculum will influence the social order seems altogether too assured. The strong vein of educational determinism in Finney's thinking, along with his advocacy of democracy, makes one question his philosophic consistency.

Finney's fundamental traditionalism runs true to form in his criticisms of present day educational practice. His forceful and just attack upon the conservatism and social innocence of educators tends somewhat to obscure certain positive principles which he lays down. He believes that education is dominantly reproductive rather than creative in function and that the prime desideratum in society is homogeneity. Since in his mind the great masses of people are beyond the reach of rational thought processes, he criticizes the present day neglect of information-getting and of what he calls the present over-emphasis of training in thinking in the schools. It is evident, in this instance, that he is arguing against the theory rather than the practice, for it would be hard to point out a public school of the present day where information absorption is sacrificed to problem-solving.

It would be difficult indeed in modern American literature of education to find an analysis of the educational process so outspokenly reactionary as in Finney's exposition. There can be no slightest doubt as to what he means and as to the fundamental philosophy which he holds. His more generalized philosophic statements about the social order and about education sometimes make him seem liberal or even progressive, but the extreme dogmatic language which he uses in referring to the nature of learning exposes him as a ruthless bitter-ender for the traditional order of things.

Finney's quarrel with Dewey and the Progressive educational theorists and practitioners is an anti-climax to his analysis of learning. It is conceivable that a little more objective perusal of Dewey's *Human Nature and Conduct* might have changed the unfortunate exposition which Finney gives in his own discussion of the relative rôles of passive and active *mentation* in social life. The cocksureness and finality with which Finney disposes of Dewey create the suspicion that Finney's analysis has been far from thorough.

The soft creed of life and the soft pedagogy of the Progressives receive the same disdain from Finney that they do in the vigorous language of Morrison and Bagley. How easy to remark about the social meleé of today that what is needed is more authority and control over individuals, and how revealing such a remark is of a strong predilection for the values of the past!

II. Educators Stressing the Ultimacy of Science

CHARLES H. JUDD

In Judd there has been violent antipathy to speculation and to the expression of personal opinion based upon experience, especially when these relate to large questions of social and educational policy. Let us examine the faith that lies behind this prejudice against philosophy. It is a faith in social institutions, by which Judd apparently means those habits which collective man has taken on since something called civilization has existed. These institutions lie locked in an accumulation called the social inheritance, and they constitute our protection against a reversion to barbarism. Until science came upon the scene, progress in the development of social institutions and in control of the social inheritance was unsure and halting. Nothing to Judd is more important than that ordered progress in the evolution of social institutions shall be assured. He, therefore, worships at the altar of science. He has assured us in as unspeculative a manner as possible that if we will but pay sufficient tribute to science, all our troubles will be ended. How this profound faith differs substantially from the earlier and more general frankly religious faith in God as ultimate guarantor of a secure destiny for mankind, it is difficult to see. Science is a wonderful thing and the perfection of its methods so recent an occurrence that in an age of declining religious faith devout men may be expected to grasp at it as a new dispensation that has the power to restore all fading values and to brighten the outlook for the future. It is not surprising therefore that Judd should revere inherited institutions as essentially beyond reproach. Will not science introduce all necessary refinements? Since we progress by evolution the present adult society must represent the best type of organization the world has yet seen. The economic virtues, under a régime of capitalistic business enterprise and the institution of property, take on, in Judd's thinking, an idealistic semblance. The most valued quality of individuals in modern society is their power to conform. So education and the school are conceived of as agencies which mold youth to the established cultural patterns including the tool pattern of scientific thinking without which prospective social evolution and control would be impossible. The emphatic opposition to speculative thought in Judd's writings seems to be somewhat on the wane. He is decidedly alert to the present social crisis, and he seems to be throwing himself energetically into the task of creating an organization of educators that will count for something in American life. The extent to which this new emphasis will cause Judd to reconsider his whole point of view, however, remains to be seen.

When we examine the nature of Judd's practical proposals for reform in the established educational machinery, we find that they are all based on one fundamental proposition—*apply scientific method to what we have and all will be well.* All the vexing, detailed questions of administration, supervision, and teaching can be solved by means of science. A centralized body of educational researchers, he believes, could best unify and direct the present sprawling educational efforts. What Judd means by social progress is fairly evident from his proposal to vest control over the schools in a body of scientists. There are few scientists as yet who do not believe in attaining social solidarity upon the foundations of present American institutions. With all major social questions thus assumed to have been satisfactorily settled, Judd proposes an orgy of investigations aiming to uncover the correct answer to every conceivable aspect of present educational practice. Perfection would be reached when the exact result upon every pupil of everything done in the classroom is known and can be planned for or against in advance by those under whom teachers serve. Traditionalism in Judd is nicely rounded out by his suggestion for teacher apprenticeship strictly under the grade-subject system, by his specific for absorbing the emotional energies of children, and by his curt dismissal of the problem of developing creativeness in children.

Judd's estimate of current educational practice consists of a long series of regrets that the régime of a thoroughly scientized education has not been attained. Despite much progress by means of school surveys, whereby our fundamentally sound educational system is being gradually refined, Judd laments the slow growth in the number of research centers and in the number of research workers in education. Characteristically Judd's concern about what is going on in American education has been limited, until quite recently, to our apparent niggardliness towards science.

In his remarks about learning Judd seems to assert, in a negative way, the prime importance of a general point of view when dealing with strictly scientific matters. Although a vast body of scientific literature has accumulated among psychologists who have explored human learning by means of concepts derived from animal experimentation, Judd will have none of it. He wants pure and unadulterated analysis of human mental processes. He wants psychological investigations which lay bare the vast influence that social institutions have upon human beings. This is clearly a blow at the absolute scientific autonomy in which Judd has such a strong faith. It is an admission that the nature of the specific basis of science depends upon the general orientations which scientists bring from outside the laboratory. When Judd rejects the principles of the so-called specific element psychology, is he not indulging in the type of speculation that he so much despises in others?

Judd has built a psychology of learning that fits very neatly the traditional point of view in education. Since children are socially incompetent at birth, and since the social inheritance is so far advanced, nothing will suffice except that children undergo long and tedious guidance. This guidance takes the form of inherited school procedures which were derived originally, according to Judd, from the characteristics of children's minds. School subjects exist because a pupil is a collection of selves. It is therefore natural to teach school subjects. The concept of the whole child and the modern problem of personality integration are consequently unnatural. This is a strange condemnation in one who rests the whole weight of civilization itself upon what is most unnatural in his own view, namely, social institutions. Judd argues that as the aims of education are clear, as the materials of education (the social inheritance and social institutions) stand ready at hand, and as the child is anti-social or non-social by nature, the only conceivable procedure leading to proper learning would be for the schools to follow a scientifically derived program which outlines every step of the way. The child's mind must be directed into the proper channels of social habituation, so that there shall be no danger of non-conformity to mores which educational researchers consider meet and respectable. Admittedly, this is difficult and distasteful to children, but the rewards in a scientifically conditioned social order are great. As further justification of prescriptive and analytic educational programs, Judd brings in the much doubted and scientifically insecure principle that mental analysis precedes by a long interval mental synthesis.

Judd preserves a calm and scientific mien when dealing with the psychological doctrines of the mechanistic school. His outward objectivity weakens somewhat at the sight of hypotheses and data which run directly counter to his own preconceptions, despite the fact that these preconceptions make little ultimate difference in the way education is conceived. Judd loses all appearance of objectivity, however, as soon as Progressive Education becomes the center of discussion. The accusations which he directs at Progressive Education are extreme, and his deliberate misinterpretations of what most Progressives stand for suggest an emotional rather than a rational origin. He is genuinely disturbed, like all dyed-in-the-wool traditionalists, when revolutionary doctrines begin to demand the attention and interest of large numbers of people. It should be clear to any unbiased student of Judd that he is as much a cult worshipper as any Progressive. And it should likewise be clear to any unbiased student of the Progressive Movement in education that the Movement does not propose an undirected school or the abandonment of the intellectual life. Judd's emphatic objection to activities as a substitute for subjects in the curriculum savors of a rigidity and dogmatism that ill comports with his scientific pretensions.

DAVID SNEDDEN

Snedden is a practical man with a dangerous touch of vision. Confident that he grasps within his mind some cognizance of every aspect of the varied cultural trends in modern America and, like Judd, possessing a profound faith in science, Snedden deals assuredly with what seem to him inevitable future outcomes in social life and in education. Like Judd, he knows that science can be trusted to refine the sum of present tendencies and so he looks fondly on the great indigenous American culture to come. Mechanization and corporateness in organization are to him in their promise and in much of their fulfillment to date unmitigated blessings. He therefore easily dismisses the hideous actualities of the past and present which have been committed in the name of these concepts. And he likewise unhesitatingly welcomes the ultimate extension of mechanization and corporateness to all phases of life under the beneficent control of science. Specialization Snedden reads into the spirit of the times, so that he must needs warn against even the use of a general term like education. The true picture of America as Snedden would like to see it is that of a knight dressed in the armor of science driving the galloping steeds of Specialization, Mechanization, and Corporate Organization into the millennium of a great culture. Presumably these chargers are securely harnessed and subjected to the discipline of the commonly accepted values which, as Snedden lists them, are none other than the virtues made so much of in theory by the typical American business man. But that is just the trouble in Snedden; what he would begin with in his eagerness for immediate scientific application are the very things most in question in the actual social life of today.

Like Morrison, Snedden begs a fundamental question when he calls the far reaching consequences of machine technique upon social life mere extensions of long-standing tendencies, and when he confidently assumes that these effects have already been complacently absorbed by the population. It seems much too early to clamp down scientific screws on the present social chaos even though practical sociologists like Snedden may possess a fascinating vision of what could be efficiently done under the authority of scientists. A population of self-conscious type-groups working and recreating according to a set formula, no matter how scientifically validated, does not seem the kind of choice America is set upon making for itself. And in spite of Snedden, there are ample reasons still for talking about *education* rather than solely about *educations*.

Notwithstanding the fundamentally different psychological backgrounds of Judd and Snedden, the latter's educational program in its main outlines almost duplicates Judd's. Specifications to the last detail are to be prepared in advance for every type of desired educational product. The main aim is social habituation and societal solidarity upon value patterns effective in the past. Every educational procedure is to bear the stamp of scientific approval. All policies and plans are made by a scientific oligarchy at the top and handed down for execution by teachers whose specialized function renders them incapable of thinking about large issues. His formula, like Judd's, is: *scientize what we have and all will be well in education.* Snedden's dogmatism about the inevitability of any other than a clear and continuing dichotomy between production and consumption with respect to all social goods, demonstrates how far his thought has been influenced by certain cultural by-products of a capitalistic economy.

Snedden rightfully calls attention to the self-centered narrowness of outlook of many influential educators. He accuses them of failing adequately to take into account the many varied educational influences of the social environment beyond the school. But his suggestion that educators should content themselves by intensively cultivating a narrow sphere of influence seems a little premature. There is still too much doubt about the future of American civilization for educators to retire from the scene of social controversy even though their past effectiveness was not a glorious one. The slow progress which science makes in fields of educational practice is as deep a matter of regret to Snedden as it is to Judd. Both men consider insufficiency of science the root of all educational evil.

Snedden's educational thinking is conditioned upon an unqualified acceptance of the Thorndike stimulus-response bond psychology taken in its most atomistic sense. In him transfer of training has lost meaning altogether. The abstract generalization so important as an educational objective in the analysis of Bagley and of Judd has vanished completely. The educational job has become the thoroughly mechanistic one of selecting from the social inheritance what is of fundamental importance, psychologizing the selections in terms of specific type pupil-groups, and teaching them in the scientifically specified way, until pupil behavior has satisfactorily altered.

It is not exactly clear from what source Snedden draws his confidence in advising radically opposed educational régimes for early childhood and for later childhood. Nothing in the annals of modern scientific child psychology could be the source of such questionable procedure. The change from a program of almost total freedom for nine years or so to one of almost no freedom while training for deferred values takes place, would appear to be conducive of some of those obscure personality upsets which Snedden so much fears are bound to ensue from Progressive educational practices. Application of his own preferred psychological principles should have made clear to him that the question of freedom or compulsion is only relevant in specific situations, which occur at all ages.

Snedden's criticisms in the field of educational theory are nearly all directed at the doctrines of Dewey and Kilpatrick. Since these two theorists represent the point of view most at variance with tradition, Snedden opposes them apparently in self-defense. We find in him the traditionalist's threadbare insistence that the Progressives advocate "the free school," that they stand for undefined and anarchic "growth," that they dabble in high sounding phrases because they like that sort of thing. To say, for instance, that Dewey does not recognize the necessity for selective treatment of the social inheritance is to fly in the face of the very heart of Dewey's contentions. Certainly it is mere quibbling to read defeatism into Kilpatrick's concern over the *unknown future*. To sum up, Snedden is against Progressivism in education because from his own quasi-authoritarian viewpoint he believes that Progressivism means an inadequate and an accidental program for nurturing the youth of America.

EDWARD L. THORNDIKE

In Thorndike the application of science to educational problems reaches its highest modern development. In him a calm mind and indefatigable industry combine to turn out a steady stream of inspired human followers and an endless procession of research studies. In him the weakness of the modern scientist is also most plainly in evidence. He takes the austere code of scientific endeavor too seriously. It is as though we were already in full control of a great progressive democratic civilization and only technical problems were left to solve. Like so many other brilliant scientists in all fields during our day, Thorndike retires from the chaotic scene of social conflict to the laboratory. He is aware of the great struggle outside, but his encyclopedic knowledge of human nature only makes him shudder at the spectacle and at what it may portend. Thorndike is too sensitive

not to speak out now and again in favor of nobility and beneficence in human affairs, but these pious mutterings of his
about religion and ethics mean little in an emergent civilization
starved for great minds willing to lend their powers to the less
technical but more significant task of social policy making. The
scientist must inevitably, like the layman, always be a partisan;
by derivation and ancestry he belongs to the new order in human
affairs. If his technical tasks become too fascinating for him
to leave at the present juncture of social evolution, then he
shirks a great duty. He becomes by forfeiture the partisan of
an ignoble *status quo*. And he perchance misses a golden opportunity to work at technical problems, within his field, of far
greater consequence than any at which he is now free to work.
It is with the non-partisan pretensions of Thorndike that we
must quarrel. In Judd and in Snedden the bias towards traditionalism of viewpoint is not so ably concealed, but Thorndike
almost succeeds in creating an illusion of real objectivity in
general outlook. When he proposes, however, that educators
analyze out in advance the amount and kind of learning needed
by various classes of the population, whether he wills it or not,
he is furnishing ammunition to those powerful interests which
desire no change in the present social order. And his use of the
term *adjustment* as the aim of education, no matter how broadly
he may wish it to be interpreted, expresses exactly what the
real powers that be most earnestly expect of the schools.

What Thorndike most desires immediately in educational practice is more scientific endeavor. This represents again the assumption that the fundamentals of educational practice are correct and that only refinements are needed. It also assumes that the
nobility of man can best be served by measuring the actual
effectiveness upon conduct of this or that subject, or this or
that educational method. There is no suggestion in Thorndike
of the possibility which is becoming ever more prominent even
to the lay mind, that the whole problem of education has been

misconceived. He wants science applied to the curriculum; he wants objectively to know what should be taught and how and to whom. He warns against prejudices which have developed against psychological and educational measurement without doubting that we are socially ready for extensive practical application of existing techniques of measurement. It is over *values* that uncertainty exists, and no amount of measurement can determine what values will eventually be approved. Thorndike need not fear that measurement will be neglected when our society knows more definitely the objectives that it wills to follow. What does all the exact data which measurers have amassed, about reading, arithmetic, and intelligence amount to in a social order where great decisions remain to be made?

Thorndike dodges the issues involved in the so-called *project method* when he facilely suggests where, in the present scheme of subjects and grades, the "method" will be most useful. He desires interest to be used as a fundamental criterion, but calls upon scientists to determine in advance what is safely interesting.

Thorndike's significant findings in the field of adult learning have apparently greatly broadened his outlook upon the larger problems of education. He now criticizes the over-intellectualization of school education and the consequent general abasement of labor. He questions the actual results in adult life of the common practices in our schools, although he apparently continues to believe that these same practices need only "scientific" refinement. As a result of his investigations upon adult learning Thorndike comes near to saying something really significant about the institutions which lie back of our present school practices, but he contents himself with an exhortation for more science instead.

Thorndike is at his best in discussing the psychology of learning. He is not bothered, as Judd and Bagley are, by the possibility that man's behavior may not be qualitatively different from that of his animal relatives a little lower on the biological scale. The evidence that man reaches his supremacy only by quantitative differences seems to Thorndike compelling, and he faces it cheerfully. This is a healthy naturalism and should not be mistaken for anti-vitalistic prejudice.

His recent extensive experiments upon human learning have enabled Thorndike to liberalize considerably his classic laws of learning. In the few inferences for education which he has had time to draw from these liberalized laws, he comes very close to the kind of thing the Progressives have been standing for. It might almost be suggested that there is an emergent conflict in Thorndike between his long-standing educational conservatism and the implications of his new supplementary principles of learning. Thorndike's approach to human personality remains, however, a dominantly static one. His investigations of human behavior are pursued upon the assumption that man is merely a summation of stimulus-response bond elements. He studies man by attempting to isolate in the laboratory more and more $S \rightarrow R$ units of behavior with the apparent hope that when all of these basic elements have been enumerated and classified, the inner mysteries of human life will have been revealed. If we grant that by refined processes of laboratory analysis this complete inventory of human behavior might possibly be made, shall we then be any the nearer an understanding of the dynamics of a normally functioning human personality? Is Thorndike really interested in studying this latter entity? One wonders, for instance, whether his impatience with the so-called Vitalists is not prompted by their exploitation of the biological approach to human nature study, as well as by the traditional religious or ethical preconceptions which frequently confuse their writings. The biological or dynamic approach in psychology opens up vistas of infinitely complex investigation, but no matter how difficult the prospect of significant results from this avenue of study may now seem, its validity as an approach is in no sense less than that of the physical and statistical approach which Thorndike emphasizes.

Unfortunately Thorndike fails a victim to anti-Progressive prejudice in his pronouncements upon general educational theory. He ought not to stoop to attack the noisy, sentimental, and self-condemnatory fringe of the Progressive Movement, for he knows well enough where the philosophic strength of the Progressives comes from. One should assume, therefore, that his critical shafts are directed upon Dewey and Kilpatrick. Where in the writings of these men does he find an emphasis upon mere experience or growth as such, directionless and anarchic? When have Dewey and Kilpatrick stood for an individual perfection that gives no thought to modern interdependence and collectivism? Have they really been saying that the child's interest is an ultimate and final guide, as Thorndike indicates? Thorndike fails thus to make any attempt at reasoned understanding of an educational viewpoint in many respects opposed to his own. His conservative orientation seems to dictate a characteristic emotionalized response of abhorrence to the new and unfamiliar.

ERNEST HORN

As another uncompromising proponent of science as the ultimate solvent of social struggle, Horn contents himself with the assurance that a felicitous answer to every one of the vexing problems of our day will be forthcoming in the analyses of trained sociologists. He is satisfied while awaiting that happy ending to social chaos, to exhort upon the need for more educational research. He dreams of a fully validated program in which every school activity shall function towards the realization of the scientifically pre-determined and supposedly, thereafter, permanent social values. Horn, like Thorndike, attempts to escape from any direct allegiance to educational conservatives or radicals by throwing a smoke screen of objectivity. His educational practice seems really to have been a happy combination of the principles of both groups. His zeal for practicality, however, suggests a heavy theoretic leaning towards the present social order and its attendant school system. Selecting and emphasizing disrespect for property as an especially dangerous present social shortage also points strongly towards *status quo* tendencies in Horn. His constant reiteration of the continuity between the interests and activities of adults and those of children as a fundamental principle suggests that he has found this a happy compromise defense, in theory at least, against radicals who see in children the promise of a markedly changed social order. In our present American society this is too simple a solution to the conflict between the idealism of youth and the weight of existing institutions. It amounts to an empty promise that if youth will only cease its rebelliousness, a paternal science will convert all adults to rationality and humaneness. Horn's child's-rights program is thus little more than an expression of the child's right to be docile while the graded school grows more benevolent.

In the discussion of Horn's practical proposals for education, the set of his mind towards tradition seems clearly demonstrated. It is scarcely a liberal touch to wish for a radically different type of school off somewhere in a laboratory. With the demands he makes upon such an experiment, it would be safely buried for generations to come. He counsels, for the common run of educators, contented submission to practical expediency and existing educational machinery. They may safely forget their real doubts about the efficacy of prevailing practices and trust to educational research for gradual improvement. Horn has little to say on the problem of how a teacher is to be friendly and stimulating to her pupils, tossed as she is at present between the two fires of a business-efficiency-mad administration and a compelling but unintelligible body of statistical educational science.

Horn finds nothing basically wrong with the public elementary school set-up. The present régime in the schools has profited greatly from the educational agitations of the past thirty years, and its faults are minor ones easily remediable by more conservatism in regard to the introduction of new subjects and by slight administrative readjustments. Language and number remain the key to education; Horn approves the conservative insistence that they be not tampered with. He frowns righteously at schools which have left the straight and narrow road to a true education, namely, the grade-subject system. These schools, according to Horn, have already demonstrated significant failure to assure transmission of fundamental social values, by which Horn apparently means the moral and ethical standards derived from the Christian-business cultural solidarity of the nineteenth century. As if these new schools really aimed in that direction! The failure of the Progressive schools up to the present is not quite so easily dismissed. Progressive schools are guided by new social and individual insights thrown against a background of breaking, but still relatively strong, traditions. Horn misses the point altogether when he accuses them of failing to preserve the very traditions against many of which they have set their course. The chaos which the Progressive schools have indisputably demonstrated is the chaos of the beginning stages of constructive effort in any period of transition from old to new social values.

Horn's formula for properly nurturing youth into a safe and sane adulthood of the most representative extant variety in American life is to trust sociologists for curriculum content, and psychologists for methods of teaching. Educational science is the result of the happy collusion of such specialists, and it can be depended upon to insure that school education shall be properly formal and informal and that pupils shall be both controlled and free. Only to a person who thinks of science as something ultimate or divinely powerful could such a vision of perfection occur. It is pure magic to believe, as Horn apparently does, that we have already within our grasp the secret of an educational program which can combine a happy childhood with felicitous social institutions.

Philosophizing about educational theory Horn thinks an eminently futile undertaking. He would not quarrel particularly with those whose intellectual tastes happen to run in that direction, but he is himself convinced that good education is always the resultant of one eternal set of principles which grows as social vision grows. He would grant that theorizing is both useful and helpful, but only as it concerns itself constructively with what now goes on in the schools. He cites the Progressive theorizing about interest as an example of speculation not only futile but actually harmful in its disturbing effects on the even tenor of school routine.

WERRETT W. CHARTERS

The hard crust of scientific determinism in social life so rigidly supported by Judd, Snedden, Thorndike, and Horn, begins to sway a little in Charters' position. Weakened on the one hand by leanings towards the values of old religion and on the other by leanings towards modern educational philosophy, Charters begins to question the ultimacy of science. He is not deserting the cause, for he continues to speak the language of these social determinists in advising advance along the lines of existing society and warning against strange new ways. He differs from the others, however, in conceding the function of the philosopher as ultimate synthesizer and clarifier of the values of life. He differs too in his insistent emphasis on adding to the predetermined content of education what he calls training in clear thinking, presumably about general matters of some importance. Charters' tone is much softer also in speaking of the curriculum; he concedes the intricacy of its problems, but he has no illusions about their complete solution in any educational research laboratory. He even dares to question, in true heretical fashion, whether the unmitigated drill on the three R's during early childhood will always be considered as righteous as at present.

Charters remains eminently safe for the old régime, nevertheless. He would build the core of American culture, to which future generations might add, out of an analysis of "cultured" minds in this generation. These "cultured" minds are undoubtedly none other than the well-educated and abundantly-leisured followers of the fading traditions of Christianity and of Capitalism. No other brand of cultured mind is as yet numerous or voluble enough to count in any such survey as Charters proposes. The doctrine of teaching to our already revolting youth what these good people believe to be the eternal verities is both dangerous and impossible. Charters speaks assuredly of the ideals of society as if they were the settled rather than the ever-emergent goods of social evolution.

Charters has a more alert mind for the genuinely practical in educational reform than any of his fellow prophets of science in the classification of the present study. To the scientific refinement of the existing school machinery he would make significant additions of genuine problem and project work. This is true compromise with no apologies for retaining the old or none for incorporating the new. If the social order changes with the slow gradualness of Charters' expectations, this may indeed prove the real method of educational reform. Charters defends his elaborate techniques of job and curricular analysis as merely improved ways of doing what would otherwise be done clumsily and haltingly. And taken in this sense with the qualifications which Charters makes upon excessive faith in objective measurement, the technical studies in which he is interested will at least accumulate data useful in any type of educational reform. He opposes traditional ideals of information-getting and also thoroughly systematized curricular programs, in the interest of more flexible school organization and greater teacher independence. Despite these liberal or radical flares in Charters' thinking, he defends the familiar grade organization, which surely, beyond the fact of its existence, bears no stamp of rational or scientific authorization. It is the homeliest truth of the ages that human institutions and customs are best served by honest critics rather than by stanch defenders, yet most of the contemporary apologists for science continue to defend the traditional ways.

Charters sounds an optimistic note when he comments on the state of educational practice today. He feels that evils are correcting themselves and cites as proof the emergence of the project method out of a background of over-formalized school procedures. The swing among educators towards widespread concern about aspects of character and personality development and the trend away from the former purely sentimental and theoretic interest in character, he regards as further evidence of healthy reform within the system. And likewise the extension of the period of teacher education is a hopeful sign. That these are improvements cannot be denied, but that they are adequate to enable education to keep pace with the rapidly changing social scene is greatly to be doubted. The haste with which Charters has himself entered the field of preparing moral and ethical lessons for the instruction of youth is decidedly premature. Better, first, to let the chaotic mores of present American society polarize towards some definite center and better to let the significant early results of modern psychiatric research accumulate in greater degree.

Like Snedden, Charters works out all his suggestions for educational reform as well as his own analysis of learning on the Thorndike specific-element, no-transfer psychology. He does not go to such lengths of vision or of dogmatism as does Snedden. He recognizes the enlarged functions of the school in modern times without feeling the necessity of Snedden's elaborate classificatory conceptions. Although he insists upon adequate and assured control of children as preparation for meeting the requirements of adult life, Charters is sensitive to a great many Progressive educational principles. The emphasis, however, which Charters places upon prepared-in-advance working units of curriculum, and his frank denial that the child has any positive function in curriculum-making renders neutral much of his apparent educational liberalism. For the adherents of a static social order the significance of a scheme of character education based upon the one-by-one learning of thousands of specific conduct items is quite clear. Charters plays right into the traditionalists' hands also when he recognizes a central core of conventional subjects and rigid training in "fundamentals." These conceptions are meaningless in any genuine understanding of what is meant by the *activity* approach in education. Charters apparently looks upon "Progressive principles or the *project method*" as methodological devices rather than as challenges to the whole accepted scheme of educational philosophy.

Charters believes himself to be aloof from partisanship towards either the left wing or the right wing of educational theory. Most men are possessed by the notion that they have attained a viewpoint which is central between extremes; no sane man will confess that he is an extremist of any kind. Being "of the center" means something different to each one who claims the affiliation. To Charters it means a mild tolerance for the principle that new views may contain elements of real value. When new views embody ideas contrary to what he considers sound, Charters characteristically moves away from his idyllic "center" to pounce upon them. So incidental instruction is called accidental instruction regardless of the intended meaning of those who use the term *incidental* constructively. And the suggestion that the school curriculum should follow normal child life is inferred by Charters to be the fruit of illusion. He is entitled to his convictions; the more clearly they are uttered the better will it be for all who think about educational problems. The author simply wishes to contend that Charters only adds to confusion by claiming non-partisanship.

FRANKLIN BOBBITT

Bobbitt's defection from the ranks of those who wish to be guided exclusively by science in their thinking about social and educational reform is even more marked than that of Charters.

In those matters where Bobbitt seems to see eye for eye with the Progressives, he does not allow any hesitant apologetics to dim his vision. Charters never quite cuts his line of communications with safe and respectable tradition. There is much, however, that is similar in the social and educational conceptions of the two men, and they belong, by virtue at least of their past, in the classification with Judd, Snedden, Thorndike, and Horn. Bobbitt appears to be much more concerned with the moving forces underlying the complex social life of today. He yearns for an all-inclusive philosophic vision with religious fervor, and he locates the root of contemporary chaos in the careless thinking of the populace upon crucial social issues.

In thinking of the function of the school under modern conditions, Bobbitt is driven, just as Charters was, to propose a detailed sociological analysis of "cultured" people as the sole way to the determination of prime and eternal values. He assumes that objectives so determined will sum up to that mysterious entity, "the good life." And once it is known what the good life is, education can be rationally and certainly planned. Granting the doubtful assumption that human values can be thus scientifically determined, and granting the still more doubtful assumption that "the good life" may be derived from a summation of these values, the building of an educational program upon such a basis would be an excellent way of preserving intact the institutions which gave the "cultured" nucleus of our population the peculiar predilections towards good and evil which they now manifest. Bobbitt seems just a little too anxious to make the future safe in terms of the present. He really fails to read the obvious implications of his own principle that *the objectives and the processes of education are one,* otherwise he would see that neither the objectives nor the processes of education are of a nature to yield to statistical treatment and thus to wholesale formulation in advance. Values, like the institutions and the customs from which they are derived, are dynamic, changing things, a cross section of a moment in their evolution, which is the best that statistical sociological analysis can yield, would be meaningless for an educational planning in which abundant present living is an important criterion. If the objectives are the processes of education, then these processes must be trusted to develop as time goes on in suitably broadening ways, and science should be employed more strategically than in statistical attempts to determine the good life once and for all.

Bobbitt holds no brief for the grade-subject school organization of the present. He concedes that the present arrangements probably must continue until plans for fundamental reorganization can be made ready. But in his attempts to point the way in curriculum reconstruction, he seems very confusing indeed. The elaborate analyses of all fields of human activity which he wishes experts to undertake are to constitute a curriculum content conceived in broader terms than merely what the school does. These analyses are to be selected and arranged in terms of the ability and interest levels of children. And yet Bobbitt insists that the child must contribute to curriculum making, because he can be effectively educated only as he participates wholeheartedly in planning his own activities! How can he do this if school activities are already planned by experts? Perhaps Bobbitt means to confine the work of experts to the exploration and collection of source materials basic to wholesome and varied environmental activities. One is led to hope that he would make these materials available to community, teacher, and child as background resources for the actual developing curriculum of daily life. Bobbitt has apparently failed to make his intentions clear on this point. It is still possible to assume that the collected curricular resources, after psychological hocus-pocus has been exercised upon them shall constitute the curriculum.

When Bobbitt attacks existing educational organization and administration, he expresses himself like a real revolutionist to whom nothing will suffice but a complete turn-over of the prevailing system of isolated schooling and the prevailing grade-subject arrangements. He moves far to the left of Charters in his willingness to question prevailing notions of what constitute the fundamental essentials of education. Bobbitt genuinely appreciates the meaning of that much maligned and much admired phrase *education is life*. He is not, therefore, greatly impressed by the educational progress of the last decade or so. Issues have not been clarified, vision is still scarce among educators, and against these basic deficiencies what matters the now universal presence of bulky syllabi?

There seems reason for assuming that Bobbitt himself has experienced a kind of conversion in educational theory such as he believes necessarily preliminary to instituting significant educational reform. In the place of former dogmatic statements about the completely preparatory nature of education, we now find Bobbitt the ardent advocate of an education in which rich present living is the main feature. He is a great apostle of "incidental" learning, despite the fact that he fails to make clear the consistency of many of his curricular proposals with "incidental" learning. Certainly in everything that he has recently said about the actual educational process, Bobbitt has moved completely away from the disciplinary analysis of the traditionalists and the elaborate but narrow calculations of the scientific enthusiasts.

Evidence that Bobbitt is still a divided mind in modern educational theory may be found in what little he has to say regarding the various points of view advanced by American educators. The Progressives he leaves strictly alone, perhaps regretting that so many of his own ideas are also expressed by them and also that they seem to possess such an adolescent gift of eloquence. Bobbitt's scientific leanings get the better of his radical philosophic faith when he contemplates a profession which still speaks so confusedly. But he reiterates his objection to the notion that scientific refinement of the existing scheme of education is all that is needed. He stands for science and he stands for a thoroughly modernized education, but he does not seem as yet to have brought the two together in any consistent and compelling wholeness of viewpoint.

III. Educators Stressing the Implications of Modern Experimental Naturalism

JOHN DEWEY

As the storm center for many years of American philosophic and educational thinking, John Dewey has proceeded steadily to build a tower of profound common sense about human nature and about human affairs. His is the sensitive, inquiring mind as completely without unexamined assumptions as it is possible to conceive. So far he seems only to have inspired a host of vociferous partisans, pro and con. Those to whom Dewey is anathema see in him only the destroyer of age-old and respectable traditions; they have not been patient enough to hear him out on the matter of traditions. And those who swear by Dewey all too evidently see him mainly as the founder of a mysteriously fascinating new cult, but these enthusiastic disciples often do not examine his work carefully enough to ascertain what its larger metaphysical significance may be. The true meaning of Dewey, therefore, awaits the penetration of his thought to the growing hordes of American people who seek light upon innumerable problems, who are shorn of undying allegiance to traditions, and who are too sophisticated to be seeking a new Messiah. Much of what Dewey has said and written will seem axiomatic and commonplace when popular awakening to the meaning of modern times occurs. The real task of building values suitable to the age of technology and the machine, as he himself has so many times patiently repeated, can be undertaken only as people grow more generally conscious that all the great inherited traditions have lost their authoritative glamour. America must create anew social institutions and social values that may have, if the people will it so, as great glamour as any created in the past. It is an undertaking in which all must consciously share in some degree and one which, in the old sense, can never be completed. No Messiah, philosopher, or strong man, or any combination of such can satisfactorily execute this task.

Rather than utter Christian and capitalistic apologetics in one form or another, Dewey has attempted to label the curious miscellany of cultural ideas and attitudes which have collected on the American scene. His works are literally a museum of Western thinking. He has penetrated to the bare rock of naturalism upon which not only American, but every modern culture, must inevitably come to rest if man is to endure as the supreme gift of Nature. Dewey is not willing to conjecture what is in the future to be built upon the bare rock of naturalistic thought; he is content in the faith that what man with simple tools has achieved in sporadic civilizations of the past, man today with perfected scientific technology can achieve with enhanced splendour.

Dewey does not surrender to any special phase of modern experience, least of all to science, in his views as to the ways out of present difficulties. Traditions to him are the raw materials which man may fabricate, and science constitutes man's set of tools. To combine the two worthily modern man must be possessed of a vision generated by enlightened thinking and by generous impulses. Dewey thus becomes, like Plato and like Rousseau, a philosopher of education. The educational principles which he evolves are radically different from those which guide the school practice of the present, because Dewey looks at tradition and at science to discover the possibility of a great evolving modern culture. His challenging proposals for educational reconstruction are impossible and impractical in even a profounder sense than radio and a thousand other modern inventions were impossible and impractical.

Dewey is an agitator not in addition to being a philosopher,

but because he is a philosopher. He thinks of his own speculations as being purposeful rather than idle, and when he recognizes some force within society which seems to him moving in
the direction of greater human beneficence and dignity, he
lends it every power that is available to him. The fact that reflective people as a whole customarily hold aloof from the scene
of social struggle suggests to Dewey the main cause of contemporary social chaos. He calls upon the university and the
intellectuals of the nation to assert themselves as social func-
tionaries, rather than as spectators or as a decorative margin to
the social order. Dewey has been almost the sole American educator of prominence to urge that school teachers ally themselves
definitely with labor groups. Characteristically he urges the
abandonment of the petty caste distinctions between educators
of different levels in the teaching function, and he shows the
dependence of any genuine academic freedom upon aggressive
professional solidarity. He calls the teaching profession to leadership in the determination of educational objectives and in the
definition of the relation of the schools to social life. In other
words, against the common theory and practice of today he is
urging the professional autonomy of teachers. In Dewey's educational thinking the teacher always occupies the strategic position; both the science and the philosophy of education exist as
service agencies to the teacher's function. He points a way
whereby the cumulations of curricular research, so blindly carried forward today, may function without effacing the personalities of teacher and pupil as they so often do in the plans of educational administrators. Scouting all thought of educational
panaceas, Dewey calls broadly for more rigidly disciplined
thinking by all engaged in the educational task as they face
their various problems.

Dewey's attack upon prevailing school practices is incisive
and direct. Granting some obvious progress in many directions,
he yet shows that the surface of needed educational reform has

scarcely been scratched. He points out the conceptual hang-overs which, by isolating fundamental human sciences from the scene of action and from each other, confuse and render futile much educational effort. He attacks ruthlessly the school board method of educational control, still so sacred almost everywhere in America, as responsible for a kind of administrative tyranny which allows almost no departures from straight-laced tradi-tional ways of doing things in schools. Despite the far-famed fruits of the new educational science, Dewey claims that the demonstrated inertia of the school machine is evidence of wide-spread lack of appreciation of the meaning of the scientific habit of mind. He asserts that those who speak loudest in praise of educational science frequently restrict the scope of scientific thinking to insignificant educational matters. Owing to the readi-ness with which unscrupulous sentimentalists claim the prestige of Dewey's name for their own loudspoken theoretic utterances, Dewey has insisted that as much futility and error may come from a total lack of adult direction in schools as from its present over-emphasis.

Dewey's position in psychological analyses of the learning process, avoiding as it does the pitfalls of philosophic concepts which hail from the pre-scientific era and likewise an easy trust in the relentless accumulation of statistically analyzable data, is the source of the soundness of much of his more generalized thinking about human nature and education. His fine sense for reality has kept his psychology close to biological facts and has made him perennially sceptical of those who would build a science of human nature upon the model of physics. He was one of the earliest critics of the attempt to create human personality and behavior out of a summation of statistically analyzable stimulus-response bond elements. And he was one of the first modern American philosophers to take as the central educa-tional principle the creative possibilities of the individual. Dewey's clarification of the discipline-freedom problem in educational theory made that issue so startlingly simple and obvious that it is no longer excusable for his opponents to repeat outworn and meaningless inherited jargon. He advocates conscious supplementation and facilitation of the social growth of children by public educational agencies in communities which recognize the educational significence of all the activities of life. Dewey insists that all such supplementation and facilitation take its cue from the ongoing experience of the individual. This is his great heresy in the eyes of both the traditionalist and the scientific group of theorists. They cannot understand how any social discipline can result from such "catering" to the individual.

The key to nearly all current controversial issues in philosophy and in education is found, according to Dewey, in the human tendency to emphasize half truths. He has with such great precision and thoroughness explored the field of theoretic double-horned dilemmas and so clearly indicated the direction of their eventual solution, that no excuse remains for polemics about problems like mind versus body, the individual versus society, the child versus the curriculum and heredity versus environment. An examination of Dewey's reaction to varying current points of view shows invariably his patient and tolerant efforts first to understand and then to combine isolated elements into a synthetic whole.

GEORGE S. COUNTS

Counts has progressed beyond any faith in either the Christian moral and spiritual tradition, or the economic tradition of capitalism in America. He has not cast himself down before the altar of tradition nor before that of science, but neither does he pay homage to the kind of liberalism under which he classifies Dewey. He claims to have moved out into the raw open spaces of modern collectivistic thought. And from there he judges the American scene with a high degree of scepticism. America to a considerable extent fades out before the blazing light of modern Russia. The primitive and powerful new religion of Communism, which is rapidly becoming a fanatic passion among the Russian masses, inspires him with revolutionary ideals for America. And although Counts is careful to point out that he has no particular predilections towards Communism in America, his attacks upon the advocates of reasoned analysis of our society seem to indicate a mind-set towards an initially complete social system which reason shall not question. He appears to believe in a kind of natural law governing the history of societies, a law which gives rise to a waxing and waning of great creative periods among nations. America, he would say, has lost the vigor of its early revolutionary enthusiasms and is awaiting leaders who will hitch its spirit to a new set of dogmas and thus cause it to enter upon a new formative period. Counts would use the schools in good engineering fashion to hasten our transition from the fading old individualism into a blossoming new collectivism.

Counts' break with Dewey comes just at this point. In Dewey there is no mystic sense of the Destiny of nations; he would be quick to point out that the appeal of Counts' point of view lies in the humaneness of the ideals it contemplates, rather than in its correct readings of the implications of modern industrialism. A Mussolini, a Spengler, and a Hitler have used the same fundamental philosophy to urge reactionary ideals. Of the men under consideration in the present study, Counts really allies himself with Briggs and Finney in his reading of social evolution and in the nature of his proposals. His divergence from Kilpatrick lies in his clearly instrumental interpretation of education. There can be no questioning Counts' assertion that the schools are at present indoctrinating the younger generation with an unworthy and fading set of human values, but to imply as Counts does, that the remedy is merely a changed set of values to be imposed by teachers seems an over-simple analysis.

In strictly educational theory Counts belongs with the Dewey-

Kilpatrick emphasis. He despises, however, the smug intellectuality and the social immuneness that have engulfed at least
the main body of Progressives. When he calls enthusiastically
for an awakening of all American educators to the reality of
social forces in the modern world, he is alive to obvious needs.
In vigorously directing attention to what Soviet Russia is doing
both socially and educationally, Counts has undoubtedly stirred
the complacency of American teachers far more in the last two
years than the less sensational theorizing of Progressive educators has in a decade. He has opened a new and wider field for all
genuine Progressives to work, and he points challengingly to the
obligations which confront them.

Counts does not fail to compliment aspects of American education that seem to him constructive, like the scientific movement and the modern emphasis upon child study. But he indicates that all these things are minor and insignificant so long as
educators fail to ally themselves with social movements that
point in the direction of an ever increasing collectivization of all
of the goods of civilization.

Counts is not so ruthless as he sounds in his suggestion that a
new set of values, cognate with modern industrial society and
mass welfare, be forged by educators and then imposed upon
the young in such a way as to generate a national spiritual
rebirth. He means to retain the real gains of Progressive education in the field of method and in analysis of the learning
process. That is, he would impose the new benevolent ideals as
benevolently as possible. Counts' positive use of such terms as
indoctrination and *imposition* is a mischievous slam at Progressive pussyfooting during a great social emergency rather than
any fundamental criticism of the main tenets of Progressive
education. Counts at his best really proposes that we indoc-
trinate our children against indoctrination. Although such a
proposal sounds inspiring, it remains meaningless until the details of its execution have been worked out.

Counts' list of doctrinal bogies which obscure educational endeavor today is forbidding enough. It would appear as though he had gathered them by listening to half-hearted discussion groups at provincial teachers' institutes. In the way he has stated them these bogies do not hail from important theoretic writings about education in America during the last decade or so. A few of them undoubtedly originate from the Progressive phrase book, but he has given them such a spiteful twist that they cannot be declared representative. To condemn as lacking in robustness the advocates of more freedom, more science, more open-mindedness, is to assume altogether too much. It is perfectly possible, as Counts well enough understands, that men can desire these things with as much passion and force as they can desire Communism or Christianity or Business Success. That certain preachers of freedom mean by it the freedom to exploit their fellowmen, that certain ardent advocates of science desire an eternal social *status quo,* and certain Progressives mean by open-mindedness the lack of any definite convictions, is far from denying the worth-whileness of the ideals themselves.

WILLIAM H. KILPATRICK

It is the repeated assertion of the traditionally inclined and of the scientifically inclined groups of educational theorists that Kilpatrick is just another ax-grinder for a particularist faith: that he has resorted to certain sentimental or sensational catch-phrases designed cleverly to win followers to his cult. The truth and justice of these accusations must be determined by every student for himself, as he takes account of the issues and the problems of modern individual and collective life. It seems fairly obvious, however, that the traditionalist is so enamored of Christian and capitalistic habits of thinking and manners of life in America that, despite lip service to the term democracy, he scarcely recognizes a social crisis when he sees one and is still less able to suggest ways out. He has a vested interest in the maintenance of what he would call the proved certainties that have come down from the past, and he can be expected to go any length in defense of the things that he holds so dear. Only the utterly innocent would think a traditionalist capable of objective evaluation of a mode of thinking that makes a sacrilegious approach to his accepted gods. And with the theorists who put their complete trust in science, the case is not far different. True, they are conscious that religion is not what it used to be, and they leave it alone, wisely or unwisely, in most of their discussions. But in their haste to do complete homage to science, they absent themselves from the social scene altogether. Though American civilization may be immediately overrun by business racketeering and criminality, the scientists are attracted only by research studies. Their vested interest is scientific research, and they can be expected to show no scruples when a Kilpatrick proposes to take away some of the pristine purity of science, nor when he questions the ultimacy of a social-science laboratory which is remote from society. Can tolerance towards philosophy, especially comparatively new philosophy, be expected from them? It is not strange, therefore, that, as was shown in the sections on "Reactions to Other Points of View" in the present study, the concern of both the traditionalist and of the scientific groups has been to discredit usually by misinterpretation the point of view of Kilpatrick. He, more than Dewey, is responsible for the publicity that Progressive educational principles have received.

Surely Kilpatrick's point of view about the world we live in proves upon intelligent examination to be a simple and obvious reading of the necessities of the times! Concisely he calls for acceptance of the existent and for exalted effort by all in shaping the present more in accord with generous human impulses. Surely by counseling greater human control of inevitable and rapid social changes, he is not making a god of change. And when he reveres and interprets democracy, he gives it an extension of meaning which discriminates between social and anti-social tendencies in the present. His conception of education as the function of building creative and integrated personalities capable of genuine sharing in communal activities, despite the magnitude of the task involved, is plainly the obligation that confronts modern society.

The easiest disposal of Kilpatrick's specific educational suggestions is to say that they are impractical. However, before we can glibly say anything is impractical, we must know what is being attempted. Do we know the aims of education in America of the twentieth century? It is exceedingly doubtful. Practices now going on in the public schools all over the land are assumed by most school people to be practical. When Kilpatrick calls attention to the fact that this practicality is dated about 1850 or earlier, how far is he wrong? America is much different today from what it was in the middle of the last century. Can it possibly be assumed that the aims of education are the same? Is it unreasonable to assert that in the emergence of enlarged educational ends, evolved theories and methods also are concomitant? Kilpatrick's preoccupation with the meaning of commonly used terms in educational theory is evidence that he is aware of this problem. His concern with the individual learner comes not from sentiment for "the child," but from a realistic reading of results in basic human sciences.

Kilpatrick sums up his criticisms upon current practice in our schools by showing that it is admirably suited to the exigencies of a static civilization. It is, of course, not a matter of theory whether American society is static or dynamic. All modern societies are dynamic, though not all in equal degree. The America of the early nineteenth century, when the ideas and practices which guided public education took shape, was vastly less dynamic in character than the America of today. The Christian tradition with its doctrine of the eternal verities was then in full bloom, and capitalism, built upon supposed natural

economic laws, was just rounding into shape. Both these traditions are decadent today, and even to the bewildered lay ob-
server the whole social scene seems to be in flux. Kilpatrick dismisses the notion that by more strongly entrenching ourselves
upon the principles of a more static period in American culture,
a fitting stability can again be attained. Has significant social
stability ever been reached by turning backward? Kilpatrick is
only calling attention to factual necessities when he says we
must re-think our educational principles and practice in thoroughgoing fashion. And when he says that we must master even
our science, he is asking only that scientists know more clearly
the social ends of their endeavor.

Kilpatrick is at his best when describing the learning process.
If there be one point at which he has concentrated his analytic
and synthetic efforts, it is on the matter of creating a theory and
a psychology of learning which fits democratic social ideals and
the known facts of human nature. In his recent "Reconstructed
Theory of the Educative Process"[6] he has put forth a document
at once clear, concise, and comprehensive—a challenge to all
who theorize about or practice education and a constructive
effort which honestly composes a naturalistic and a democratic
philosophic vision with what seem the most reliable conclusions
in the basic human sciences. Kilpatrick early compromised his
acceptance of Thorndike's main formulations upon human learning by extensive supplementation from the biological and the
psychiatric approaches to problems of personality development.
He has always placed the problem of the development of an
integrated individual character central in his psychological
thinking. This explains his impatience at undertakings like the
extensive researches into the teaching of school subjects, which
look only to the cultivation of narrow aspects of personality
growth.

The key to Kilpatrick's criticisms of other educational theo-

[6] *Teachers College Record*, XXXII, March 1931, 530-58.

rists is found in the way in which he connects particular educational theories and principles with basic outlooks upon life. He attacks especially theories which imply a preconceived acceptance of present social institutions as they are now or as they have been in the past. He attacks also theories which imply preconceived notions of what the future should be like. This leaves him the advocate of theories based upon a critical analysis of present social institutions in the interest of more genuinely thoroughgoing democracy.

Despite the broadness of sweep which his writings show, Kilpatrick does not quite break the academic bounds of the professor who is concerned with problems of learning. To every issue of life he would seem to apply the same intellectualistic estimate, the same conscious urge towards improvement, towards ever more refined *activity*. Of stopping places, consummatory finalities in life, he speaks but seldom. The cross-fertilization of his creative pedagogy with developing native strains of culture along other lines, particularly in art and literature and drama is apparently not attempted. A philosophy and methodology of education, to be lastingly influential should synthesize these emotional strivings within the native soul. Kilpatrick's writings are challenges to fundamental educational reform, but do not seem to emphasize sufficiently the need for rich cultural attainments on the part of those who are to do the reforming. It is to be suspected that many students who are profoundly influenced by Kilpatrick and who resolve to provide creative opportunities for the children whom they teach, are unaware of their own narrow cultural horizons. With the breakdown of the old institutional loyalties among teachers it becomes exceedingly important that theorists who urge them to marked departures from commonly accepted principles and techniques of educating shall also provide enlightening guidance towards the attainment of sufficiently varied aesthetic and spiritual experience. While Kilpatrick has successfully communicated a high standard of conscientiousness to his students, it is doubtful whether he has much clarified their more vital perplexities. The phrase "activity leading to further activity" is for many teachers little more than a stylistic expression for educational modernity because they have never felt its full significance in their own narrowly circumscribed and over-academic experience. Analysis, experimental attack, even the attitude of open-mindedness, are after all but instrumentalities in the service of self-realization, enhanced enjoyments, and richer leisure. These instrumentalities become ends in themselves only for the comparatively few who are of an exclusively intellectualistic temper. Kilpatrick does not appear to emphasize enough the transcendent value of experience in its non-intellectual aspects.

Again, anyone reading or listening to Kilpatrick cannot fail to be convinced that he preaches a radical social philosophy. But why are conservative teachers seemingly so little disturbed by it? Many thousands of American teachers have been constructively influenced by Kilpatrick, but what indications are there that these teachers have positively altered the prevailing aimlessness and aloofness of the profession as a whole? What happens to Kilpatrick's radicalism when it meets a conservative force? In the past, at least, it seems to have been shunted into rather strictly methodological attempts by individual teachers to create a more sympathetic school environment for children. This is obviously not unimportant, but does it meet the case before American education? Kilpatrick's strategy for educational and social reform has been that of "boring from within." He hopes that the needed changes will be gradually attained through the interpenetration of the influence of wise educators among conflicting groups in American social life. The implication is never drawn that conflict between various groups or classes within our society is already so advanced as to preclude effectiveness of integrative attempts by a professedly classless group like the teachers. Where is the significance of a viewpoint with broad social implications, if it does not lead to bold aggressive united stands by teachers on critical major issues of social change? Kilpatrick affords a theoretic glimpse into more perfected democracy, but he does not seem to supply the driving challenge to effective action. Theoretic commitment of the teaching profession to complete ethical democracy is not enough to break the teacher's inveterate habits of qualification and compromise in the face of situations whose range exceeds professional or technical considerations.

The time seems to have come in the development of American culture when teachers must have done with certain customary and verbal allegiances and declare their real sympathies in no uncertain terms. If they are to share in the constructive shaping of emerging tendencies, they cannot continue to face away from direct attack upon forces deliberately hindering social advance, and to refrain from applying openly such pressure as proper organization may make them capable of. Kilpatrick does not appear to be willing to take sides definitely and without qualification in the waxing social struggle of the present. His theoretic analyses point towards radical change but his suggested methodological strategy seems no longer very realistic.

The criticism noted above should not in any sense be allowed to obscure Kilpatrick's contributions in the field of educational theory. Let us state these clearly in summary fashion. First, he has worked out, upon a truly elaborate scale, the implications of the experimentalist or naturalistic point of view for the various aspects of educational practice. In doing this he has immeasurably extended the professional field of philosophy of education and clearly defined the meaning of research in that field. Second, by mastering the technique of educative communication and of conference truly shared, he has created for the experimentalist point of view a bond of understanding which links in coöperative endeavor important educational centers all over the world.

HAROLD RUGG

Rugg, like Counts, attempts to be a marked critical variant from the experimentalist positions of Dewey and Kilpatrick. Whereas Counts revolts against what he calls the domination of experimentalist thinking by an innocuous nineteenth century Liberalism, Rugg pins upon experimentalists the accusation of a narrowly intellectualistic interpretation of life. Like Counts, however, Rugg by virtue of his deliverance from Christian, capitalistic, and scientific apologetics and by virtue of his adherence to fundamental Progressive educational principles, seems legitimately to belong in this third category of the present study.

It is strange indeed that Rugg should be the first American educational theorist of prominence to call attention to certain strains of unmistakably virile native cultural products which began to appear under the sway of the Christian-Business cultural solidarity during the nineteenth century. But even in Rugg's consciousness this phenomenon of a growing American artistic and intellectual independence bears all the earmarks of a recent discovery at secondhand. He seems to have been completely under the influence of the artistic enthusiasms and the emotional entanglements of that self-conscious group in American letters who launched *The Seven Arts* magazine a short time before America's entrance into the World War. Rugg, nevertheless, has genuine feeling for the possibilities of an American art and culture built out of native social backgrounds and a native vision of glorified individual self-expression.

So enthusiastic does Rugg become over the meaning of this insight for the theory of education, that he makes an attack upon one of the chief products of American native talent up to the present time, namely the writings of John Dewey. This philosophic source of guidance in reconstructing American culture out of all the promising strands of the past and present Rugg seems to have grossly misunderstood. If there be one designation that sums up the deeper meanings of Dewey's philosophy, it is *creative artistry.* Rugg seems to miss this note completely and goes on to discuss ineffectively something he calls the artist's "way of knowing." As if "knowing" may be anything else than a technical tool in the case of either the artist or the scientist. It is to be regretted that Rugg's significant turning of educational theory to perhaps the most fundamentally constructive aspect of American traditions should have been given this peculiar twist. He tries to be a seer pointing the way to ultimate salvation, when really he is uttering only stale Kantian sentiments about the world within and the world without.

Rugg's vision of educational reconstruction is of a far different order. Believing profoundly that children attending the public schools must be intelligent about the social life of which they are a part, Rugg has single-handedly taken the responsibility of putting together in educationally usable form a prodigious amount of compounded history, geography, sociology, and economics relevant to the American scene.[7] Through the dark forest of theoretic ponderings over the educative function of the social sciences he has cleared a way which will be a lasting example to hesitant workers in these fields. And he has in this same venture shown educational theorists how to assume some practical responsibility. Rugg has committed himself clearly also in the matter of the reform of teacher training. Nowhere in the literature of teacher training has this problem been analyzed so clearly and with such vision as in Rugg's discussion.

Rugg's ideal school program, despite its comprehensive grasp of social forces at work on the American scene, remains essentially a compromise. He has so far shown himself unable to get

[7] I *An Introduction to American Civilization* (New York: Ginn), 1929.
II *Changing Civilizations in the Modern World* (Ginn), 1930.
III *A History of American Civilization: Economic and Social* (Ginn), 1930.
IV *A History of American Government and Culture* (Ginn), 1931.
V *An Introduction to Problems of American Culture* (Ginn), 1931.
VI *Changing Governments and Changing Cultures* (Ginn), 1932.

clear of the traces of contemporary educational research. The psychology of the elementary school subjects is too much with him and except for his passionately conceived productions in the social science field he seems to have surrendered to the traditional common branches. No amount of concern for creativity in the school life of children can ever make up for the failure to see the problem of modern education wholly in terms of integrated personality growth. Rugg remains intent upon diluting his school program with the fruits of objective studies on school subjects. It is not to be assumed that the accumulated research studies on school subjects are of no value in educational reform—they may prove highly useful—but they were not conceived and carried on in the interest of fundamental reform. These multitudinous studies should not, therefore, be allowed to obscure efforts at radical revision of educational theory and practice.

Rugg seems to think of the school as an advance agent of social progress without asking penetrating questions about the social chaos in America today. He shows conclusively that the school has always been built in the image of past social conditions. Can the school by means of the vision of educators move itself, and then society, out from under the pressing weight of the past? Community mutuality centered around the educational establishment cannot be attained without serious social struggle. Educators will have to forget their "nonpartisan" professional pretentions long enough to make common cause with the masses out of whose final triumph only can the American culture of the future be built. Rugg hopes that present resources in enlightenment will be applied in the establishment of modern school nuclei such as he so enthusiastically describes and he apparently expects that the contagion spread by them will cause the emergence of a new social order. The attention which Rugg gives to technical curricular problems is eloquently expressive of a faith which is as basic in him as it is in Judd and Thorndike—namely, that the researcher is the ultimate guarantor of general beneficence.

Rugg's discussions of learning indicate that he is eager to have his cake and eat it as well. When he speaks in the visionary philosophic vein, nothing seems more important than that every individual shall express himself creatively in wholesome educative activities. Only thus, he avers, can wholesome personality integration ensue. When he speaks in the scientific psychological vein, the matter of greatest educational importance to him is a program of planned activities graded to age, mental, and interest levels, and prepared for teaching purposes by experts. Rugg does not synthesize these two aspects of his thinking in any clearly uncompromising fashion. His thinly veiled Kantianism will probably cause him to be accepted by school people as the earnest advocate of a supplementation of present educational practice by aesthetics in various forms.

It has already been suggested that Rugg's attack upon Dewey is a misguided one. That he was motivated perhaps by experimentalist followers of Dewey, who have in some cases been guilty of an intellectualism without benefit of intuition, is no good excuse for not examining closely enough Dewey's own writings.

The New Technology shows Rugg dealing with the present prolonged economic depression and with what it portends. He shares the vision of the engineering group known as Technocracy, which for a short spasm allowed the American public to dream of a rapidly approaching millennium of plenty and luxury. Rugg, however, dares to venture where the Technocrats feared to tread. He suggests how a social order which combines economic plenty with high culture may be ushered in. This proposal marks him as a major prophet of the waning American middle class. Despite all his well-documented strictures upon the rich and powerful rulers of contemporary America, and upon the economic system which they represent, he comes to the truly remarkable conclusion that these men and the governmental agencies which they control will finance and promote the radical reconstruction of American society by means of a comprehensive educational program! Rugg enthusiastically desires the revolution, but he refuses even to think about revolutionary processes except in hopelessly Utopian terms.

BOYD H. BODE

Bode in his social and in his educational philosophy represents the conservative wing of the followers of Dewey. He has not attempted to build particularly upon any of the general propositions which Dewey has suggested as basic to educational reconstruction. He has rather from the vantage point of Dewey's general position in modern philosophy attempted with quite devastating success to direct criticism at current educational and psychological theories. He seems, however, not to understand the nature of Kilpatrick's efforts to build a really functional set of educational concepts, by means of which teachers may understand better just what it is they are trying to do with children, with themselves, and with the social order. Like some others of Kilpatrick's critics, he thinks of Kilpatrick as representing a kind of primitive Rousseauian tangent in modern educational theory. It is probable that Bode and Kilpatrick would agree rather completely in their criticisms of theorists of the traditional and the scientific schools of thought because each of these schools imply denial of the full meaning of social democracy. But Bode revolts at Kilpatrick's attempt, by means of the project method, to state the positive educational meaning of thoroughgoing social democracy.

As Bode states his own general point of view, it seems at once naïve and realistic; naïve in the sense that he is full of the wordy idealism that has characterized so many ineffective liberals in American life; realistic in his insistence that democracy be detailed into a program of action capable of guiding educators out of their present theoretic confusion. Except in a moralistic and rhetorical sense, Bode seems not to respond to this latter challenge himself. He has no positive program to offer beyond well spoken sentiments calculated not to offend vested interests in society or in the public school system. The discipline of thinking upon which he sets such store may conceivably prove our eventual salvation, but Bode's own thinking as an educator appears to fall short of including social forces operating decisively on the contemporary American scene, like the stir created by Soviet Russia, the rapid disintegration of established religion, the emergence of racketeering as a fatal cancer upon the business system, the emblazoned publicity for matters formerly closely censored or circumscribed, and the insurgency of American art in its various forms.

True, Bode proposes the building of a philosophy which shall synthesize and give direction or meaning to all social forces. No one could object to this as a worthy proposal, but what are the specifications to be followed? Surely no concert of educators can accomplish it, nor can any concert of best minds from various fields. The outlook which will guide the American masses in the future can emerge only from the vital and incisive conflicts of viewpoint among men who are unafraid to take account of actual crises, and unafraid to speak out in ringing accents what they think and propose. Most Progressives, as Counts points out, have been content to keep their tongues in their cheeks, and Bode seems not to be an exception. In outline Bode's suggestions for a thoroughly integrated school program adapted to contemporary civilization are both interesting and constructive. But it is confusing when he attempts to synthesize democratic social ideals with what he calls scientific organization of subject matter. Apparently the whole present set-up of educational machinery and method can by some little philosophic hocus-pocus be adjusted to realize the everlasting golden age that Bode believes is promised in the future. His fear that the cultivation of purely intellectual interests will become a lost art, if educators do not plan directly and in detail for it, bespeaks a limited understanding of human nature.

Bode's attempt to straddle a middle ground between extreme current tendencies in American education, and thus to appear at once progressive and practical, is a profoundly safe conservative strategy. It is an out-of-date and over simple analysis, however, to say that the main educational issue now lies between those who wish adult compulsion and those who wish complete childhood freedom. The main issue today lies rather between those educators who respect their professional integrity enough to accept social responsibility commensurate with their powers and those who will continue to allow themselves to be used slavishly in the service of fading and ignoble ideals.

Bode has accomplished notable results in undermining much current psychological theory as it is applied to education. Like Kilpatrick and Dewey, he builds his analysis of learning upon a biological base. Although he seems to have overemphasized the purposive nature of human behavior as contrasted with that of animals lower in the scale, he nevertheless has contributed a very clear and revealing account of the relation between human behavior or intelligence and the environmental background in interaction with which it is built. In identifying thinking and learning, Bode builds far beyond the educational researchers who seem to be satisfied that the elements of school subjects, which their techniques isolate so effectively, make learning an exceedingly simple matter for both the teacher and the pupil. As in the case of Rugg, however, Bode's analysis is weakened by the effort to give school subjects an important place. They still make up a large part of what Bode thinks of as education and are by no means purely instrumental curricular materials as in Dewey and Kilpatrick. Insistent concern for school subjects assures the theorist an audience among "practical" educators but Bode's special pleading implies a sense of deeper righteousness.

IV. The Issues Confronting American Educators Today

The analysis of the more recent thinking of the seventeen educators considered in Sections Two and Three would seem to indicate that American education is in a state of disturbed equilibrium, vacillating at the present time between several centers of attraction. American educators apparently refuse to proceed in whole-hearted fashion to carry out a program of Christian education like that of Herman H. Horne; they refuse to let a Judd or a Snedden frame a completely scientific program for them; and they refuse to accept the practical educational implications of a naturalistic philosophy like that of John Dewey. The first is a way to explore the future in terms of a great religious tradition; the second is a way to refine the *status quo* by means of science; and the third is a way to explore the future in terms of intelligent human adaptation and control. Let us analyze each a little more deeply.

Upholders of the so-called traditional viewpoint cast a fond eye towards a cultural solidarity that existed in the past; they see the vision of an American Christian Utopia which, provided that God grant man grace and guidance, may really be brought to pass. An orientation of this kind entails a host of consequences in the way of attitude and behavior. There is a tendency to accept the essential religious, philosophic, ethical, social, and economic formulations of the past as only slightly inadequate today—a few slight adjustments and the chaos of today will turn into the order of yesterday. The revolutionary changes in the more objective sciences are readily accepted since the relations they bear to fundamental social institutions are not blatantly apparent. Educators may look to the future with great inspiration, for has not universal education only just come into its own? Democratic ideals, closely tied up in America with the accepted religious and ethical standards, afford critical tools with which to view educational organization and techniques. The educator is thereby enabled to appear with a revamped educational program, guaranteed, if carried through, to realize adequately the best that is in the old ideals—which to the traditionalist means the best that can ever be. The upholders of this viewpoint react with profound misunderstanding or with exhausted patience to those who would question the revered scheme of traditional values. The basic assumption seems to be that any educational program based on scepticism towards traditional ideals and practices must be a thoroughly mistaken one.

The upholders of the second outlook have had enough training in fields of modern science so that the old religious values tend to generate discomfort and to be pushed into the background. But since man's spiritual nature abhors a vacuum, science takes on a religious aspect. The vision is that of a perfected social order reached through the ceaseless, minute, self-sacrificing labor of devoted scientists. There seems to be nothing fundamentally wrong with the moral, religious, and economic values which have come down from the past—did not science itself spring out of the same social matrix? Only the utterly mythological or the scientifically invalidated materials of the old tradition are rejected. Education is regarded as a proper field for science also. What a wide future opens up for education when every principle and every practice shall have been statistically validated! Speculations which reach beyond the frontier of the already accomplished validations are taboo, especially those speculations which question the adequacy of educational practices which existing educational science has helped refine.

In the third outlook thinking does not crystallize upon the old religious center or upon its scientific substitute. Speculation arises out of the uncharted chaos of modern life. Human experience is viewed as it actually functions in an environment such as never was seen before—an environment which changes almost before it can be known. Is there nothing on the horizon by which a course may be laid? The vision appears of a complete passing beyond old values, of a scientific attack upon human problems which is directed by a philosophically criticized scheme of values relevant to the contemporary world. Life in all of its manifestations is recognized as alternately precarious and secure. The total effect of human effort has been, and may increasingly continue to be, that of diminishing precariousness and of increasing security. All human institutions are measured against the criterion of social usefulness and of release of individuality. Education means the actualization of distinctly human potentialities. Every present school practice is suspected of being tied to a vested habit which limits rather than frees human nature. Ceaseless criticism is showered upon theoretic defenders of tradition and upon theoretic advocates of a blind science.

The tenets of the several positions thus briefly summarized are never completely maintained by any of the individuals classified in the present study, but the positions as outlined are assumed to describe adequately enough the *orientations* out of which the thinking of the seventeen educators emerges. There have been evident many obvious exceptions to complete consistency between any one individual's general outlook, as analyzed, and his suggestions and criticisms on current educational practice, his theory of the learning process, and his reactions to other theorists; the author, nevertheless, believes that on the whole the classifications are warranted. It seems proper therefore to assert that American education will emerge from its present theoretic confusion when educators face more squarely than they have in the past the fundamental issues of social life and human destiny as they apply to the American scene and to the problems of education.

Dare traditionalists look with a cold analytic gaze at the traditions which they revere? Dare scientists emerge from the busy-work of research laboratories to air their souls in philosophy? And dare philosophers of the new dawn unite to shape a program which shall at once combine tradition and science into enlightened practice?

SUGGESTIVE STRATEGIC CONSIDERATIONS
FOR AMERICAN EDUCATORS

SUGGESTIVE STRATEGIC CONSIDERATIONS FOR AMERICAN EDUCATORS

PREFATORY NOTE

IN SECTION TWO an analysis was made of the points of view of seventeen American educational theorists. Section Three criticized and interpreted these viewpoints in the light of the orientation evident in the opening section of the study. In the final section which immediately follows, the author ventures upon an analysis of certain considerations which appear to him to be strategic to the assumption, by educators and teachers generally, of genuine professional solidarity and integrity.

I. SOCIAL AIMS

It would seem a commonplace to declare that the most fundamental duty of teachers is to be adequately comprehensive of the meanings of the modern world and in satisfactory adjustment to it. But the modern world is so new, so undefined, so subversive of "fundamental" traditions, and the counsels offered for its understanding and for personal adjustment in it are so varied, that many sincere people seeking for wholesome integration become only the worse confused. A few generations back "getting right with God" under the careful tutelage of the Christian ministry opened all the doors of understanding and brought the soul into harmonious relations with the outer world. Today God, in the old sense at least, has retired from the scene, and the human race, arrived at apparent physical maturity, faces the vast implications of the future without the assurance of transcendental grace and beneficence.

About the middle of the nineteenth century the last claims of Western Christianity to complete hegemony over all the fields of life were finally invalidated. Only a few highly sensitive intellectuals grasped the significance in the immediacy of its cumulative impact of what had been happening in many obscure scientific cloisters all over Christendom. With all the age-old values of a Christian religious interpretation of the universe apparently menaced, the climate surrounding these sensitive intellectuals turned suddenly frigid. The shudders which they spread through volume after volume of discourse and poetry and story during the later nineteenth century amounts to a vast and pathetically melancholic literature. The scientists, whose dogged curiosity had created all the havoc, fought back at first but gradually lost interest in polemics and concentrated upon their minute but nevertheless devastating labors. By the end of the nineteenth century a world whose physical aspect had profoundly changed was the result. Gone were the handicrafts and small-scale industry, gone the independent isolated nations, gone the old barriers of time and space and sea and land, gone agricultural supremacy, gone petty trade. In their stead had come Big Business, the ceaseless fecundity of the machine, and interdependence between nations. People in their deeply seated mental and emotional attitudes, however, remained anchored to a world which had already disappeared over the horizon of time. They refused to be moved from their moorings. The greatest war in human history ensued when the new century had barely turned the first decade. Still the minds of the ruling elder statesmen held fast to the traditional conceptions of the true, the good, and the beautiful that had demanded the sacrifice of millions of young men to the destructive propensities of the aeroplane, the submarine, poison gas, the howitzer, and the machine gun. The present day witnesses the race brought to the crowning absurdity of a world of plenty faced with economic ruin! Frenzy stalks through Europe and the Far East, and deaf ears are turned to councils of liberal moderation. America fortunately drags on behind, her situation not quite so desperate, her people still capable of a kind of credulity which those of other nations would mock.

Such in brief is the world that educators face today. It is this world that they must seek to understand and in understanding assist to control. How much longer will American educators remain complacent—secure in the haven of empty assurances that they are leaders and that their luckless busy-work will bring prosperity and happiness finally to all?

Economy measures which the powerful financial groups of the nation are forcing upon the public are beginning to ruffle somewhat the surface of this educational complacency. The time seems opportune for the growing discontent of educators to ripen into broadly conceived social attitudes and definite political action. Can educators attain truer bearings in the days and months of moderation which remain before America also swings to Fascism or some similar stop-gap organization? Are they brave and intelligent enough to search earnestly for new centers around which to build their personal integrity and their professional endeavors?

This means putting aside resolutely such irreparably damaged entities as the Christian tradition and capitalism, to which even now the allegiance of educators is rather verbal than real. The Christian tradition has contributed much to the upward struggle of man toward civilization, but it was itself a synthesis of many traditions and many movements, and it must give way in turn to a new synthesis of outlook—the achievement of more mature men in the modern world. The things of highest value for individual experience and for ethical standards in modern America will not, however, be found out so long as intellectual leaders maintain a sensitivity over the supernatural significance of Christian mythology or a sentimental personal attachment to the character of Jesus. It may as well be frankly recognized by

American educators that the days of Christian cultural solidarity in America are over. The task of reclaiming from the old tradition what may be significantly valuable for American social purpose in the twentieth century is thus rendered somewhat less arduous.

Obviously the same attitude of appreciative creative reconstruction applies when modern capitalism, or the so-called business régime, is considered. Since decay seems even farther advanced in the case of the traditional economic institutions, it will be more difficult to find much of permanent value or relevant to modern economic requirements. It is the boast of contemporary business leaders that economic individualism has given America its superb machinery of production and distribution—an equipment more than adequate to high standards of consumption among the populace. With that boast we are not concerned; the scientists working in social causation may some day unearth better insight as to the relation between the wisdom of business men and technological triumphs. Today even the famed "good will" of business is too often a technique of exploitation, self-interest, and profit at whatever cost. The opportunity confronts educators to do as a few religious organizations have already done, namely, renounce every semblance of allegiance to the economic régime of business for profit. Educators must prepare themselves and the younger generation whose ideas and attitudes are to some considerable degree in their trust for the task of bringing industry and technology to full functioning in the interest of a classless society. The conflict with politicians, business men, and financiers who wish to save capitalism at all costs must be honestly faced.

Again, the most constructive opportunity of all faces educators in the startling cultural miscellany that is American civilization today. In the light of their own generous educational ideals, they can assist in the selection of tendencies that point in the direction of a new and beautiful America of which only poets formerly have dreamed. A prompt and effective declaration of war upon the baser tendencies in American culture which are the despair of today is the educator's manifest obligation.

These are tasks in the eager execution of which educators may build new loyalties more relevant, more promising, more secure, and perhaps more enduringly productive. Technological equipment even in the social sciences exists already in surprising abundance. The resolution to use this equipment in the construction of a new social order will open realms of social technology of still broader scope and of greater adequacy.

It has been the attempt of this study in some degree to demonstrate that the skeletal framework of a mental and spiritual orientation sufficient to the new day in America exists in the philosophic formulations of experimental naturalism. The name most significantly attached to this edifice of modern attitudes is, of course, that of John Dewey. He is to many perhaps better known as the philosopher of Progressive Education. As such, his phrases have been quoted, admired, and reviled until attitudes towards him have hardened almost beyond the reach of thought. This is peculiarly unfortunate because his methodological suggestions for educational reform are important only in their relation to the deeper social attitudes from which they spring. If the so-called philosophy of John Dewey bears any relevance to the large social problems by which educators are confused today, this relevance lies in its bed-rock analysis of human nature in the modern environmental setting. To minds in which the social institutions that evolved on the American scene of yesterday have crystallized into ideal constructs this philosophy can have only negative significance; its educational formulations can mean only anarchy. But to minds elastic enough to appreciate the institutional miscellany of history, and American enough to honor revolutionary traditions and the spirit of the frontier, Dewey's philosophic writings afford an invaluable insight into the meaning and the methodology of human progress. For those who really think and understand within this philosophic vein, every-day experience takes on a new significance; behavior is explained by its antecedents and by its consequences inseparably connected in intricate ways; dichotomies are resolved as mind is linked in intimate continuity with nature; the way to more and better assured human consummations is clearly pointed out; and ethics is shown as the form of a social life in which experience is consciously shared among all men. Perhaps the greatest significance of the viewpoint under discussion is in the challenge made to the creative effort of man. It is ever central in Dewey's thought that man is the creator *par excellence,* upon this is built the abiding faith that out of man's creative efforts the world may be made anew in the image of ideals suggested by present experience but reaching beyond present experience.

The question has been raised as to whether there is a place in this modern naturalism for religion and art and the higher life. It is not possible by loudly acclaiming them or by expressing concern for them to order these fruits of the human spirit to appear. The best insight of the present seems to indicate, however, that religion, art, and the higher life grow naturally in an environment where men are free from the oppressive dominance of organic needs.

The educator, like the member of other professions, or like the intellectual, the artist, the engineer, the tradesman, the farmer, the office worker, and the unskilled laborer has in the past exercised only technical or incidental significance in American life. He has been content like the others to take his orders from administrators who exercised power chiefly in the interest of entrepreneurs. Educators up to the present time have been satisfied that all was for the best and that an eventually better future would crown their poorly rewarded efforts. Like the other productive American workmen in almost all lines of endeavor teachers have formed organizations and by a truly marvelous ingenuity preserved them against political contamination. Non-partisanship has been a kind of sacred entity in American professional and trade organizations generally. The great reward of these noble efforts and of the worship of non-partisanship today is a social order in which the productive workers as a class are faced with greater insecurity than ever before and a social order in which all forms of idealism have been rather thoroughly debunked. Truly the times are overripe for an intelligent reconstruction of the aims and ideals of all organizations of productive workers. Educators as workers upon human attitudes, which lie at the root of all of our present troubles, may well honor their calling by being among the first to throw their energies into the building of a new society. This would mean the emergence in their organizations of a Higher Partisanship, in which the power of associations of educators would be openly exercised in the interest of all groups of productive workers holding to the same unselfish major aim—namely, the early ordering of an environment in which all men may enjoy and create the fruits of the human spirit to the measure of their capability.

Reverberations of broader social thinking have already stirred the medical profession, the clergy, the engineers, and the farm and labor organizations. The very use of the term "social medicine," though it still strikes shudders of horror in the breast of the successful private physician, is a sign that ideas of broad scope are fermenting within the medical profession. The increasingly bold sallies of Christian and Jewish religious organizations against the profit motive and against capitalism in general represent significant assaults upon purely individualistic types of religion. The sensational publicity that the engineering "technocrats" have received over some of their startling promises is both an indication of a readiness for unconventional thinking in economic matters on the part of the populace and a sign that engineers have begun to comprehend the fact that technology bears some responsibility in the problems of human excellence and human misery. The increasing militancy of the unemployed and of sporadic groups of farmers shows signs already of stimulating far-reaching reconstructions of aim and policy on the part of labor and farm organizations. Is there no challenge to educators and to associations of educators in all this? Must they calmly await such social changes as other groups of workers bring to pass and then docilely take instructions from the masters of a new social order? Or can they, too, participate cooperatively and significantly in the shaping of that new social order?

Shall we, then, have a Soviet of educators driving to dictatorial power in the American state? That would be both impossible and absurd. We can have, however, if educators prove not utterly spineless, a professional organization which shall wield an equal share of power with all other productive groups in the shaping of a new State. And more than that—since educators as a class supposedly represent the depository of culture and the frontiers of knowledge, a superb opportunity exists to bring these influences to play realistically in the great coöperative reconstruction of American civilization.

The social aims of educators grow out of a world brought to an absurdly desperate situation. The foundations of a philosophy adequate to modern times have already been laid though they are somewhat obscured by the welter of decaying fragments of traditional social institutions. The educational aims fitting to an emerging social situation cannot escape the designation of partisan. When given detailed expression by an organization of educators conscious of its share of real power, we may hope that they shall represent a Higher Partisanship, a declaration of faith and an eagerness to act coöperatively and creatively towards replacing our present business civilization with a civilization in which first things will be really first. Shall educators be among the last to realize that science, technology, modern industry, and the machine, are *social* products, conditioned upon the coöperative endeavor of many individuals and not private possessions called into existence at the signal of wealthy "men of affairs"? Technologists have amassed data indicating that man's control of power and energy today is sufficient so that a few hours of work on the part of every adult will assure a standard of living far in excess of that now common among the American population. Have educators no stake in the social revolution which shall realize such a possibility?

II. TEACHING AIMS

Textbooks and printed curricula in schools and colleges throughout the nation are full of long lists of both general and specific educational aims. The general aims abound in fine-sounding phrases relative to character and health and vocation and culture. The specific aims are in terms of reading, arithmetic, geography, civics, and other common or abstruse subjects. The general aims usually take up a few scant pages in the front of the book and the specific aims together with elaborate subject matter and methodological suggestions make up its body. The common assumption is that if we follow carefully enough the specific aims relating to subject matter the general aims must necessarily also be reached.

The American people and American educators in particular, during recent years, have not been lacking in rhetoric with which to describe the type of citizen which the schools should be engaged in preparing. Most of the more generalized formulations which have been suggested during the past twenty years are much the same and few people would object to them as well meant efforts to deal with an ever present and most difficult problem of education in a democracy. There is an increasing awareness among laymen and within the teaching profession, however, that all these so-called general aims have meant little to teachers and less to pupils. Character education inquiries, programs of moral instruction, the development of measuring devices for character and personality, and the establishment of psychiatric clinics for children are all evidences of a growing restlessness over the problem of realizing the general aims of education.

It is possible that there may be something wrong with the way the whole problem of aims has been conceived by the majority of school people. The proverbial remark that greatest time and attention are given to that which is valued highest is not without bearing in this connection. How does it come about that our educational curricula and textbooks devote so much space to specific aims and purposes and so little to general or more ideal ends? Or put in another way, why is there no clearly apparent relation between the teaching of subject matter and the growth of character? Some insight comes if we glance briefly at the historical rôle of the school in American life. At first the school's main purpose was to guarantee memorization of some form of religious catechism. Later with the development of universal free public education, it was to teach facility with letters and with figures and to assure patriotic sentiments. Under both these older aims the personality and character growth of children were managed with satisfying success by the home and the church. In the modern era these larger functions of education have more and more been pushed into the circle of the school. But the school has had no adequate philosophy and psychology with which to handle them. It is not surprising therefore that the measure of the school's actual functioning in matters of character and personality is found largely in the few pages of introductory rhetoric in text-books and curricula and in convention oratory. We *literally* don't know what to do about these things.

Another complicating factor has been the rapid rise of educational science and of professional specialization before the enlarging functions of the school in modern life had been fully appreciated by educators. Until recently most of the efforts of scientists and specialists within the field of education have been given over to the problems bearing on literacy and mastery of factual information. Educational scientists have extended and enlarged the old subjects, added new subjects, developed and validated new teaching devices and techniques, and revamped school administration, supervision, and organization in terms of larger programs of subjects. When vocational education edged in a few years back, that was conceived in terms of subjects as far as possible. And serious attempts are now being made to put morals on a subject basis. There is no blinking the fact that schools have been subject mad. The working philosophy and psychology of teachers held more consciously because of broader professional training, is almost completely in terms of subjects. In the minutely specific, prepared-and-stated-in-advance objectives, which educational science has made possible under the subject scheme, it is to be expected that general objectives should not function in any but a decorative way.

What, then, is the alternative? It is now recognized by educators that the modern school must do something about personality and character growth. Committees of specialists from related fields of social science are actively thinking and working on the problem. Parent-teacher groups everywhere discuss the matter endlessly. The air seems truly astir with the psychology of personality. Will the outcome be the reversal of customary emphases which is clearly called for? Will our school curricula of the future consist mainly of suggestive approaches to problems of personality integration, and provisions for the genuine discipline which comes from broad social participation, allowing only comparatively small space to briefly statable, because universally recognized, standards of literacy or information absorption? It seems in time a likely eventuality. Frank recognition of the nature and meaning of present educational inconsistencies can hasten appropriate reconstructive action.

What should be a teacher's aims with youth? Let us first make certain assumptions which are only in small degree justified by the present educational situation:

1. A community in which institutional and industrial activities are thrown open for the educative participation of youth.
2. A type of school administration which exists solely to render teaching more autonomous.
3. Teachers adequately fitted and happy in their professional choice.
4. An educational science which brings to teachers the resources of basic related sciences.
5. Curricula constantly reconstructed to needs nominated by teachers and to needs indicated by changes in community life.

Little as we know about the deeper problems of teaching, we are, nevertheless, certain that teachers can be effective in two ways basic to personality integration, character growth, and mental discipline. Almost nothing is known about the details of how these effects are obtained or why they are obtained. But about the reality of this effectiveness every able adult can testify. A successful teacher calls into question in a student's consciousness facts, attitudes, feelings and desires, principles and habits of action, all of which he has been accustomed to take for granted. This may be called the *negative* teaching effect. A successful teacher causes a student to take on new interests which lead to the learning of facts, the formation of attitudes, the awakening of desires, the deduction of principles, the building of habits of conduct, all of which never before have occupied the center of his attention. This may be called the *positive* teaching effect. Persons who have these effects upon students should be defined as teachers, and only such.

It is impossible at the present time for a teacher to aim consciously and so to direct his behavior that these *negative* and *positive* effects shall with any certainty be of a desirable kind. All he can do is hope that success will crown efforts made almost completely in the dark. There is no royal road to teaching effectiveness. An environment indifferent to man teaches him superbly, illiterate parents often have admirable results with children, companions good and ill have deep and abiding educational effects, and individuals learn lasting lessons from their enemies. The most formal teacher who sternly makes his pupils "toe the mark" in the most abstruse subject matter has his appreciative advocates as well as the genial teacher who works upon the modern doctrine of interest. These are truths which any sane person thinking about the more important problems of education must admit. They are the real starting points of an educational science and until the conditions and the structures which cause them are laid bare, teaching must remain an unanalyzed art.

Are no aims, therefore, to be formulated for classroom procedure? The aims of teachers should be more modest and more individualized than they have been in the past. Under the basic assumptions made above, such must clearly be the case. A teacher will have aims for his students in accordance with his own temperament, mentality, scale of interests and the way in which he conceives his duties. He will change these in the course of shared study with his pupils, with other teachers and with the lay public as the developing situations of life require. He must, however, make the actual decision about what seems good policy for him and for his group else there is no art to teaching whatever. As has been pointed out in the section on social aims of teachers, the teacher is a strategically important member of the community as a whole. His relations with the community must therefore be intimate and analytic, and what goes on in his classroom must be in accordance with the developing community ideals. The teacher is also a member of a professional association or guild which has a clearly stated responsibility in community problems involving the general welfare and which holds at an increasingly high level the qualitative standards for admission into the profession. Operating constantly between the limiting factors of community and professional association, the teacher should be free from any further restrictions or responsibilities.

III. Conclusion

It has seemed evident in the course of the present study that a large amount of the theorizing of prominent American educators about the relations of society and education has been limited by too much concern for social institutions which are manifestly decadent or by undue concentration upon technical scientific problems with consequent neglect of more important social considerations. In the discussions of individual men wherein the varying views were presented, analyzed, and interpreted, it became apparent that a genuine source of enlightened guidance for the contemporary educational situation might be found in philosophic speculation along the lines of modern experimental naturalism. In the minds of the men who think experimentally, America is conceived as having a destiny which bursts the all too obvious limitations of Christian religious sanctions and of capitalistic profit economy. Although differing variously in specific interpretations, the experimental naturalists all think in terms of an emergent culture controlled by human efforts. They appear to understand what is going on in the modern world without becoming frantically desperate about the destruction of inherited values or over-enthusiastic about the possibilities of a science which has rejected philosophy. They see the educator in terms of what he might become when free from the shackles which hold him to his established routines. Experimental naturalists are not saviors; they are simply men who have done considerable hard disillusioned thinking. Their message to teachers of the present is not that of blindly accepting whatever ideas they may have given expression to, but rather that of examining closely the world of the present and of giving expression to more ideas.

From the vantage point of the present study, the following

objectives for educators are suggested. They, in no sense, purport to be all-comprehensive or final. They do, however, lay claim to be along the line of much needed strategy if educational workers are to play any important part in the society which is building in America.

1. The maturing of personal viewpoint by reading and discussion, by scrutiny of contemporary civilization, and by self-examination.[1]

2. A continuing effort to clarify the vision of an educator's function in American civilization. In what degree does he carry the responsibility for controlled social evolution? To what extent is he more than a mere public servant engaged in carrying out orders issued by executives?

3. The blotting out of the "brass halo" which teachers have long suffered under. This means a will not to be affected by the slushy epithets of public apologists for existing social institutions and a will to assist youth constantly towards ready discernment of apologetics in any form.

4. Immersion into the budding native culture by steady enlargement and cultivation of professional and non-professional cultural opportunities available in the social environment. This is really the highest obligation of an intelligent teacher, because the value of any form of specialized professional endeavor can be gauged only by reference to the extent and depth of the individual's participation in and appreciation of existing social life.

5. Active participation by educators and teachers in various organizations of the lay public agitating for social reforms whose realization would be in harmony with evolving ideals of American society.

[1] See appendix for a tentative list of questions to be asked and answered by educators. These were derived from examination of the writings of the seventeen men discussed in this study.

6. The thoroughgoing renovation of existing professional organizations of educators so that in aim and principle they shall be intelligently militant in criticism of all vested interests in society and similarly militant in support of evolving modern standards of value in all fields of human interest.

7. Amalgamation of existing professional educational organizations for the purpose of united action on all questions of broad social import at any time before the public anywhere in the land.

8. Promotion of the spiritual solidarity of all classes of intellectuals in the interest of enlightening and possibly of guiding inevitable future mass movements within the population.

9. Active participation of individual educators and of professional organizations of educators in the gradually crystallizing public effort to create out of prevailing chaos and confusion in economic, political, spiritual, ethical, and artistic realms a culture which is under no continuing obligations to past American or foreign cultural patterns.

10. A teacher-training program conceived in the light of the changing aims and functions of education in contemporary America. This implies the critical re-examination of all established precedents in teacher-training organization.

11. A system of school administration constructed under the guidance of experimental social philosophy with the major aim of meeting the professional needs of teachers. This implies relegating the elaborate administrative technology modeled after business practice and capitalistic finance to the background where it may be drawn upon when needed in reconstruction programs.

12. The attitude of creative inquiry to be clearly recognized as essential in all people of the teaching profession. The trained specialists and the elaborate scientific technology of educational research, as conceived at present, to be made available as sup-

plementary service agencies in the solution of the actual problems of teaching.

13. The incorporation of graduate and undergraduate schools of education into a general plan of public education, so that their resources in experts and in experimental facilities may be used effectively in continuing educational reconstruction.

14. A program of public elementary and secondary education organized in the interest of collective ideals and emphasizing the attainment of economic equality as fundamental to the detailed determination of more broadly cultural aims.

15. Centralized organization in public education to an extent which will not only guarantee provision of the most valid knowledge together with adequate facilities for incorporating it into educational practice in every local community throughout the country, but promote as well the construction of attitudes, in the populace, conducive to enlightened reconstruction of social institutions.

16. A program of public vocational, professional, and higher education integrally organized in terms of a social order wherein all natural resources and the entire industrial structure is controlled by governmental agencies and operated for the equal benefit of all. This portends educational planning in terms of broadly cultural and creative motives and the final disappearance of programs of education based upon the motive of individual monetary success.

17. Gradual amalgamation of all cultural forces in community life, including industry, radio, motion pictures, newspapers, libraries, art galleries and museums, the theater, the opera, musical organizations, book publication, and the school itself into an educational program as wide and as continuous as life.

18. Such autonomy for every classroom teacher, from the nursery school through the university as accords with true ar-

tistic integrity. This implies that teachers shall be answerable for their professional conduct to their own professional organizations which, in turn, shall be fully responsible to the public.

19. The abolition of the present supervisory system in public education and its replacement by higher professional qualifications for teachers and by public teacher service bureaus equipped to continue on a voluntary basis the in-service education of teachers.

20. Gradual abolition of specified grades, subjects, textbooks, testing, and promotion schemes as conceived under the present administrative-supervisory set-up in public education. The development of a series of flexible organizational schemes and teaching programs by local faculties under the guidance and sanction of professional associations and of the lay public.

21. Domination of all specific teaching aims for an indefinite period by the general aim of rendering the attitudes of all normal individuals toward all the problems of life sufficiently tentative to allow for growth and change.

22. Determination of all directly functional teaching aims in and during the educational process by reference to the needs and possibilities of pupils as determined by professionally qualified and socially conscious teachers.

APPENDIX

APPENDIX

The following list of questions about general philosophic and specific educational issues was developed in the course of the examination of source materials for the present study.

A consistent position with regard to the issues raised is considered fundamental to a clear view of modern America and the relation of education to the social order. For it is upon such issues that the line of cleavage in the educational philosophy of the present and of the future must continue to be drawn.

The teacher who wishes in some way to be influential in molding a better America out of the assets and the liabilities of present day America must increasingly be conscious of his attitude and relation to the questions raised in the following list.

The questions are numbered to accord roughly with an order from the more general to the more specific.

1. What is the place of God in modern life?
2. How shall the Christian religion, or any other organized religion, be regarded today?
3. What is meant by Nature, and what is man's relation to Nature?
4. To what extent is inevitability of either civilizational advance or civilizational decay an adequate assumption?
5. To what extent is change an aspect of modern life?
6. What is meant by mind?
7. What is the function of thinking?
8. Is scientific method a means or an end or both?
9. Does modern science make philosophy unnecessary?

10. What attitude shall be taken to the institutions under which social life is ordered?

11. To what extent is a pervasive common culture desirable?

12. What is the purpose and function of ideals?

13. How shall democracy be regarded?

14. What is meant by social integration?

15. Should collectivism replace individualism?

16. What is the relation between industrialism and social planning?

17. What shall be said about indoctrination and imposition as methods used by a self-conscious social order?

18. Are the interests of the individual as such, fundamentally opposed to those of society?

19. Can "good" in the broadest sense come from the masses of men and women?

20. Do the masses need a compelling faith?

21. How is originality distributed among human beings?

22. What is meant by leadership?

23. When shall a man or woman be called cultured?

24. Are there possibilities latent in the American scene?

25. Is a distinctive high-type American culture likely to appear in the future?

26. What is the relation between business and industry?

27. How desirable is criticism of existing social institutions?

28. Is the small local community a distinctly passing phase of modern life?

29. What ought education accomplish?

30. How shall the teacher look at the social inheritance?

31. What should be the relation between the school and society?

32. Are vocation and culture fundamentally opposed?

33. Is education chiefly transmission?

34. Is education chiefly preparation?

35. Is education of value in itself?

36. When is a person educated?

37. Who shall determine educational objectives?
38. To what extent is education a science?
39. To what extent is education an art?
40. What are the assets and liabilities of the present American educational "system?"
41. What should be the relation of the Federal Government to education?
42. Is administrative centralization, local, state, or national, desirable in education?
43. To what extent should education and educators be autonomous?
44. What type of school administration is desirable?
45. What is the function of job or activity analysis in education?
46. How much specialization is desirable among teachers?
47. Do intelligence test results warrant some form of educational determinism?
48. How specialized should learning be?
49. Where are educational standards or norms of performance to be found?
50. What is the relation between adult standards and childhood education?
51. What is meant by curriculum?
52. To what extent should the curriculum be systematized?
53. Is organization of education by subjects indispensable?
54. What are the "minimum essentials" of education?
55. What is the meaning and the rôle of supervision?
56. What are the ethical and moral bearings of school instruction?
57. What is the meaning and function of art in education?
58. Ought a teacher pursue practical reformist strategies in his lay relations to the community?
59. How shall teacher training be conceived?
60. Is research beyond a teacher's ken?

61. Can a teacher be genuinely creative?
62. Should teachers organize for social action?
63. What is the place of the university in the total educational program?
64. How shall elementary education be conceived?
65. How shall secondary education be conceived?
66. How shall liberal arts education be conceived?
67. What type and what extent of adult education is necessary?
68. What are the relations between heredity and environment?
69. What is meant by a *unit* or an *element* of mental activity?
70. When may an individual personality be considered satisfactorily integrated?
71. Need the school concern itself about personality development?
72. Under what conditions does learning best go on?
73. What is the relation between interest and discipline?
74. What is the relation between effort and discipline?
75. How important are language activities in education?
76. What means shall a teacher use to hold the attention of his pupils?
77. What is the place of objective measurement in education?
78. How shall educational method be conceived?
79. What is meant by study?
80. Under what circumstances may we legitimately direct children toward deferred goals?
81. What is the relation between analysis and synthesis in a child's developing experience?
82. Are adequately mastered primary learnings the most that teachers may hope for?
83. How much transfer of training occurs in conscious educative endeavor and under what specific conditions?
84. What is the relation between size of class and education?
85. In what circumstances and for what purposes should homogeneous grouping of pupils be resorted to?

86. Is consistent and conscious variation among all known teaching methods desirable?
87. When shall coercion be used in learning?
88. What is the meaning of the *project* method?
89. What function does drill serve in education?
90. In what matters and to what degree are educators justified in being dogmatic?

BIBLIOGRAPHIES

I. GENERAL BIBLIOGRAPHY OF SECTION ONE

World Civilization

ADAMS, M. (ed.): The Modern State, Century, 1933.

ALLEN, D. (ed.): Pacifism in the Modern World, Doubleday, 1932.

ANGELL, N.: Unseen Assassins, Harper, 1932.

ANGELL, N.: From Chaos to Control, Century, 1933.

BEARD, C. A. (ed.): A Century of Progress, Harper, 1933.

BEARD, C. A. (ed.): Toward Civilization, Longmans, 1930.

BEARD, C. A. (ed.): Whither Mankind, Longmans, 1928.

BOSSARD, J. H. S., AND OTHERS: Man and His World, Harper, 1932.

BRAILSFORD, H. N.: Olives of Endless Age, Harper, 1928.

BURNS, C. D.: Leisure in the Modern World, Century, 1932.

BURY, I. D.: The Idea of Progress, Macmillan, 1932.

BRIFFAULT, R.: Breakdown: The Collapse of Traditional Civilization, Brentano, 1932.

CABOT, C. Q.: The Year of Regeneration, Harper, 1932.

COHEN, M. R.: Law, Reason, and the Social Order, Harcourt, 1933.

COLE, G. D. H.: A Guide Thru World Chaos, Knopf, 1932.

COLUMBIA UNIVERSITY FACULTY: An Introduction to Contemporary Civilization in the West (Syllabus), Columbia University Press, 1929.

CONDLIFF, J. B. (ed.): World Economic Survey, 1931-32, World Peace Foundation, 1933.

COTTLER, J., AND J. HAYM: Heroes of Civilization, Little, Brown, 1932.

COUNTS, G. S., AND OTHERS: Bolshevism, Fascism, and Capitalism, Yale University Press, 1932.

DAVIES, J. L.: Man and His Universe, Harper, 1930.

DAVIS, J. (ed.): The New Russia, Day, 1933.

DOBB, M.: Soviet Russia and the World, Sidgwick and Jackson, 1933.

DORSEY, G. A.: Man's Own Show: Civilization, Harper, 1931.

DRINKWATER, J.: This Troubled World, Columbia University Press, 1933.

EDDY, S.: The Challenge of Europe, Farrar, 1933.

FISCHER, LOUIS: Machines and Men in Russia, H. Smith, 1932.
FLETCHER, B. A.: Youth Looks at the World, Stokes, 1933.
FRANK, W.: Dawn in Russia, Scribner, 1932.
FRIEDELL, E.: Cultural History of the Modern Age, 3 volumes, Knopf, 1932.
GOLDENWEISER, A.: History, Psychology, and Culture, Knopf, 1933.
GASSET, J. O.: The Modern Theme, Norton, 1933.
GASSET, J. O.: The Revolt of the Masses, Norton, 1932.
GIBBS, P.: The Way of Escape, Harper, 1933.
HANSEN, A. H.: Economic Stabilization in an Unbalanced World, Harcourt, 1932.
HARDING, T. S.: Man and His Fictions, Dial, 1933.
HAUSLEITER, L.: World Dance of the Machines, Century, 1933.
HODSON, H. V.: Economics of a Changing World, H. Smith and R. Haas, 1933.
HOOK, S.: Towards the Understanding of Karl Marx, Day, 1933.
LANGSAM, W. C.: The World Since 1914, Macmillan, 1933.
LASKI, H. J.: Democracy in Crisis, University of North Carolina Press, 1933.
LENIN, V. I.: State and Revolution, International, 1933.
LENIN, V. I.: Toward the Seizure of Power, International, 1933.
LIPPMANN, W.: Interpretations 1931-32, Macmillan, 1932.
LIPPMANN, W. The United States in World Affairs, 1932, Harper, 1933.
MACIVER, R.: Society: Its Structure and Changes, Long and Smith, 1931.
MARX, K.: Capital, Modern Library, 1932.
MOWRER, E. A.: Germany Puts the Clock Back, Morrow, 1933.
MALAPARTE, C.: Coup D'Etat: The Technique of Revolution, Dutton, 1932.
MOULTON, H. G., AND L. PASVOLSKY: War Debts and World Prosperity, Century, 1932.
MUIR, R.: The Interdependent World and Its Problems, Little, Brown, 1933.
MURRY, J. M.: The Necessity of Communism, J. Cape, 1933.
NEWFANG, O.: Capitalism and Communism, Putnam, 1933.
PAGE, K.: National Defense, Farrar, 1932.
POWERS, J. H.: Years of Tumult: The World Since 1918, Norton, 1932.
RANDALL, J. H., JR.: Our Changing Civilization, Stokes, 1929.
REEVE, S. A.: The Natural Laws of Social Convulsion, Dutton, 1933.

SCHUMAN, F. L.: International Politics, McGraw-Hill, 1933.

SELDES, G.: World Panorama: 1918-1933. Little, Brown, 1933.

SHAW, C. G.: The Surge and Thunder, American, 1933.

SMITH, N. C., AND J. C. M. GARNETT: The Dawn of World Order, Oxford, 1933.

STRACHEY, J.: The Coming Struggle for Power, Covici, Friede, 1933.

SWAIN, J. W.: Beginning the Twentieth Century, Norton, 1933.

THOMAS, C. W. (ed.): Essays in Contemporary Civilization, Macmillan, 1931.

TODD, A. J.: Industry and Society, Holt, 1933.

VAN LOON, H.: What I Have Learned From History, Boni, 1933.

VILLARD, O. G.: The German Phoenix, H. Smith and R. Haas, 1933.

WARD, H. F.: In Place of Profit, Scribner, 1933.

WASHBURNE, C.: Remakers of Mankind, Day, 1932.

WEYL, H.: The Open World, Yale University Press, 1932.

WILLIAMS, F. E.: Youth and Russia, Farrar, 1933.

WINTER, E.: Red Virtue, Harcourt, 1933.

WOODY, T.: New Minds: New Men?, Macmillan, 1932.

WORLD PEACE FOUNDATION: Armaments Yearbook of the League of Nations, World Peace Foundation, 1933.

AMERICAN CIVILIZATION

ADAMIC, L.: Laughing in the Jungle, Harper, 1932.

ADAMS, J. T.: Epic of America, Little, 1931.

ADAMS, J. T.: Our Business Civilization, Boni, 1930.

ADAMS, J. T.: The March of Democracy, 2 volumes, Scribner, 1932.

ALLEN, D.: Adventurous Americans, Farrar, 1932.

ALLEN, F. L.: Only Yesterday, Harper, 1931.

AMERICAN SOCIOLOGICAL SOCIETY: Social Conflict, University of Chicago Press, 1931.

ANONYMOUS: High-Low Washington, Lippincott, 1933.

BARRETT, C. (ed.): Contemporary Idealism in America, Macmillan, 1933.

BEARD, C. A. (ed.): America Faces the Future, Houghton, 1932.

BEARD, C. A., AND W. BEARD: American Leviathan, Macmillan, 1930.

BEARD, C. A.: Rise of American Civilization, Macmillan, 1933.

BEARD, M. R.: America Through Women's Eyes, Macmillan, 1933.

BLANCHARD, C. E.: A New Day Dawns, Medical Success Press, 1932.

BLANCHARD, C. E.: Our Altruistic Individualism, Medical Success Press, 1932.

BLANCHARD, C. E.: Our Unfinished Revolution, Medical Success Press, 1933.

BLANKENSHIP, R.: American Literature as an Expression of the National Mind, Holt, 1931.

BONN, M. J.: The Crisis of Capitalism in America, Day, 1932.

BORSODI, R.: This Ugly Civilization, Harper, 1933.

BOWDEN, R. D.: In Defense of Tomorrow, Macmillan, 1931.

BOWERS, C. G.: Beveridge and the Progressive Era, Houghton, 1932.

CALVERTON, V. F.: The Liberation of American Literature, Scribner, 1932.

CANTOR, N. F.: Crime, Criminals, and Criminal Justice, Holt, 1932.

CHAMBERLAIN, J.: Farewell to Reform, Liveright, 1932.

CHAPMAN, J. J.: New Horizons in American Life, Columbia University Press, 1932.

COUNTS, G. S.: The American Road to Culture, Day, 1930.

CROSS, C.: A Picture of America, Simon and Shuster, 1932.

DARROW, C.: The Story of My Life, Scribner, 1932.

DEVOTO, B.: Mark Twain's America, Little, 1932.

DEWEY, J.: Individualism Old and New, Minton, Balch, 1930.

DEWEY, J.: The Public and Its Problems, Holt, 1927.

DOUGLAS, P. H.: The Coming of a New Party, McGraw-Hill, 1932.

FLYNN, J. T.: God's Gold: Rockefeller and His Times, Harcourt, 1932.

FOSTER, W. Z.: Toward Soviet America, Coward-McCann, 1932.

FRANK, G.: Thunder and Dawn, Macmillan, 1932.

FURNAS, C. C.: America's Tomorrow, Funk and Wagnalls, 1933.

GERLING, C. J.: Advancing Our Civilization, Meador, 1933.

HACKER, L. M., AND B. B. KENDRICK: The United States Since 1865, Crofts, 1932.

HELM, W. P.: Washington Swindle Sheet, Boni, 1932.

HILL, E. C.: The American Scene, Witmark, 1933.

HILL, F. E.: What Is American, Day, 1933.

HOFFMAN, R.: Masses vs. Classes, University of California Press, 1932.

HOPKINS, E. J.: What Happened in the Mooney Case, Putnam, 1932.

HUBERMAN, L.: We The People, Harper, 1933.

KALLEN, H. M.: Individualism: An American Way of Life, Liveright, 1933.

KALLET, A., AND F. J. SCHLINK: 100,000,000 Guinea Pigs, Vanguard, 1933.

KILPATRICK, W. H.: Our Educational Task, University of North Carolina Press, 1930.

KILPATRICK, W. H. (ed.): The Educational Frontier, Century, 1933.

LANDIS, B. Y., AND J. D. WILLARD: Rural Adult Education, Macmillan, 1933.

LEWISOHN, L.: Expression in America, Harper, 1932.

LYND, R. S., AND H. M. LYND: Middletown, Harcourt, 1929.

MARKEY, M.: This Country of Yours, Little, 1932.

McKEE, H. S.: Degenerate Democracy, Crowell, 1933.

MERRIAM, C. E.: The Written Constitution and the Unwritten Attitude, R. Smith, 1931.

MILLER, H. A.: The Beginnings of Tomorrow, Heath, 1933.

MOLEY, R.: Tribunes of the People, Yale University Press, 1932.

MOWRER, E. A.: This American World, Sears, 1928.

ODEGARD, P.: The American Public Mind, Columbia University Press, 1930.

OGBURN, F., AND A. GOLDENWEISER (eds.): The Social Sciences, Houghton, 1927.

ORTON, W. A.: America in Search of Culture, Little, Brown, 1933.

O'SHEEL, S.: It Never Could Happen, Coventry, 1932.

PAGE, K. (ed.): Recent Gains in American Civilization, Chautauqua Press, 1928.

PARRINGTON, V. L.: Main Currents in American Thought, 3 volumes, Harcourt, 1927.

PATON, STEWART: Prohibiting Minds and the Present Social and Economic Crisis, Hoeber, 1932.

PHELPS, P.: America On Trial, McKay, 1933.

QUINN, A. H.: The Soul of America, University of Pennsylvania Press, 1932.

REGIER, C. C.: The Era of the Muckrakers, University of North Carolina Press, 1932.

RINGEL, F. J. (ed.): America as Americans See It, Harcourt, 1932.

ROOSEVELT, F. D.: Looking Forward, Day, 1933.

ROSS, M.: Machine Age in the Hills, Macmillan, 1933.

RUGG, H.: Culture and Education in America, Harcourt, 1931.

RUGG, H.: The Great Technology, Day, 1933.

SCHLESINGER, A. M.: The Rise of the City, 1878-1898, Macmillan, 1933.

260 BIBLIOGRAPHY OF SECTION ONE

SCHMALHAUSEN, S. D.: Our Neurotic Age; A Consultation, Farrar, 1932.

SCHNEIDER, H. W.: The Puritan Mind, Holt, 1931.

SELDES, G.: The Years of the Locust, Little, 1933.

SINCLAIR, U.: American Outpost, Farrar, 1932.

SINCLAIR, U.: Upton Sinclair Presents William Fox, U. Sinclair, 1933.

SKINNER, R. D.: Our Emerging Generation, Dial, 1932.

STEFFENS, L.: The Autobiography of Lincoln Steffens, Harcourt, 1931.

STRUNSKY, S.: The Rediscovery of Jones, Little, 1931.

TERPENNING, W. B.: Village and Open Country Neighborhoods, Century, 1931.

TERRETT, C.: Only Saps Work, Vanguard, 1930.

TUGWELL, R. G.: The Industrial Discipline, Columbia University Press, 1933.

TURNER, F. J.: Significance of Sections in American History, Century, 1932.

WALDMAN, S.: Death and Profits, Putnam, 1933.

WALLACE, W. K.: Our Obsolete Constitution, Day, 1932.

WATERS, W. W.: B.E.F., Day, 1933.

WERNER, M. R.: Tammany Hall, Garden City, 1932.

WEYGANDT, C.: A Passing America, Holt, 1932.

WILBUR, R. L. (ed.): Medical Care for the American People, University of Chicago Press, 1933.

WILSON, E.: The American Jitters, Scribner, 1932.

WRIGHT, F. L.: An Autobiography, Longmans, 1932.

Recent Social Trends in the United States, McGraw-Hill, 1933.

THE PROBLEM OF RELIGION

ADLER, F.: The Reconstruction of the Spiritual Ideal, Appleton, 1924.

AMES, E. S.: Religion, Holt, 1929.

BARNES, E. W.: Scientific Theory and Religion, Macmillan, 1933.

BLOCK, M.: The New Church in the New World, Holt, 1932.

BOOTH, H. K.: The World of Jesus, Scribner, 1933.

BRADEN, C. S.: Modern Tendencies in World Religions, Macmillan, 1933.

BURTT, E. A.: Religion in an Age of Science, Stokes, 1929.

DURANT, W.: On the Meaning of Life, Long and Smith, 1932.

EMBREE, E. R.: Prospecting for Heaven, Viking, 1932.

FRIESS, H. L., AND H. W. SCHNEIDER: Religion in Various Cultures, Holt, 1932.

FOSDICK, H. E.: As I See Religion, Harper, 1932.

HAAS, J. A. W.: Christianity and Its Contrasts, Falcon, 1932.

HALDANE, J. B. S.: Science and Human Life, Harper, 1933.

HORTON, W. M.: Theism and the Modern Mood, Harper, 1930.

HUME, R. E.: Treasure-House of the Living Religions, Scribner, 1933.

KALLEN, H. M.: Judaism at Bay, Bloch, 1932.

KUHN, A. B.: Theosophy, Holt, 1930.

LAMONT, C.: Issues of Immortality, Holt, 1932.

LEARY, L. G.: Problems of Protestantism, McBride, 1933.

LUNN, A., AND C. E. M. JOAD: Is Christianity True? Lippincott, 1933.

LYMAN, E. W.: The Meaning and Truth of Religion, Scribner, 1933.

MACFARLAND, C. S.: Christian Unity in Practice and Prophecy, Macmillan, 1933.

MACINTOSH, D. C. (ed.): Religious Realism, Macmillan, 1931.

MARTIN, A. W.: Seven Great Bibles, World Unity, 1931.

MAXIM, H. P.: Life's Place in the Cosmos, Appleton, 1933.

MEAD, G. H.: The Philosophy of the Present, Open Court, 1932.

MENCKEN, H. L.: Treatise on the Gods, Knopf, 1930.

MORE, P. E.: The Catholic Faith, Princeton University Press, 1931.

NIEBUHR, R.: Leaves from the Notebook of a Tamed Cynic, Norton, 1931.

OXNAM, G. B. (ed.): Preaching and the Social Crisis, Abingdon, 1933.

PLANCK, M.: Where is Science Going, Norton, 1933.

POTTER, C. F.: The Story of Religions, Simon and Shuster, 1929.

RANDALL, J. H., AND J. H. RANDALL, JR.: Religion and the Modern World, Stokes, 1929.

RECKITT, M. B.: Faith and Society, Longmans, 1932.

RUSSELL, B.: A Free Man's Worship, Mosher, 1923.

SCHMIDT, N.: Evolution of Religion, Holt, 1933.

SHAW, G. B.: The Adventures of the Black Girl in Her Search for God, Dodd, Mead, 1933.

SULLIVAN, J. W. N.: The Limitations of Science, Viking, 1933.

SWIFT, A. L.: Religion Today, McGraw-Hill, 1932.

SWIHART, A. K.: Since Mrs. Eddy, Holt, 1931.

TILLICH, P.: The Religious Situation, Holt, 1932.

WARD, H. F.: Which Way Religion?, Macmillan, 1931.

WARD, H. F.: Our Economic Morality and the Ethic of Jesus, Macmillan, 1929.

WEBER, H. C.: Yearbook of American Churches, Round Table Press, 1933.

WESTCOTT, G.: A Calendar of Saints for Unbelievers, Minton, Balch, 1933.

WIEMAN, H. N.: Religious Experience and Scientific Method, Macmillan, 1926.

WIEMAN, H. N.: Wrestle of Religion with Truth, Macmillan, 1927.

WIEMAN, H. N., AND OTHERS: Is There a God?, Willett, 1933.

ECONOMIC PROBLEMS

American Labor Year Book, Vol. XIII (1932), Rand Book Store, 1932.

ANDREWS, J. B.: Labor Problems and Labor Legislation, American Association for Labor Legislation, 1932.

ARKWRIGHT, F.: The A.B.C. of Technocracy, Harper, 1932.

ARMSTRONG, B. N.: Insuring the Essentials, Macmillan, 1933.

BERLE, A. A., JR., AND G. C. MEANS: The Modern Corporation and Private Property, Macmillan, 1933.

BOND, F. D.: Wall Street, Appleton, 1933.

BOUCKE, F.: Laissez Faire and After, Crowell, 1932.

CHASE, S.: A New Deal, Macmillan, 1932.

CHASE, S.: The Nemesis of American Business, Macmillan, 1932.

COLE, G. D. H.: Economic Tracts for the Times, Macmillan, 1932.

COUNTS, G. S.: The Soviet Challenge to America, Day, 1931.

CUMMINS, E. E.: The Labor Problem in the United States, Van Nostrand, 1933.

DABNEY, T. E.: Revolution or Jobs, Dial, 1933.

DAHLBERG, A.: Jobs, Machines, and Capitalism, Macmillan, 1932.

DENNIS, L.: Is Capitalism Doomed?, Harper, 1932.

DONHAM, W. B.: Business Adrift, McGraw-Hill, 1931.

DONHAM, W. B.: Business Looks at the Unforeseen, McGraw-Hill, 1932.

DURANT, W.: A Program for America, Simon and Shuster, 1931.

ELIOT, T. D.: American Standards and Planes of Living, Ginn, 1932.

EPSTEIN, A.: Insecurity: A Challenge to America, Smith and Haas, 1933.

ERNST, M. L.: America's Primer, Putnam, 1931.

FAIRCHILD, H. P.: Profits or Prosperity, Harper, 1932.

FEDERAL COUNCIL OF CHURCHES OF CHRIST IN AMERICA: Our Economic Life in the Light of Christian Ideals, Association Press, 1932.

FLYNN, J. T.: Graft in Business, Vanguard, 1931.
GOLDSTEIN, J. M.: The Agricultural Crisis, Day, 1933.
GRUENING, E. H.: The Electric Challenge, Day, 1933.
GRUENING, E. H.: The Public Pays, Vanguard, 1931.
HAZLITT, H. (ed.): A Practical Program for America, Harcourt, 1932.
HENDERSON, F.: The Economic Consequences of Power Production, Day, 1933.
HOBSON, J. A.: Poverty in Plenty, Macmillan, 1932.
HOLLANDER, J. H.: Want and Plenty, Houghton, 1933.
ILIN, M.: New Russia's Primer, Houghton, 1931.
KEYNES, J. M.: Essays in Persuasion, Harcourt, 1932.
KNICKERBOCKER, H. R., AND OTHERS: Red Economics, Houghton, 1932.
KRESS, A. J.: Capitalism, Cooperation, Communism, Randall, Inc., 1932.
LAIDLER, H. W.: Concentration of Control in American Industry, Crowell, 1931.
LAIDLER, H. W.: The Road Ahead, Crowell, 1932.
LAIDLER, H. W. (ed.): Socialist Planning and a Socialist Program, Falcon, 1932.
LEVIN, J.: Power Ethics, Knopf, 1931.
LOEB, H.: Life in a Technocracy, Viking, 1933.
MAXWELL, S. R.: Plenocracy, Citizens Universal Service, 1933.
MILLS, F. C.: Economic Tendencies in the United States, National Bureau of Economic Research, 1933.
MITCHELL, B.: A Preface to Economics, Holt, 1932.
MORLEY, F. (ed): Aspects of the Depression, University of Chicago Press, 1932.
NEARING, S.: Must We Starve?, Vanguard, 1932.
RAUSHENBUSH, S.: The Power Fight, New Republic, Inc., 1932.
RENATUS, K.: The Twelfth Hour of Capitalism, Knopf, 1932.
RICHARDSON, D.: Will They Pay?, Lippincott, 1933.
SALTER, J. A.: Recovery, The Second Effort, Century, 1932.
SCHMALHAUSEN, S. D. (ed.): Recovery Through Revolution, Covici, Friede, 1933.
SMITH, J. G. (ed.): Facing the Facts, Putnam, 1932.
SODDY, F.: Wealth, Virtual Wealth and Debt, Dutton, 1926.
SOULE, G.: A Planned Society, Macmillan, 1932.

TAGGART, R. V.: Thorstein Veblen, University of California Press, 1933.

THOMAS, N.: America's Way Out, Macmillan, 1931.

THOMAS, N.: As I See It, Macmillan, 1932.

THOMPSON, C. D.: Confessions of the Power Trust, Dutton, 1933.

VAN DEVENTER, J. (ed.): For and Against Technocracy, Business Bourse, 1933.

VEBLEN, T. B.: Absentee Ownership, Viking, 1923.

VEBLEN, T. B.: Vested Interests and the State of the Industrial Arts, Viking, 1919.

VEBLEN, T. B.: The Engineers and the Price System, Viking, 1933.

WEISHAAR, W., AND W. W. PARRISH: Men Without Money, Putnam, 1933.

WELLS, H. G.: The Work, Wealth and Happiness of Mankind, Doubleday, 1931.

WILSON, W.: Forced Labor in the United States, International, 1933.

WOODWARD, W. E.: Money for Tomorrow, Liveright, 1932.

WORMSER, J. M.: Frankenstein Incorporated, McGraw-Hill, 1931.

YOUNG, V.: A Fortune to Share, Bobbs-Merrill, 1932.

SOCIAL AND MORAL PROBLEMS

ADAMS, J. T.: Tempo of Modern Life, Boni, 1931.

ALEXANDER, F. M.: Man's Supreme Inheritance, Dutton, 1918.

BARNES, H. E.: Can Man Be Civilized?, Brentano, 1932.

BARNES, H. E.: Living in the 20th Century, Long and Smith, 1931.

BERNARD, L. L., AND OTHERS: Social Attitudes, Holt, 1932.

BLOCK, I.: Sexual Life of Our Times, Blackfriars, 1932.

BOOTH, M.: Youth and Sex, Morrow, 1933.

COE, G. A.: The Motives of Men, Scribner, 1928.

COHEN, F. S.: Ethical Systems and Legal Ideals, Falcon, 1933.

DEVINE, E. T.: Progressive Social Action, Macmillan, 1933.

DEWEY, J.: Characters and Events, 2 volumes, Holt, 1929.

DEWEY, J.: Reconstruction in Philosophy, Holt, 1920.

DEWEY, J., AND J. H. TUFTS: Ethics (revised edition), Century, 1932.

DRAKE, D.: The New Morality, Macmillan, 1928.

EDMAN, I.: The Contemporary and His Soul, Cape and Smith, 1931.

EINSTEIN, A., AND OTHERS: Living Philosophies, Simon and Shuster, 1931.

FLANDERS, R. E.: Taming Our Machines, R. Smith, 1931.

GRANT, P.: Youth Fights Alone, Long and Smith, 1933.

HADER, J. J., AND E. C. LINDEMAN: Dynamic Social Research, Harcourt, 1933.

HALE, W. H.: Challenge to Defeat, Harcourt, 1932.

HART, J. K.: Inside Experience, Longmans, 1927.

HOLMAN, C. T.: The Cure of Souls, University of Chicago Press, 1932.

HUXLEY, J.: What Dare I Think, Harper, 1931.

KANDEL, I. L.: Comparative Education, Houghton, 1933.

KILPATRICK, W. H.: Education and the Social Crisis, Liveright, 1932.

KILPATRICK, W. H. (ed.): The Educational Frontier, Century, 1933.

KOPF, M. E.: Birth Control in Practice, McBride, 1933.

LEE, G. S.: Heathen Rage, R. Smith, 1931.

LINDSAY, B. B., AND W. EVANS: The Revolt of Modern Youth, Boni and Liveright, 1925.

LIPPMANN, W.: Preface to Morals, Macmillan, 1929.

LUMLEY, F. E.: The Propaganda Menace, Century, 1933.

MAGOUN, F. A.: Problems in Human Engineering, Macmillan, 1932.

MARITAIN, J.: Theonas, Scribner, 1932.

MARTIN, E. D.: Civilizing Ourselves, Norton, 1932.

MURPHY, G., AND F. JENSEN: Approaches to Personality, Coward, McCann, 1932.

NIEBUHR, R.: Moral Man and Immoral Society, Scribner, 1932.

NIETZSCHE, F.: Thus Spake Zarathustra, Macmillan, 1916.

OVERSTREET, H. A.: The Enduring Quest, Norton, 1931.

RILEY, W.: Men and Morals, Doubleday, 1929.

ROBINSON, J. H.: Mind in the Making, Harper, 1921.

ROBINSON, J. H.: The Humanizing of Knowledge, Doran, 1924.

SHAW, G. B.: Too True to Be Good, Dodd, Mead, 1934.

SMITH, T. V.: American Philosophy of Equality, University of Chicago Press, 1927.

SMITH, T. V.: The Democratic Way of Life, University of Chicago Press, 1926.

TAWNEY, R. H.: Equality, Harcourt, 1931.

WELLS, H. G.: What Are We To Do With Our Lives? Doubleday, 1931.

WESTERMARCK, E.: Ethical Relativity, Harcourt, 1932.

WOODWORTH, R. S.: Adjustment and Mastery, Century, 1933.

MISCELLANEOUS

ADAMIC, L.: Dynamite, Viking, 1931.

CAHILL, H.: American Folk Art, Norton, 1933.

DELL, F.: Love Without Money, Farrar, 1931.

EASTMAN, M.: The Literary Mind, Scribner, 1931.

ELMER, M. C.: Family Adjustment and Social Change, Long and Smith, 1931.

FERRISS, H.: The Metropolis of Tomorrow, Ives Washburne, 1932.

FRANKL, P. T.: Machine Made Leisure, Harper, 1932.

GEDDES, N. B.: Horizons, Little, 1932.

HARDING, T. S.: The Joy of Ignorance, Day, 1932.

HEALY, W., AND OTHERS: Reconstructing Behavior in Youth, Knopf, 1929.

HOPKINS, E. J.: Our Lawless Police, Viking, 1931.

KEPPEL, F. P., AND R. L. DUFFUS: The Arts in American Life, McGraw-Hill, 1933.

LICHTENBERGER, J. P.: Divorce: A Social Interpretation, McGraw-Hill, 1931.

MASON, D. G.: Tune In, America, Knopf, 1931.

PERRY, C. A.: The Work of the Little Theatres, Russell Sage Foundation, 1933.

PITKIN, W. B.: Short Introduction to the History of Human Stupidity, Simon and Shuster, 1932.

ROURKE, C.: American Humor, Harcourt, 1931.

SAYLOR, O. M.: Revolt in the Arts, Brentano, 1930.

SIMONSON, L.: The Stage is Set, Harcourt, 1932.

THORNDIKE, A. H.: The Outlook for Literature, Macmillan, 1931.

VAN DOREN, M.: American Poets, 1630-1930—Anthology, Little, 1932.

VAN DOREN, M.: The Oxford Book of American Prose, Oxford, 1932.

WALLER, W.: The Old Love and the New, Liveright, 1930.

WRIGHT, F. L.: Modern Architecture, Princeton University Press, 1931.

WRIGHT, F. L.: The Disappearing City, Payson, 1932.

II. SOURCES OF THE ANALYSES MADE IN SECTION TWO

HERMAN H. HORNE

General Viewpoint and Its Relation to Education

The Democratic Philosophy of Education: Macmillan, 1932, pp. 42, 48, 70-71, 72, 83, 101, 113, 177, 185, 236, 270, 288, 304-5, 307, 325, 359, 367, 402, 410, 490, 501, 503, 528.

This New Education: Abingdon Press, 1931, pp. 10, 11, 108, 109, 125, 141, 142, 152, 154, 217, 218, 220, 236, 267, 270.

The Philosophy of Education: Macmillan, 1930, pp. 1, 2, 4, 5, 6, 13, 41, 50, 53, 86, 102, 105, 111, 113, 114, 122, 126, 134, 135, 146, 155, 159, 160, 221, 226, 240, 250, 255, 261, 262, 264, 265, 266, 268, 270, 271, 273, 280-285, 292, 296, 291, 301, 303, 316.

Nature of Practical Proposals

This New Education, pp. 73, 82, 87, 89, 90, 121, 122, 123, 124, 151, 153, 171, 192, 199, 204, 206, 270.

The Philosophy of Education, pp. 9, 12, 69, 73, 74, 78, 79, 83, 125, 126, 146, 148, 165, 166, 185, 220, 306.

Estimate of Current Educational Practice

This New Education, pp. 53, 63, 73, 86, 99, 186.

The Philosophy of Education, pp. 83, 87, 88, 158, 192.

The Nature of Learning

The Democratic Philosophy of Education, pp. 19, 31, 32, 173, 175, 178, 207, 223, 375, 427, 489, 517.

This New Education, pp. 38, 85, 86, 89.

The Philosophy of Education, pp. 4, 49, 55, 57, 68, 69, 70, 75, 78, 79, 80, 81, 82, 89, 101, 106, 108, 144, 158, 162, 166, 171, 175, 182, 183, 191, 193, 196, 198, 199, 202, 204, 206, 209, 210, 211, 214, 215, 216, 218, 221, 222, 223, 224, 232, 233, 273, 274, 275.

Reactions to Other Points of View

The Democratic Philosophy of Education, pp. 69, 94, 109, 166, 185, 208, 261, 268, 276, 303, 327, 336, 345, 361, 381, 382, 421,

429, 433, 434, 450, 451, 454, 472, 474, 487, 491, 499, 501, 503, 516, 518.
This New Education, pp. 71, 72, 74, 95, 96, 103, 104, 106, 107.
The Philosophy of Education, pp. 152, 310, 311, 314, 315.

HENRY C. MORRISON

General Viewpoint and Its Relation to Education

School Revenue: University of Chicago Press, 1930, pp. 7, 8, 12, 41, 52, 62, 63, 64, 120, 127, 222.
The Practice of Teaching in the Secondary School (2d rev. ed.): University of Chicago Press, 1931, pp. 37, 38, 62, 91, 164, 171, 341, 343, 349, 400, 401, 420, 596, 667, 678, 680.
The Evolving Common School, Inglis Lecture, 1933, Harvard University Press, 1933, pp. 1, 5, 38-40, 43, 57, 60, 62.
"The Secondary Period and the University," *School Review*, Vol. XXXVII, Jan., 1929, p. 20.

Nature of Practical Proposals

The Practice of Teaching in the Secondary School (2d. rev. ed.), pp. 7, 13, 25, 60, 61, 70, 80, 81, 92, 93, 94, 96, 97, 168, 198, 438, 580, 581, 605, 667, 610, 629, 636.
The Evolving Common School, pp. 44-49, 52, 59.
"The Secondary Period and the University," *School Review*, Vol. XXXVII, Jan., 1929, pp. 26, 27.

Estimate of Current Educational Practice

School Revenue, 1930, pp. 61, 69, 78, 86, 101, 109.
The Practice of Teaching in the Secondary School (2d rev. ed), pp. 69, 74, 99, 100, 323, 471, 472, 580.
The Evolving Common School, pp. 2-4, 10, 16, 19-21, 27.
"Planning for the Whole School Period," *English Journal*, Vol. XX, April, 1931, p. 294.
"Definition of the Secondary School and Its Implications," *High School Quarterly*, Vol. XVII, p. 113.

The Nature of Learning

The Practice of Teaching in the Secondary School (2d. rev. ed.), pp. 19, 31, 51, 92, 107, 108, 179, 262, 269, 274, 276, 277, 279, 281, 282, 284, 285, 301, 313, 314, 325, 327, 328, 383, 404, 405, 417.
The Evolving Common School, p. 55.

"Planning for the Whole School Period," *English Journal*, Vol. XX, April, 1931, p. 294.

"Definition of the Secondary School and Its Implications," *High School Quarterly*, Vol. XVII, p. 116.

Reactions to Other Points of View

School Revenue, 1930, pp. 107, 236.

The Practice of Teaching in the Secondary School (2d rev. ed.), pp. 110, 111, 161, 348, 418, 590, 599, 600, 604.

"The Secondary Period and the University," *School Review*, Vol. XXXVII, Jan., 1929, p. 23.

WILLIAM C. BAGLEY

General Viewpoint and Its Relation to Education

Education, Crime, and Social Progress: Macmillan, 1931, pp. 3, 4, 7, 32, 73, 83, 125, 133.

Determinism in Education: Warwick and York, 1925, pp. 26, 27, 31, 32, 34, 38, 45, 111, 159.

Eurich, A. C. (ed.): The Changing Educational World: University of Minnesota Press, 1931, pp. 84, 85.

Schilpp, P. A. (ed.): Higher Education Faces the Future: Liveright, New York, 1930, p. 141.

The Twenty-Sixth Yearbook, Part II, National Society for the Study of Education: Public School Publishing Co., 1926, pp. 29, 37, 38.

"The Teacher's Contribution to Modern Progress," *Teachers' Journal and Abstract*, Vol. IV, Oct., 1929, pp. 449, 450, 451, 453.

"The Profession of Teaching in the United States," *School and Society*, Vol. XXIX, 1929, p. 110.

"The Future of American Education," *Proceedings* of the National Education Association, 1930, p. 219.

Nature of Practical Proposals

Education, Crime, and Social Progress, pp. vii, 5, 13, 38, 40, 64, 77, 84, 85, 86, 93, 139.

Determinism in Education, p. 112.

Eurich, A. C. (ed.): The Changing Educational World, pp. 82, 84.

Schilpp, P. A. (ed.): Higher Education Faces the Future, pp. 136, 148, 149.

The Twenty-Sixth Yearbook, Part II, pp. 33, 35, 37.

"The Teacher's Contribution to Modern Progress," *Teachers' Journal and Abstract*, Vol. IV, Oct., 1929, p. 453.

"The Profession of Teaching in the United States," *School and Society,* Vol. XXIX, 1929, pp. 108, 109.

"Professors of Education and Their Academic Colleagues," *Mathematics Teacher,* Vol. XXIII, May, 1930, pp. 284, 285, 286.

"Teaching as a Fine Art," *Journal of Educational Method,* Vol. IX, May, 1930, p. 461.

"The Future of American Education," *Proceedings* of the National Education Association, 1930, pp. 223, 225.

Estimate of Current Educational Practice

Education, Crime, and Social Progress, pp. vii-x, 15, 38, 67, 84, 87, 104, 105, 112.

Determinism in Education, p. 35.

Eurich, A. C. (ed.): The Changing Educational World, pp. 84, 85, 87, 88.

Schilpp, P. A. (ed.): Higher Education Faces the Future, pp. 144, 147.

The Twenty-Sixth Yearbook, Part II, pp. 30, 36.

"The Profession of Teaching in the United States," *School and Society,* Vol. XXIX, 1929, pp. 106, 108, 109.

"The Future of American Education," *Proceedings* of the National Education Association, 1930, p. 223.

"The Place of Applied Philosophy in Judging Student Teaching," *Educational Administration and Supervision,* Vol. XVII, May, 1931, p. 334.

The Nature of Learning

Education, Crime, and Social Progress, pp. 61, 115, 117, 119, 121, 122.

Determinism in Education, p. 189.

"Suggestions Relative to the Functions of the National Council on Education," *Proceedings* of the National Education Association, 1930, p. 203.

Reactions to Other Points of View

Education, Crime, and Social Progress, pp. ix, xi, 32, 70, 74, 82, 89, 91, 92, 97, 99.

Determinism in Education, pp. 39, 146.

Eurich, A. C. (ed.): The Changing Educational World, pp. 146, 147.

The Twenty-Sixth Yearbook, Part II, p. 36.

"Modern Educational Theories and Practical Considerations," *School and Society*, Vol. XXXVII, April 1, 1933, pp. 409-14.

ELLWOOD P. CUBBERLEY

General Viewpoint and Its Relation to Education

Introduction to the Study of Education and to Teaching: Houghton, Mifflin Co., 1925, pp. 29, 30, 39, 61, 86, 156, 158, 230, 351, 373, 432, 453, 464, 481.
Introduction to the Study of Education (rev. ed., Cubberley and Eels): Houghton, Mifflin Co., 1933, pp. 29, 32, 42, 45, 48, 51, 146, 159, 255, 521.

Nature of Practical Proposals

Introduction to the Study of Education and to Teaching, pp. 86, 100, 110, 117, 121, 135, 145, 150.
Public School Administration: Houghton, Mifflin Co., 1929, pp. 87, 89, 412, 413, 416.
"Professional Relationships in the School Family," *Illinois Teacher*, Vol. XIX, March, 1931, p. 21.
Introduction to the Study of Education (rev. ed.), pp. 49, 107, 112, 140.

Estimate of Current Educational Practice

Introduction to the Study of Education and to Teaching, pp. 64, 151, 184, 259, 273, 348, 457.
Public School Administration, pp. 39, 417.

The Nature of Learning

Introduction to the Study of Education and to Teaching, pp. 42, 84, 132, 155, 174, 175, 182, 183, 204, 205, 218, 219, 225, 226, 235, 239, 248, 262, 266, 267, 269, 278, 281.
Public School Administration, pp. 88, 512.
Introduction to the Study of Education (rev. ed.), pp. 172, 234-52.

Reactions to Other Points of View

Introduction to the Study of Education and to Teaching, pp. 160, 243.
Introduction to the Study of Education (rev. ed.), p. 269.

THOMAS H. BRIGGS

General Viewpoint and Its Relation to Education

Inglis Lecture, 1930: Harvard University Press, pp. 8, 9, 22, 23,

25, 28, 29, 43, 46, 47, 49, 58, 65, 74, 78, 86, 96, 97, 102, 107, 110, 133, 142.

Curriculum Problems: The Macmillan Co., 1927, pp. 14, 18, 26, 30, 41, 45, 48, 49, 50, 64, 65, 66, 79, 86, 95, 124, 126, 127, 129, 130, 132.

"The Fetish of the Physical," *School and Society*, Vol. XXXIII, May, 1931, p. 683.

"Articulation: Some Fundamental Purposes and Its Ideals," *Bulletin* 30, Department Secondary School Principals, March, 1930, pp. 182, 183.

"Jeremiah Was Right," *Teachers College Record*, Vol. XXXII, May, 1931, pp. 688, 691, 692, 693, 694, 695.

"Responsibility of Supervision," *Bulletin* 25, Department Secondary School Principals, March, 1929, p. 9.

"Treason, Costs, and Industry," *Educational Review*, Vol. LXIX, March, 1925, pp. 131, 132.

"Cooperating in Economy," *School and Society*, Vol. XXXIV, Nov. 18, 1932, p. 719.

"Interests as Liberal Education," *Teachers College Record*, Vol. XXIX, May, 1928, p. 673.

Nature of Practical Proposals

Inglis Lecture, 1930, pp. 15, 31, 51, 54, 61, 71, 83, 91, 104, 108, 109, 111, 114, 123.

Curriculum Problems, pp. 7, 9, 10, 11, 19, 20, 21, 23, 24, 25, 27, 35, 37, 38, 39, 47, 127, 131.

"The Fetish of the Physical," *School and Society*, Vol. XXXIII, May, 1931, pp. 682, 683.

"Jeremiah Was Right," *Teachers College Record*, Vol. XXXII, May, 1931, pp. 683, 685, 689, 690, 693.

"Why Do We Do It?" *Teachers College Record*, Vol. XXXII, April, 1931, p. 593.

"Articulation: Some Fundamental Purposes and Its Ideals," *Bulletin* 30, Department Secondary School Principals, March, 1930, p. 179.

"Responsibility of Supervision," *Bulletin* 25, Department Secondary School Principals, March, 1929, p. 8.

"Cooperating in Economy," *School and Society*, Vol. XXXIV, Nov. 28, 1931, pp. 721, 722, 723.

"Special Functions of Secondary Schools," National Education Association, Department of Supt., Seventh Yearbook, p. 191.

Estimate of Current Educational Practice

Inglis Lecture, 1930, p. 21, 24, 27, 37, 42, 63, 81, 87, 88, 90, 94, 118, 141.
Curriculum Problems, pp. 3, 37, 74, 104.
"Interests as Liberal Education," *Teachers College Record,* Vol. XXIX, May, 1928, pp. 668, 671, 672.
"Why Do We Do It?" *Teachers College Record,* Vol. XXXII, April, 1931, pp. 591, 595, 596.
"Jeremiah Was Right," *Teachers College Record,* Vol. XXXII, May, 1931, pp. 681, 682, 683, 689.
"Articulation: Some Fundamental Purposes and Its Ideals," *Bulletin* 30, Department Secondary School Principals, March, 1930, pp. 177, 182.
"Cooperating in Economy," *School and Society,* Vol. XXXIV, Nov. 28, 1931, p. 719.

The Nature of Learning

Curriculum Problems, pp. 16, 38, 45, 51, 53, 56, 58, 70, 72, 73, 80, 81, 97, 98, 99, 100, 101, 102, 103.
"Interests as Liberal Education," *Teachers College Record,* Vol. XXIX, May, 1928, p. 671.
"Special Functions of Secondary Schools," National Education Association, Department of Supt., Seventh Yearbook, pp. 199, 202.

Reactions to Other Points of View

Curriculum Problems, pp. 6, 7, 51.
"Jeremiah Was Right," *Teachers College Record,* Vol. XXXII, May, 1931, pp. 685, 686.
"Articulation: Some Fundamental Purposes and Its Ideals," *Bulletin* 30, Department Secondary School Principals, March, 1930, p. 178.

ROSS L. FINNEY

General Viewpoint and Its Relation to Education

A Sociological Philosophy of Education: The Macmillan Co., 1928, pp. 4, 10, 74, 87, 103, 108, 109, 110, 116, 117, 118, 119, 124, 141, 161, 170, 239, 252, 268, 311, 312, 383, 398, 411, 421, 428, 435, 463, 485, 486, 532.
"The Tide Is Turning," *Journal of Educational Sociology,* Vol. IV, June, 1931, p. 624.

"Major Educational Trends and Vocational Guidance," *Vocational Guidance Magazine*, Vol. X, April, 1932, p. 299.

Nature of Practical Proposals

A Sociological Philosophy of Education, pp. 12, 95, 166, 240, 249, 261, 281, 337, 355, 371, 515, 517, 549, 552, 556.

Estimate of Current Educational Practice

A Sociological Philosophy of Education, pp. 11, 55, 115, 175, 180, 181, 286, 346, 453, 502, 536, 548, 550.

The Nature of Learning

A Sociological Philosophy of Education, pp. 48, 58, 60, 61, 82, 97, 159, 160, 188, 285, 288, 364, 365, 366, 395, 396, 422, 437, 467, 469, 480.
"Major Educational Trends and Vocational Guidance," *Vocational Guidance Magazine*, Vol. X, April, 1932, pp. 291, 293.

Reactions to Other Points of View

A Sociological Philosophy of Education, pp. 60, 145, 156, 188, 461, 471, 478, 488.

CHARLES H. JUDD

General Viewpoint and Its Relation to Education

The Unique Character of American Secondary Education (Inglis Lecture, 1928): Harvard University Press, pp. 10, 15, 23.
Psychology of Secondary Education: Ginn and Co., 1927, pp. 20, 27, 28, 29, 110, 294, 333, 385, 414, 419.
Psychology of Social Institutions: Macmillan, 1926, pp. 17, 32, 33, 73, 217, 274, 287, 322, 327, 333, 335.
The Twenty-Sixth Yearbook, Part II, National Society for the Study of Education, Public School Publishing Co., 1926, p. 113.
"How Can American Educational Forces Cooperate More Effectively," *School and Society*, Vol. XXXIII, March, 1931, p. 91.
"Achievements of American Education: Instruction," *Proceedings* of the National Education Association, 1930, p. 666.
"Understanding Our Hindrances," *Journal of Adult Education*, Vol. II, June, 1930, pp. 243, 244.
"Value of Existing Social Tendencies in Education," *School and Community*, Vol. XVI, Jan., 1930, p. 46.
"Why Adult Education?" *School and Society*, Vol. XXXII, Dec., 1930, pp. 744, 747.
"Social Psychology and the Curriculum," *Texas Outlook*, Vol. XVI,

March, 1932, pp. 19-20.
"Education, the Nation's Safeguard," N.E.A. Dep't. of Superintendence Official Report, 1932, pp. 36, 37, 39, 41.

Nature of Practical Proposals
The Unique Character of American Secondary Education, pp. 44, 47, 51, 62, 63.
Psychology of Secondary Education, pp. 51, 63, 115, 154, 158, 166, 268, 322, 355.
Psychology of Social Institutions, pp. 209, 331, 340.
Eurich, A. C. (ed.): The Changing Educational World: University of Minnesota Press, 1931, p. 75.
Recent Social Trends, McGraw-Hill, 1933, pp. 348, 349.
"How Can American Educational Forces Cooperate More Effectively?" *School and Society*, Vol. XXXIII, March, 1931, pp. 81, 88.
"Achievements of American Education: Instruction," *Proceedings* of the National Education Association, 1930, p. 668.
"Value of Existing Social Tendencies in Education," *School and Community*, Vol. XVI, Jan., 1930, p. 43.
"Good Administration Anticipates Educational Problems," Department of Elementary School Principals, *Bulletin* 9, April, 1930, pp. 170, 172.
"Why Adult Education?" *School and Society*, Vol. XXXII, Dec., 1930, p. 750.
"Training of Teachers for a Progressive Educational Program," *Elementary School Journal*, Vol. XXXI, April, 1931, pp. 576, 584.
"Social Studies in the High School," *High School Clearing House*, Vol. IV, June, 1930, pp. 573, 574.
"Examples of Scientific Procedure in Supervision," *Proceedings* of the National Education Association, 1929, p. 585.
"Education, the Nation's Safeguard," N.E.A. Dep't. of Superintendence Official Report, 1932, pp. 39, 41, 42.
"Curriculum: A Paramount Issue," *Proceedings* of the National Education Association, 1925, p. 811.
"National Survey of Teacher Training," *Journal* of the National Education Association, Dec., 1930, p. 291.
"Education and Politics," *Educational Record*, Vol. XII, July, 1931, pp. 254, 259, 260, 261, 264.

Estimate of Current Educational Practice
The Unique Character of American Secondary Education, pp. 31, 41, 45, 49, 56, 57, 58.

Psychology of Secondary Education, pp. 162, 356, 508.

Eurich, A. C. (ed.): The Changing Educational World, pp. 68, 69, 77.

The Twenty-Sixth Yearbook, Part II, p. 116.

Recent Social Trends, pp. 325-381.

"How Can American Educational Forces Cooperate More Effectively," *School and Society,* Vol. XXXIII, March, 1931, p. 89

"Achievements of American Education: Instruction," *Proceedings* of the National Education Association, 1930, p. 665.

"Why Adult Education?" *School and Society,* Vol. XXXII, Dec., 1930, p. 748.

"Production of Good College Teaching," Association of American Colleges, *Bulletin* 15, March, 1929, p. 91.

"Can High School Supervision Be Made Scientific?" *Proceedings* of the National Education Association, 1928, pp. 735, 737, 739, 740.

"Fallacy of Treating School Subjects as Tool Subjects,": *Proceedings* of the National Education Association, 1927, p. 251.

"National Survey of Teacher Training," *Journal* of the National Education Association, Dec., 1930, p. 291.

"Education, the Nation's Safeguard," N.E.A. Dep't. of Superintendence, Official Report, 1932, p. 40.

The Nature of Learning

Psychology of Secondary Education, pp. 14, 56, 142, 145, 157, 344, 408, 443, 448, 462, 467, 523, 531.

Psychology of Social Institutions, pp. 298, 324, 328.

The Twenty-Sixth Yearbook, Part II, pp. 114, 115.

"How Can American Educational Forces Cooperate More Effectively?" *School and Society,* Vol. XXXIII, March, 1931, p. 89.

"Why Adult Education?" *School and Society,* Vol. XXXII, Dec., 1930, p. 744.

"Early Emotions and Early Reactions as Related to Mature Character," *School and Society,* Vol. XXV, March, 1927, p. 359.

"Training of Teachers for a Progressive Educational Program," *Elementary School Journal,* Vol. XXXI, April, 1931, pp. 577, 580, 581.

"Social Studies as the Core of the Junior High School Curriculum," *Proceedings* of the National Education Association, p. 776.

Reactions to Other Points of View

Psychology of Secondary Education, p. 28.

Psychology of Social Institutions, pp. 330, 336.

The Twenty-Sixth Yearbook, Part II, pp. 115, 117.
Recent Social Trends, Vol. I, pp. 349, 356.
"How Can American Educational Forces Cooperate More Effectively," *School and Society*, Vol. XXXIII, March, 1931, p. 89.
"Training of Teachers for a Progressive Educational Program," *Elementary School Journal*, Vol. XXXI, April, 1931, pp. 578, 579, 582.
"Curriculum of the Teacher's College," *Proceedings* of the National Education Association, 1926, p. 912.

DAVID SNEDDEN

General Viewpoint and Its Relation to Education

Towards Better Educations: Bureau of Publications, Teachers College, Columbia University, 1931, pp. 17, 65, 234, 237, 267, 281, 323, 328, 332, 333, 339, 353, 363, 370, 372, 406, 408.
School Educations: Bureau of Publications, Teachers College, Columbia University, 1930, pp. 1, 26, 50, 58, 59, 67, 74, 108, 109, 112, 115, 116, 130, 131, 142, 143, 149, 166, 172, 173, 178.
Second Yearbook of the National Society for the Study of Educational Sociology: Bureau of Publications, Teachers College, Columbia University, 1929, pp. 30, 97, 109, 112.
What's Wrong With American Education?: Lippincott, 1927, pp. 19, 54, 58, 83, 189, 241.
"Specialization of Educative Processes: Some Anticipations," *School and Society*, Vol. XXXV, March 26, 1932, p. 413.
"Education for a Changing Social World," *School and Society*, Vol. XXXV, March 14, 1932, pp. 655, 656, 657, 658, 661.

Nature of Practical Proposals

Towards Better Educations, pp. 16, 30, 33, 48, 66, 79, 137, 161, 186, 187, 189, 198, 199, 277, 315, 324, 382, 420.
School Educations, pp. 12, 16, 24, 25, 54, 79, 88, 120, 132, 163, 164, 165, 178, 181.
Second Yearbook of the National Society for the Study of Educational Sociology, pp. 28, 77, 84, 152.
What's Wrong With American Education? pp. 130, 207.
"Specialization of Educative Processes: Some Anticipations," *School and Society*, Vol. XXXV, March 26, 1932, p. 415.

Estimate of Current Educational Practice

School Educations, p. 62.
Second Yearbook of the National Society for the Study of Educa-

tional Sociology, pp. 96, 100, 104, 111, 132.
What's Wrong With American Education? pp. iv, v, 7, 17, 18, 32, 33, 37, 38, 40, 41, 62, 87.

The Nature of Learning

Towards Better Educations, pp. 17, 95, 200, 207.
School Educations, pp. 35, 35.
Second Yearbook of the National Society for the Study of Educational Sociology, pp. 11, 13, 17, 20, 81, 82, 83.
What's Wrong With American Education? pp. 42, 140, 212, 296, 338.

Reactions to Other Points of View

Towards Better Educations, pp. 123, 133, 207, 343, 367, 373, 374, 379.
School Educations, pp. 58, 76, 80, 119, 157, 158, 176.
Second Yearbook of the National Society for the Study of Educational Sociology, pp. 28, 84.
What's Wrong With American Education? pp. 129, 133, 163.

EDWARD L. THORNDIKE

General Viewpoint and Its Relation to Education

Human Learning: Century Co., 1931, pp. 193, 200.
Adult Learning: Macmillan, 1928, pp. 192, 193, 194.
Thorndike and Gates, Elementary Principles of Education: Macmillan, 1929, pp. 6, 10, 11, 16, 31, 37, 44, 59, 169, 199, 207, 303, 304, 308, 323.
"The Right Use of Leisure," *Journal of Adult Education,* Vol. II, Jan., 1930, p. 45.
"Curriculum Research," *School and Society,* Vol. XXVIII, 1928, p. 576.
"The Distribution of Education," *School Review,* Vol. XL, May, 1932, p. 345.

Nature of Practical Proposals

Thorndike and Gates, Elementary Principles of Education, pp. 12, 38, 164, 166, 172, 178, 183, 204, 225, 226, 229, 230, 271, 277, 286, 300.
"Curriculum Research," *School and Society,* Vol. XXVIII, 1928, pp. 570, 572, 573, 576.
"Need of Fundamental Analysis of Methods of Teaching," *Elementary School Journal,* Vol. XXX, Nov., 1929, pp. 190, 191.

Estimate of Current Educational Practice

Adult Learning, pp. 193, 194.

Thorndike and Gates, Elementary Principles of Education, pp. 81, 202, 213, 311, 317.

"Curriculum Research," *School and Society,* Vol. XXVIII, 1928, pp. 573, 574, 576.

"The Testing Movement in the Light of Recent Research," *Journal of Educational Research,* Vol. XVII, 1928, p. 349.

The Nature of Learning

Human Learning, pp. 5, 7, 29, 46, 89, 100, 103, 117, 121, 122, 132, 139, 167, 168, 182, 189.

Thorndike and Gates, Elementary Principles of Education, pp. 79, 80, 95, 100, 101, 104, 105, 107, 161, 171, 181.

Reactions to Other Points of View

Human Learning, pp. 15, 176.

Thorndike and Gates, Elementary Principles of Education, pp. 22, 24, 26, 181, 271.

"Curriculum Research," *School and Society,* Vol. XXVIII, 1928, p. 575.

ERNEST HORN

General Viewpoint and Its Relation to Education

The Twenty-Sixth Yearbook, Part II (National Society for the Study of Education): Public School Publishing Co., 1926, pp. 104, 105, 106, 108, 109.

The Twenty-Sixth Yearbook, Part I, p. 293.

"The Principles of Activity Programs," Baltimore Bulletin of Education, Sept., 1931, p. 3.

"Educating for Freedom and Responsibility," Religious Education, Vol. XXV, Sept., 1930, pp. 632, 634.

"A Platform for Progress in Classroom Teaching," *School and Community,* Vol. XVI, May, 1930, pp. 296, 297.

"What are the Most Important Recent Contributions in the Field of Elementary Education?" Ninth Yearbook of American Association of Teachers Colleges, pp. 905, 906.

"The Curriculum Problem Attacked Scientifically," *Proceedings,* National Education Association, 1925, p. 812.

"New Emphases in Elementary Education." Univ. of Kentucky. Eighth Annual Educational Conference, 1931, p. 17.

Nature of Practical Proposals

The Twenty-Sixth Yearbook, Part II (National Society for the Study of Education), pp. 105, 108, 110, 111, 112.

The Twenty-Sixth Yearbook, Part I (National Society for the Study of Education), pp. 291, 292, 293, 294, 295, 296.

"The Principles of Activity Programs," *Baltimore Bulletin of Education,* Sept., 1931, p. 2.

"Differentiated Courses for Bright Pupils," *Official Report,* Dept. of Supt., N.E.A., 1931, p. 268.

"Educating for Freedom and Responsibility," *Religious Education,* Vol. XXV, Sept., 1930, pp. 634, 635, 636.

"A Forum on the Fundamental Problems of the Junior High School," *Proceedings,* National Education Association, 1927, p. 784.

"A Platform for Progress in Classroom Teaching," *School and Community,* Vol. XVI, May, 1930, p. 298.

"What are the Most Important Recent Contributions in the Field of Elementary Education?" Ninth Yearbook, American Association of Teachers Colleges, pp. 906, 907.

"The Curriculum Problem Attacked Scientifically," *Proceedings,* National Education Association, 1925, pp. 812, 814.

"New Emphases in Elementary Education," Univ. of Kentucky, Eighth Annual Educational Conference, 1931, pp. 19, 20, 157.

Estimate of Current Educational Practice

The Twenty-Sixth Yearbook, Part II (National Society for the Study of Education), pp. 100, 101, 107, 108.

The Twenty-Sixth Yearbook, Part I (National Society for the Study of Education), p. 296.

"The Principles of Activity Programs," Baltimore Bulletin of Education, Sept., 1931, p. 1.

"Educating for Freedom and Responsibility," Religious Education, Vol. XXV, Sept., 1930, p. 632.

"What are the Most Important Recent Contributions in the Field of Elementary Education?" Ninth Yearbook, American Association of Teachers Colleges, p. 904.

The Nature of Learning

The Twenty-Sixth Yearbook, Part II (National Society for the Study of Education), pp. 100, 102, 103, 105, 107, 108.

The Twenty-Sixth Yearbook, Part I (National Society for the Study of Education), pp. 294, 295.

"Freedom and Responsibility," *School and Community*, Vol. XVI, Jan., 1930, p. 45.
"A Platform for Progress in Classroom Teaching," *School and Community*, Vol. XVI, May, 1930, p. 299.
"What are the Most Important Recent Contributions in the Field of Elementary Education?" Ninth Yearbook, American Association of Teachers Colleges, pp. 905, 907.

Reactions to Other Points of View
The Twenty-Sixth Yearbook, Part II (National Society for the Study of Education), pp. 99, 106.
"Suggested Uses for This Yearbook," Second Yearbook, National Conference of Supervisors and Directors of Instruction, p. 293.
"Freedom and Responsibility," *School and Community*, Vol. XVI, Jan., 1930, p. 37.

WERRETT W. CHARTERS

General Viewpoint and Its Relation to Education
The Teaching of Ideals: Macmillan, 1928, pp. 29, 31.
Curriculum Construction: Macmillan, 1923, pp. 4, 16, 27, 31, 32, 42, 43, 63, 74, 79, 80, 148.
"Articulating the School With Life," *Ohio University Educational Research Bulletin*, No. 8, April, 1929, pp. 150, 151.
"Adult Education," *Ohio University Educational Research Bulletin*, No. 7, Nov., 1928, p. 370.
"Better Schools," *Ohio University Educational Research Bulletin*, No. 14, Oct., 1931, p. 382.
"Education," *Ohio University Educational Research Bulletin*, No. 11, May, 1931, p. 300.
"Next Steps," *Journal of Adult Education*, Vol. II, Oct., 1930, pp. 370, 375.
"The Curriculum and the Future," *Journal of Educational Research*, Vol. XIX, July, 1929, p. 142.
"Who Should Make the Curriculum?" Kentucky University Proceedings of the Fifth Annual Educational Conference, pp. 14, 15, 17.
"Education for a Changing Civilization," *Journal of Educational Research*, Vol. XVII, 1928, p. 216.

Nature of Practical Proposals
The Teaching of Ideals, pp. 165, 181, 259, 335, 355.
Curriculum Construction, pp. 102, 141, 146, 150, 155, 157.

"Testing," *Ohio University Educational Research Bulletin*, No. 8, Nov., 1929, p. 386.

"Next Steps," *Journal of Adult Education*, Vol. II, Oct., 1930, p. 370.

"Who Should Make the Curriculum?" Kentucky University Proceedings of the Fifth Annual Educational Conference, p. 16.

"Use of Activity Analysis in Curriculum Construction," New York (State) University Proceedings of the 64th Convocation, 1928, pp. 45, 46, 50.

Estimate of Current Educational Practice

The Teaching of Ideals, pp. 112, 161, 184.

Curriculum Construction, pp. 61, 77, 149.

"Next Steps," *Journal of Adult Education*, Vol. II, October, 1930, p. 374.

The Nature of Learning

The Teaching of Ideals, pp. 15, 16, 20, 28, 38, 47, 106, 110, 185, 215, 315, 318, 321, 338, 341, 347.

Curriculum Construction, pp. 30, 57, 59, 60, 100, 106, 111, 140, 153, 154.

"Director of Character Education," *Ohio University Educational Research Bulletin*, No. 8, July, 1929, p. 10.

"Articulating the School with Life," *Ohio University Educational Research Bulletin*, No. 8, April, 1929, p. 150.

"Larger Classes," *Ohio University Educational Research Bulletin*, No. 8, Sept., 1929, p. 276.

"Morons," *Ohio University Educational Research Bulletin*, No. 7, April, 1931, p. 188.

"Character Development Through Classroom Procedures," *School and Community*, Vol. XVI, Oct., 1930, p. 434.

"Success, Personality and Intelligence," *Journal of Educational Research*, Vol. XI, 1925, p. 172.

"Who Should Make the Curriculum?" Kentucky University Proceedings of the Fifth Annual Educational Conference, p. 14.

Reactions to Other Points of View

The Teaching of Ideals, p. 164.

Curriculum Construction, p. 152.

"Fads," *Ohio University Educational Research Bulletin*, No. 7, Oct., 1928, p. 327.

"Use of Activity Analysis in Curriculum Construction," New York (State) University Proceedings of the 64th Convocation, 1928, p. 46.

FRANKLIN BOBBITT

General Viewpoint and Its Relation to Education

The Twenty-Sixth Yearbook, Part II National Society for the Study of Education: Public School Publishing Co., 1926, pp. 42, 43, 45, 50, 54.

"Rebuilding the Curriculum in Line with its True Function," *Nation's Schools*, Vol. III, Jan., 1929, pp. 15, 16.

"Objectives of Modern Education," *Journal of Education*, Vol. X, Nov., 1929, p. 200.

"Education as a Social Process," *School and Society*, Vol. XXI, April, 1925, pp. 453, 455, 456, 459.

"Difficulties to be Met in Local Curriculum Making," *Elementary School Journal*, Vol. XXV, May, 1925, pp. 656, 660.

"Are there General Principles that Govern the Junior College Curriculum?" In *Proceedings*, Institute for Administrative Officers of Higher Institutions, 1929, pp. 20, 25.

Curriculum Investigations (Supplementary Educational Monographs): University of Chicago Press, 1926, pp. 2, 4.

How to Make a Curriculum: Houghton, Mifflin Co., 1924, pp. 8, 30, 54, 81, 150, 281, 283.

"The Relation Between Content and Method," *Journal of Educational Sociology*, Vol. V, Sept., 1931, p. 8.

Nature of Practical Proposals

The Twenty-Sixth Yearbook, Part II, National Society for the Study of Education, pp. 45, 46, 47, 49, 50, 51, 52, 53.

"Objectives of Modern Education," *Journal of Education*, Vol. X, Nov., 1929, p. 247.

"Education as a Social Process," *School and Society*, Vol. XXI, April, 1925, p. 458.

"Difficulties to be Met in Local Curriculum Making," *Elementary School Journal*, Vol. XXV, May, 1925, pp. 657, 659, 663.

"Are there General Principles that Govern the Junior College Curriculum?" *Proceedings*, Institute for Administrative Officers of Higher Institutions, 1929, p. 27.

Curriculum Investigations, p. 6.

How to Make a Curriculum, pp. 2, 6, 8, 35, 37, 39, 42, 61, 96.

Estimate of Current Educational Practice

"Rebuilding the Curriculum in Line with its True Function," *Nation's Schools*, Vol. III, Jan., 1929, p. 14.

"Difficulties to be Met in Local Curriculum Making," *Elementary School Journal*, Vol. XXV, May, 1925, pp. 654, 655, 659, 660, 661, 662.

"Are there General Principles that Govern the Junior College Curriculum?" *Proceedings*, Institute for Administrative Officers of Higher Institutions, 1929, p. 14.

"Education as a Social Process," *School and Society*, Vol. 21, April, 1925, p. 457.

Curriculum Investigations, pp. 22, 28, 31.

How to Make a Curriculum, pp. 5, 44, 45, 50, 150.

The Nature of Learning

The Twenty-Sixth Yearbook, Part II, National Society for the Study of Education, pp. 46, 47, 53.

"Education as a Social Process," *School and Society*, Vol. XXI, April, 1925, pp. 456, 457, 459.

"Difficulties to be Met in Local Curriculum Making," *Elementary School Journal*, Vol. XXV, May, 1925, p. 655.

"Are There General Principles That Govern the Junior College Curriculum?" *Proceedings*, Institute for Administrative Officers of Higher Institutions, 1929, p. 18.

How to Make a Curriculum, pp. 30, 47, 247.

"The Relation between Content and Method," *Journal of Educational Sociology*, Vol. V, No. 1, Sept., 1931.

Reactions to Other Points of View

The Twenty-Sixth Yearbook, Part II (National Society for the Study of Education), pp. 47, 49.

"Education as a Social Process," *School and Society*, Vol. XXI, April, 1925, p. 454.

How to Make a Curriculum, pp. 4, 5, 33.

JOHN DEWEY

General Viewpoint and Its Relation to Education

Philosophy and Civilization: Minton, Balch, 1931, pp. 10, 11, 297, 304, 305, 315, 316, 317, 318, 319, 320, 321, 323, 325, 327, 328, 329, 330.

Inglis Lecture, 1931: Harvard University Press, 1931, pp. 1, 26, 40, 41.

A Credo (pamphlet): Simon and Schuster, 1931, pp. 4, 6, 7, 10, 13, 16.

Individualism Old and New: Minton, Balch, 1930, pp. 30, 31, 32, 33, 36, 52, 55, 56, 57, 64, 65, 67, 70, 72, 80, 86, 89, 90, 91, 94, 96, 97, 109, 110, 114, 121, 124, 127, 131, 132, 133, 134, 135, 137, 143, 148, 150, 153, 155, 166, 167, 169, 170.
Construction and Criticism (pamphlet): Columbia University Press, 1930, pp. 3, 7, 9, 24.
The Quest for Certainty: Minton, Balch, 1929, pp. 7, 9, 31, 40, 77, 169, 210, 215, 252, 255, 256, 268, 272, 273, 299, 307, 311, 313.
Characters and Events: Henry Holt, 1929, Vol. I, pp. 412, 413, 416; Vol. II, p. 800.
The Sources of a Science of Education: Horace Liveright, 1929, pp. 74, 75.
The Public and Its Problems: Henry Holt, 1927, pp. 31, 32, 34, 61, 68, 109, 113, 126, 131, 133, 134, 137, 139, 142, 144, 146, 147, 149, 166, 167, 172, 173, 183, 184, 199, 200, 201, 203, 204, 207, 208, 209, 210, 211, 214, 216, 217.
Beard, C. A. (ed.): Whither Mankind? Longmans, 1928, pp. 313, 314, 315, 316, 317, 319, 324.
Kallen, H. M. (ed.): Freedom in the Modern World, Coward-McCann, 1928, p. 266.
Page, Kirby (ed.): Recent Gains in American Civilization; The Chautauqua Press, 1928, pp. 257, 271, 272, 273, 274, 275.
Schilpp, P. A. (ed.): Higher Education Faces the Future, pp. 278, 279, 281, 282.
Kilpatrick, W. H. (ed.): The Educational Frontier, Century, 1933, pp. 32, 35, 39, 42-44, 46-50, 52-59, 61-65, 68-72, 287, 288, 291, 292, 294, 295, 297, 303, 304, 306, 308-311, 314-319.
"Some Aspects of Modern Education," School and Society, Vol. XXIV, Oct., 1931, pp. 581, 582, 583, 584.
"The Direction of Education," School and Society, Vol. XXVII, April, 1928, p. 496.
"A Key to the New World," (book review), The New Republic, Vol. XLVI, May, 1926, p. 410.
"The Manufacturer's Association and the Public Schools." Journal of National Education Association, Vol. XVII, Feb., 1928, p. 62.
"Art in Education and Education in Art," The New Republic, Vol. XLVI, Feb., 1926, p. 282.
"Practical Democracy," (book review), The New Republic, Vol. XLV, Dec., 1925, p. 54.
"Social Science and Social Control," The New Republic, Vol. LXVII, July, 1931, p. 277.

"The Economic Situation, A Challenge to Education," *Journal of Home Economics,* 1932, Vol. XXIV, pp. 498, 499.
"Education and Our Present Social Problems," *School and Society,* Vol. XXXVII, April 15, 1933, p. 473-76.

Nature of Practical Proposals

Philosophy and Civilization, p. 326.
Inglis Lecture, 1931, pp. 29, 30, 36, 37, 38, 39, 40.
Individualism Old and New, pp. 139, 141, 144, 154, 155, 164, 165.
The Sources of a Science of Education, pp. 12, 13, 19, 26, 30, 31, 33, 36, 42, 46, 47, 48, 49, 50, 51, 56, 58, 59, 74, 77.
Schilpp, P. A. (ed.): Higher Education Faces the Future, pp. 279, 280.
Dewey, J., and others: Art and Education, Barnes Foundation, 1929, pp. 180, 183.
Kilpatrick, W. H. (ed.): The Educational Frontier, p. 36-38, 51, 59, 71, 72, 288.
"The Direction of Education," *School and Society,* Vol. XXVII, April, 1928, p. 496.
"General Principles of Educational Articulation," *School and Society,* Vol. XXIX, March, 1929, pp. 401, 403, 404.
"Duties and Responsibilities of the Teaching Profession," *School and Society,* Vol. XXXII, Aug., 1930, pp. 189, 190, 191.
"How Much Freedom in New Schools?" *The New Republic,* Vol. LXIII, July, 1930, p. 206.
"The Bankruptcy of Modern Education," *School and Society,* Vol. XXVII, Jan., 1928, p. 23.
"Social Science and Social Control," *The New Republic,* Vol. LXVII, July, 1931, p. 277.
"Teachers as Citizens," *American Teacher,* Vol. XVI, Oct., 1931, p. 7.
"The Economic Situation—A Challenge to Education," *Journal of Home Economics,* 1932, Vol. XXIV, pp. 501.
"Education and Our Present Social Problems," *School and Society,* Vol. XXXVII, April 15, 1933, pp. 476-78.

Estimate of Current Educational Practice

Philosophy and Civilization, pp. 296, 316, 326.
Inglis Lecture, 1931, pp. 6, 14, 15, 27.
Individualism Old and New, pp. 127, 128.
Construction and Criticism (pamphlet), pp. 9, 10.
The Sources of a Science of Education, pp. 40, 41, 69, 71.

The Public and Its Problems, pp. 171, 198, 200.
Kilpatrick, W. H. (ed): The Educational Frontier, pp. 33, 34, 66, 67, 300, 301.
"Some Aspects of Modern Education," *School and Society*, Vol. XXXIV, Oct., 1931, p. 580.
"General Principles of Educational Articulation," *School and Society*, Vol. XXIX, March, 1929, pp. 403, 404.
"How Much Freedom in New Schools?" *The New Republic*, Vol. LXIII, July, 1930, p. 205.
"The Direction of Education," *School and Society*, Vol. XXVII, April, 1928, p. 494.
"Art in Education and Education in Art," *The New Republic*, Vol. XLVI, Feb., 1926, p. 11.
"The Bankruptcy of Modern Education," *School and Society*, Vol. XXVII, January, 1928, p. 23.
"The Economic Situation—A Challenge to Education," *Journal of Home Economics*, 1932, Vol. XXIV, p. 498.

The Nature of Learning
Philosophy and Civilization, pp. 119, 253, 256, 275, 289, 290, 291, 294, 295, 296, 307, 308, 309.
Inglis Lecture, 1931, pp. 12, 13.
Individualism Old and New, p. 168.
Construction and Criticism (pamphlet), pp. 11, 18, 20, 21.
The Quest for Certainty, pp. 138, 234, 235, 242, 243, 254, 267.
The Sources of a Science of Education, pp. 49, 64, 65, 68.
The Public and Its Problems, pp. 159, 160, 161, 162.
Dewey, J., and others, Art and Education, pp. 177, 178, 182.
Ogburn and Goldenweiser (eds.): The Social Sciences and Their Interrelations, Houghton, Mifflin, 1927, p. 34.
Kilpatrick, W. H. (ed.): The Educational Frontier, p. 305.
"General Principles of Educational Articulation." *School and Society*, Vol. XXIX, March, 1929, pp. 401, 402, 403, 406.
"How Much Freedom in New Schools?" *The New Republic*, Vol. LXIII, July, 1930, p. 205.
"Social Science and Social Control," *The New Republic*, Vol. LXVII, July, 1931, p. 277.

Reactions to Other Points of View
Philosophy and Civilization, p. 12.
Inglis Lecture, 1931, pp. 17, 18, 31, 32.

A Credo (pamphlet), p. 8.
Individualism Old and New, pp. 85, 134.
The Sources of a Science of Education, pp. 60, 62, 66, 67, 68, 72, 73.
Dewey, J., and others, Art and Education, pp. 180, 181.
Kilpatrick, W. H. (ed.): The Educational Frontier, pp. 51, 289, 290, 301, 302, 311-13.

GEORGE S. COUNTS

General Viewpoint and Its Relation to Education

Dare the School Build a New Social Order? (pamphlet): John Day, 1932.
The Soviet Challenge to America: John Day, 1931, pp. 66, 218, 300, 301, 313, 314, 315, 325, 329, 333, 334, 335, 339.
The American Road to Culture: John Day, 1930, pp. 12, 13, 17, 18, 19, 67, 121, 134, 172, 175, 177, 181, 182, 184, 189.
Inglis Lecture, 1929: Harvard University Press, pp. 3, 30, 37, 45, 46, 64, 66.
The Twenty-Sixth Yearbook, Part II (National Society for the Study of Education): Public School Publishing Co., 1926, pp. 73, 74, 75, 81, 85.
"Secondary Education and the Social Problem," *School Executives' Magazine*, 1932, Vol. LI, pp. 499, 500, 501.

Nature of Practical Proposals

Dare the School Build a New Social Order? (pamphlet).
The American Road to Culture, pp. 54, 55, 95, 108, 154, 169, 193.
Inglis Lecture, 1929, pp. 19, 49, 53, 69.
The Twenty-Sixth Yearbook, Part II (National Society for the Study of Education), pp. 75, 76, 77, 80, 83, 84, 86, 87, 90.
"Secondary Education and the Social Problem," *School Executives' Magazine*, 1932, Vol. LI, p. 520.

Estimate of Current Educational Practice

Dare the School Build a New Social Order? (pamphlet).
The Soviet Challenge to America, pp. 179, 180.
The American Road to Culture, pp. 22, 23, 49, 50, 52, 65, 91, 109, 156, 158, 194.
Inglis Lecture, 1929, p. 17.
The Twenty-Sixth Yearbook, Part II (National Society for the Study of Education), p. 81.

"Secondary Education and the Social Problem," *School Executives'*
Magazine, 1932, Vol. LI, p. 519.

The Nature of Learning

Dare the School Build a New Social Order? (pamphlet).
The Soviet Challenge to America, pp. 317, 325.
The American Road to Culture, pp. 148, 149, 177.
The Twenty-Sixth Yearbook, Part II (National Society for the Study
of Education), pp. 79, 80, 82.

Reactions to Other Points of View

Dare the School Build a New Social Order? (pamphlet).
The Soviet Challenge to America, p. 332.
The American Road to Culture, pp. 114, 126, 129, 138, 187, 192.
Inglis Lecture, 1929, p. 68.
The Twenty-Sixth Yearbook, Part II (National Society for the
Study of Education), pp. 77, 90.

WILLIAM H. KILPATRICK

General Viewpoint and Its Relation to Education

The Educational Frontier, Century, 1933, pp. 122-26, 130-32, 134-40,
144-46, 152, 153, 155, 156, 159, 259, 260, 263, 268, 285.
Education and the Social Crisis, Liveright, 1932, pp. 13, 14, 17, 20,
22-24, 27, 31, 35, 38, 40, 57, 59, 79.
Our Educational Task: University of North Carolina Press, 1930,
pp. 8, 15, 17, 28, 66, 69, 80, 81, 89, 90, 92, 95, 96, 101, 102, 113.
Education for a Changing Civilization: Macmillan, 1927, pp. 9, 15,
21, 28, 38, 40, 49, 61, 62, 71, 83, 84, 85, 86, 110, 132.
The Twenty-Sixth Yearbook, Part II (National Society for the Study
of Education): Public School Publishing Co., 1926, p. 121.
Ogburn and Goldenweiser (eds.): The Social Sciences and Their
Interrelations: Houghton Mifflin, 1927, pp. 426, 429.
"Thinking in Childhood and Youth," *Religious Education*, Vol.
XXIII, Feb., 1928, pp. 132, 136.
"Our Changing Schools," *Journal of Adult Education*, Vol. I, April,
1929, pp. 148, 151.
"Relations of Philosophy and Science in the Study of Education,"
School and Society, Vol. XXX, July, 1929, p. 47.
"The Task Confronting Adult Education," *Journal of Adult Educa-
tion*, Vol. I, Oct., 1929, pp. 407, 408, 411.

"What is Good Education?" *Educational Council Bulletin,* Nov., 1931, pp. 12, 13.

"Social Factors Influencing Educational Methods in 1930," *Journal of Education Society,* Vol. IV, April, 1931, pp. 488, 489.

"A Theory of Progressive Education to Fit the Times," *Progressive Education,* Vol. VIII, April, 1931, pp. 288, 290, 291, 293.

"Universities, American, English and German," *Journal of Higher Education,* Oct., 1931, p. 358.

"Hidden Philosophies," *Journal of Educational Sociology,* Vol. IV, Oct., 1930, pp. 36, 37.

"First Things in Education," *School and Society,* Vol. XXXIV, Dec., 1931, pp. 847, 849, 850.

"The American Elementary School," *Teachers College Record,* Vol. XXX, March, 1929, pp. 521, 522.

"The Philosophy of American Education," *Teachers College Record,* Vol. XXX, Oct., 1928, pp. 14, 16.

"Some Basic Considerations Affecting Success in Teaching Art," *Teachers College Record,* 1931, Vol. XXXII, p. 356.

"A Reconstructed Theory of the Educative Process," *Teachers College Record,* 1931, Vol. XXXII, pp. 532, 536, 544, 554, 555, 558.

Nature of Practical Proposals

The Educational Frontier, pp. 125, 127, 128, 129, 134, 136, 138, 141, 143-45, 147-50, 155, 158, 260-62, 264, 265, 267, 269-73, 275-83.

Education and the Social Crisis, pp. 36, 43, 44, 46, 47, 48, 49, 51, 53, 54, 58, 60, 61, 63, 65, 74, 75, 76, 78, 79.

Our Educational Task, pp. 101, 104, 107, 109, 115, 116, 118.

Education for a Changing Civilization, pp. 68, 69, 77, 100, 112, 113, 116, 118, 125, 128, 135, 136.

The Twenty-Sixth Yearbook, Part II (National Society for the Study of Education), pp. 123, 125, 129, 130, 131, 132, 133, 137, 139, 140.

Essays in Honor of John Dewey: Holt, 1929, p. 190.

Ogburn and Goldenweiser (eds.): The Social Sciences and Their Interrelations: Houghton, 1927, pp. 424, 430.

"Thinking in Childhood and Youth," *Religious Education,* Vol. XXIII, Feb., 1928, pp. 138, 139.

"The Task Confronting Adult Education," *Journal of Adult Education,* Vol. I, Oct., 1929, p. 406.

"How Can We Help Our Prospective Teachers to Be and to Remain Eager to Learn?" *Proceedings,* Eastern States Association of Professional Schools for Teachers, 1930, p. 77.

"A Theory of Progressive Education to Fit the Times," *Progressive Education*, Vol. VIII, April, 1931, p. 292.

"First Things in Education," *School and Society*, Vol. XXXIV, Dec., 1931, pp. 851, 853, 854.

"The Philosophy of American Education," *Teachers College Record*, Vol. XXX, Oct., 1928, pp. 17, 19, 21.

"The American Elementary School," *Teachers College Record*, Vol. XXX, March, 1929, pp. 524, 525.

"Some Basic Considerations Affecting Success in Teaching Art," *Teachers College Record*, Vol. XXXII, Jan., 1931, pp. 354, 355.

"A Reconstructed Theory of the Educative Process," *Teachers College Record*, Vol. XXXII, March, 1931, pp. 550, 552, 556.

Estimate of Current Educational Practice

The Educational Frontier, pp. 147, 266, 273, 274, 284-86.
Education and The Social Crisis, pp. 18, 28, 55, 56.
Our Educational Task, pp. 19, 20, 109, 114.
Education for a Changing Civilization, pp. 57, 76, 92, 126.
The Twenty-Sixth Yearbook, Part II (National Society for the Study of Education), p. 141.
Essays in Honor of John Dewey, pp. 175, 183, 189.

"Our Changing Schools," *Journal of Adult Education*, Vol. I, April, 1929, p. 149.

"How Can We Help Our Prospective Teachers to Be and to Remain Eager to Learn?" *Proceedings*, Eastern States Association of Professional Schools for Teachers, 1930, p. 77.

"Social Factors Influencing Educational Method in 1930," *Journal of Educational Sociology*, Vol. IV, April, 1931, p. 490.

"Training Teachers for Progressive Education," National Education Association, Dept. of Supt., *Official Report*, 1931, p. 793.

"The Philosophy of American Education," *Teachers College Record*, Vol. XXX, Oct., 1928, p. 20.

"The American Elementary School," *Teachers College Record*, Vol. XXX, March, 1929, pp. 517, 527.

"A Reconstructed Theory of the Educative Process," *Teachers College Record*, Vol. XXXII, March, 1931, pp. 544, 545, 547, 549.

The Nature of Learning

The Educational Frontier, pp. 132, 133, 264, 267, 268, 271, 272, 275, 277, 278.
Education and the Social Crisis, pp. 63, 64.

Our Educational Task, pp. 88, 105, 106, 107.

Education for a Changing Civilization, pp. 97, 98, 102, 103, 104, 105, 113, 119, 121, 123, 129.

How We Learn: Associated Press, Calcutta, 1929, pp. 8, 15, 75.

Foundations of Method: Macmillan, 1925, pp. 98, 159, 291.

The Twenty-Sixth Yearbook, Part II (National Society for the Study of Education), p. 144.

Ogburn and Goldenweiser (eds.), The Social Sciences and Their Interrelations: Houghton, 1927, pp. 422, 423.

"A Reconstructed Theory of the Educative Process," *Teachers College Record*, Vol. XXXII, March, 1931, pp. 532, 533, 534, 535, 536, 537, 538, 539, 541, 542, 543, 544, 553, 555, 557.

"Some Basic Considerations Affecting Success in Teaching Art," *Teachers College Record*, Vol. XXXII, Jan., 1931, pp. 351, 357.

"Our Changing Schools," *Journal of Adult Education*, Vol. I, April, 1929, p. 152.

"The Task Confronting Adult Education," *Journal of Adult Education*, Vol. I, Oct., 1929, p. 410.

"What is Good Education?" *Educational Council Bulletin*, Nov., 1931, pp. 14, 16.

"First Things in Education," *School and Society*, Vol. XXXIV, Dec., 1931, pp. 850, 851.

Reactions to Other Points of View

The Educational Frontier, pp. 145, 146, 151, 259.

Education and the Social Crisis, pp. 62, 73, 74.

Our Educational Task, p. 109.

Education for a Changing Civilization, pp. 134, 135.

The Twenty-Sixth Yearbook, Part II (National Society for the Study of Education), pp. 142, 144.

"Relations of Philosophy and Science in the Study of Education," *School and Society*, Vol. XXX, July, 1929, pp. 43, 46.

"What Do We Mean by Progressive Education?" *Progressive Education*, Vol. VII, Dec., 1930, p. 383.

"Social Factors Influencing Educational Method in 1930," *Journal of Educational Sociology*, Vol. IV, April, 1931, p. 487.

"Hidden Philosophies," *Journal of Education Society*, Vol. IV, Oct., 1930, p. 37.

"A Theory of Progressive Education to Fit the Times," *Progressive Education*, Vol. VIII, April, 1931, p. 292.

BIBLIOGRAPHY OF SECTION TWO 293

"First Things in Education," *School and Society*, Vol. XXXIV, Dec.,
1931, p. 852.
"The American Elementary School," *Teachers College Record*, Vol.
XXX, March, 1929, pp. 527, 528.
"Some Basic Considerations Affecting Success in Teaching Art,"
Teachers College Record, Vol. XXXII, Jan., 1931, p. 356.
"The Relation of Philosophy to Scientific Research," *Journal of Edu-
cational Research*, Vol. XXV, Oct., 1931, pp. 97-114.

HAROLD RUGG

General Viewpoint and Its Relation to Education
Culture and Education in America: Harcourt, Brace, 1931, pp. 10,
11, 13, 58, 59, 72, 73, 76, 83, 86, 92, 93, 177, 208, 215, 234, 236,
239, 242, 243, 252, 254, 255, 259, 260, 269, 270, 276, 284, 286,
288, 289, 297, 298, 333, 346, 355, 398, 399, 400, 401.
The Great Technology: John Day, 1933, pp. 14-16, 18, 21, 23, 24,
26, 38, 67-69, 71-77, 84-86, 102-05, 126, 127, 140, 164, 167, 169,
170, 172, 173, 180, 181, 186, 190, 191, 195, 201-03, 206, 208, 209,
211, 212, 215-18, 228, 229, 241, 257-60, 283-88.

Nature of Practical Proposals
Culture and Education in America, pp. 74, 75, 283, 289, 294, 295,
303, 308, 309, 313, 321, 323, 334, 340, 342, 351, 352, 353, 358, 385,
386, 390, 391, 392, 393, 394, 395, 396.
The Great Technology, pp. 233-236, 251-256, 261-273, 277-280.

Estimate of Current Educational Practice
Culture and Education in America, pp. 58, 59, 61, 63, 66.
The Great Technology, pp. 238-40, 243-51.

The Nature of Learning
Culture and Education in America, pp. 189, 230, 231, 233, 299, 301,
305, 307, 309, 310, 312, 317, 322, 324, 337, 362, 363, 366, 389.
The Great Technology, pp. 275-277.

Reactions to Other Points of View
Culture and Education in America, pp. 104, 111, 155, 156, 209, 210,
216, 217, 218, 219, 220, 221, 224, 225, 226, 227, 228, 229, 251, 361.

BOYD H. BODE

General Viewpoint and Its Relation to Education
Conflicting Psychologies of Learning: Heath, Boston, 1929, pp. 265,
274, 287, 293, 294, 295, 302.

Modern Educational Theories: The Macmillan Co., 1927, pp. 9, 15, 19, 20, 34, 93, 233, 238, 243, 259, 264, 265, 269, 284, 288, 297, 320, 346.

Kilpatrick, W. H. (ed.): The Educational Frontier, Century, 1933, pp. 6-10, 15, 22-31.

Journal of Philosophy (book review), Vol. XXIII, p. 388.

"The New Education: 10 Years After," *The New Republic*, Vol. LXIII, Jan., 1930, p. 62.

"So Many Paths," *Independent Education*, Vol. II, June, 1929, p. 14.

"Relation of Philosophy of Education to the Scientific Study of Education and Modern Educational Practices," *Proceedings*, 6th Annual Educational Conference, Kentucky University, p. 24.

"Currents and Cross Currents in Higher Education," *Journal of Higher Education*, Oct., 1931, p. 379.

"Education Through Freedom in Learning," N.E.A. Dept. of Superintendence, *Official Report*, 1932, pp. 191, 192.

Nature of Practical Proposals

Conflicting Psychologies of Learning, pp. 272, 274, 298, 299.

Modern Educational Theories, pp. 28, 38, 46, 56, 70, 89, 106, 172, 213, 217, 305, 323, 345.

Kilpatrick, W. H. (ed.): The Educational Frontier, pp. 16, 29, 31.

"Determining Principles of Curriculum Construction," *Educational Administration and Supervision*, Vol. XII, April, 1926, p. 223.

"Where Does One Go For Fundamental Assumptions in Education?" *Educational Administration and Supervision*, Vol. XIV, Sept., 1928, p. 368.

"The Most Outstanding Next Steps for Curriculum Makers in the United States," *Teachers College Record*, Vol. XXX, p. 189.

"So Many Paths," *Independent Education*, Vol. II, p. 12, 13.

"Relation of Philosophy of Education to the Scientific Study of Education and Modern Educational Practices," *Proceedings*, 6th Annual Educational Conference, pp. 24, 26.

New Problems in Secondary Education, *Proceedings*, 6th Annual Educational Conference, p. 48.

"Education for Character," Indiana University School of Education, *Bulletin* 5, Nov., 1928, p. 48.

"What Educational Principles Will Guide Teachers to Appreciate Vital Values for Children in the Kindergarten Primary," *Proceedings*, National Education Association, 1930, pp. 371, 372, 375.

"Problems of Liberal Education," *Educational Administration and Supervision*, Vol. XVI, Nov., 1930, p. 636.
"Modern Trends in Education," Kansas Teacher, Vol. XXXIII, April, 1931, p. 190.

Estimate of Current Educational Practice
Conflicting Psychologies of Learning, pp. 41, 58, 284, 300.
Modern Educational Theories, pp. 33, 37, 134, 239, 254, 279, 280, 347, 348.
Kilpatrick, W. H. (ed.): The Educational Frontier, pp. 3-5, 11, 14, 15, 22, 31.
Journal of Philosophy (book review), Vol. XXIII, p. 386.
"Conflicting Ideals," *School and Community*, March, 1931, p. 123.
"The New Education: 10 Years After," *The New Republic*, Vol. LXIII, pp. 61, 64.
"So Many Paths," *Independent Education*, Vol. II, p. 13.

The Nature of Learning
Conflicting Psychologies of Learning, pp. 161, 228, 238, 246, 247, 249, 258, 259, 261, 275, 281, 282.
Modern Educational Theories, pp. 65, 186, 199, 200, 202, 205, 213, 214, 217, 218, 324.
"So Many Paths," *Independent Education*, Vol. II, pp. 11, 14.
"New Problems in Secondary Education," *Proceedings*, 6th Annual Educational Conference, Kentucky University, p. 48.
"Education for Character," Indiana University School of Education, *Bulletin* 5, Nov., 1928.
"What Educational Principles Will Guide Teachers to Appreciate Vital Values for Children in the Kindergarten Primary," *Proceedings*, National Education Association, 1930, p. 371.
"Modern Trends in Education," *Kansas Teacher*, Vol. XXXIII, April, 1931, p. 12.

Reactions to Other Points of View
Conflicting Psychologies of Learning, pp. 140, 189, 209, 267, 268.
Modern Educational Theories, pp. 33, 40, 85, 89, 91, 100, 107, 132, 150, 164, 165, 302.
Kilpatrick, W. H. (ed.): The Educational Frontier, pp. 17, 18, 20.
"Where Does One Go For Fundamental Assumptions in Education?" *Educational Administration and Supervision*, Vol. XIV, Sept., 1928, pp. 364, 366.

"John Dewey," *Ed. Res. Bull.* 8, Ohio State University, Oct., 1929, p. 343.

"The New Education: 10 Years After," *The New Republic*, Vol. LXIII, p. 63.

"So Many Paths," *Independent Education*, Vol. II, June, 1929, pp. 11, 12.

"What Educational Principles Will Guide Teachers to Appreciate Vital Values for Children in the Kindergarten Primary," *Proceedings*, National Education Association, 1930, p. 370.

INDEX

INDEX

Academic freedom, 31

Adult Education movement, 34

Aims of education, 235-36

America, 18-20, 28-29, 41, 43, 229-30, 240, 247

American Association for the Advancement of Science, 33

American Association of University Professors, 31

American civilization (bibliography), 257-60

American Civil Liberties Union, 31

American culture, 28-29, 31, 35-36, 230-31

American Economics Association, 33

American Historical Association, 33

American institutions, viii, 5, 25, 30, 229-30

American mind, 36, 39, 40-41

American opportunity, 42-43

American Philosophical Society, 33

American philosophy, 36, 231-32

American Psychological Association, 34

American society, 15, 27, 36, 41, 45, 229, 230, 234-35

Art, 232

Assumptions basic to education, 238

Atheist, 4, 14

Bagley, W. C.,
analysis of viewpoint, 59-64
interpretive criticism, 165-68

Bellamy, Edward, 29

Bible, 5-7

Big Business, 17-18, 23-24, 34, 230

Bobbitt, F.,
analysis of viewpoint, 112-18
interpretive criticism, 196-200

Bode, B.,
analysis of viewpoint, 147-53
interpretive criticism, 218-20

Briggs, T. H.,
analysis of viewpoint, 70-75
interpretive criticism, 171-75

Business enterprise, 9, 15, 18-21, 25-27, 29, 38, 41, 230

Business régime, decline of, 15-28

Capitalism, 19, 27, 229-30

Captains of industry, 16-17, 20-21

Catholic faith, 10

Catholic Welfare League, 19

Catholics, 4, 8

Challenge to educators, 223, 229-31, 234-35

Character education, 235-37

Charity, 23

Charters, W. W.
analysis of viewpoint, 106-12
interpretive criticism, 193-96

Censorship, 37

Chicago, University of, 29

Christian tradition, decline of, 3-15, 227, 229-30, 233

Christianity, Protestant, 4, 8

Churches, 6-8, 10-15, 19-20, 41

Civilization, American (bibliography), 257-60
world (bibliography), 255-57

Class struggle, 24

Classical economics, 16-17, 22-23, 29, 31